"There could not have been a more opportune time for the publication of *Who's* Left *in Israel?* Dan Leon has done a good job of selecting the fifteen contributors and editing this unusual anthology. It appears at a time when even rightists in Israel are waking up to the political reality of what is called 'the two-state solution' – the State of Palestine alongside the State of Israel. This a political necessity for which most of the authors, and Dan Leon himself, have been struggling for decades." *Ari Rath, former editor of the Jerusalem Post*

"This important book illustrates the heterogeneity of contemporary Israeli society. It offers comprehensive descriptions and analyses of particular groups within the structure of the society. In clarifying the various discourses which contribute to the complexity of the society, it provides the reader with illuminating and often painful information and insights. This knowledge should be made available to anyone striving to become better acquainted with Israeli society." *Professor Daniel Bar-tal, Tel Aviv University*

"In tackling complex questions on Israel's official policies, past and present, *Who's* Left *in Israel?* challenges much of the 'conventional wisdom' which has stymied so many initiatives for peace. This thought-provoking work is essential reading for all those who seek peace and justice in Israel/Palestine." *Latif Dori, Secretary of the Committee for Israeli–Palestinian Dialogue, founded by Israelis of Oriental origin; recipient of the Kreisky Prize for Peace and Human Rights*

"The special quality of Dan Leon's convincing anthology is that it flows from his long experience both as an activist in the Israeli left and as a writer with unusual ability to view its history and prospects in broad perspective. *Who's* Left *in Israel* deserves to be read by all those interested in the dilemmas facing the Israeli left in our times." *Knesset Member Ran Cohen*

"Dan Leon's *Who's* Left *in Israel* is an insightful and seminal collection of essays on why the Left faltered and what serious alternatives it can now offer to an Israel beset with profound problems growing out of its conquest and occupation." *Murray Polner, a peace activist, and past editor of* Present Tense *magazine and the newsletters* Shalom *and* PS: The Intelligent Guide to Jewish Affairs

"Dan Leon is to be commended on having amassed such an extraordinary collection of essays on all aspects of the political left in Israel, a country which, until 1977, was regarded as a society built by socialists and run on socialistic lines. The essays, by a wide variety of writers with special interests ranging from the 'woman question' through education to Zionism and the Palestinians, are an eye-opener, and a wake-up call, for anyone who cares about Israel – not just leftists. This book should be given the widest possible distribution among Jews and non-Jews, Israelis and others, politicians and lay people alike. It will bring them sharply, and often dismayingly, up-to-date on the deadly stalemate that the state has fallen into in the last 25 years." *Lynne Reid Banks, author of* The Indian in the Cupboard

WHO'S *LEFT* IN ISRAEL?

In memory of my friend and mentor
Aharon Cohen
(1910–1980)

Who's *Left* in Israel?

RADICAL POLITICAL ALTERNATIVES FOR THE FUTURE OF ISRAEL

Edited by

DAN LEON

sussex
ACADEMIC
PRESS

BRIGHTON • PORTLAND

The right of Dan Leon to be identified as Editor of the Introduction and Editor of the editorial Organization of this work has been asserted in accordance with the Copyright, Designs and Patents Act 1988.

2 4 6 8 10 9 7 5 3 1

First published 2004 in Great Britain by
SUSSEX ACADEMIC PRESS
PO Box 2950
Brighton BN2 5SP

and in the United States of America by
SUSSEX ACADEMIC PRESS
920 NE 58th Ave   Suite 300
Portland, Oregon 97213-3786

British Library Cataloguing in Publication Data
A CIP catalogue record for this book is available from the British Library.

Library of Congress Cataloging-in-Publication Data
Who's left in Israel? : radical political alternatives for the future of Israel / edited by Dan Leon.
   p. cm.
Includes bibliographical references and index.
ISBN 1-903900-56-5 (h/c, alk. paper) — ISBN 1-903900-57-3 (p/b, alk. paper)
   1. National characteristics, Israeli.   2. Israel—Civilization.
3. Israel—Politics and government—20th century.   4. Israel
—Social   conditions—20th century.   5. Israel—Ethnic
relations.   6. Arab–Israeli conflict—1993—Peace.
I. Leon, Dan.
DS112.W43   2004
956.9405'4—dc22
                                                     2004000499
                                                     CIP

Typeset and designed by G&G Editorial, Brighton
Printed by MPG Books Ltd, Bodmin, Cornwall
This book is printed on acid-free paper.

Contents

❖ ∨ ❖

Contents

Acknowledgments

First and foremost I want to express my appreciation to the fifteen writers who agreed so readily to write chapters in *Whose* Left *in Israel?* Without their contribution of time and energy, the implementation of the idea behind this book would have remained on paper. It was their commitment which gave it flesh and blood and for this I am indebted to them.

Second, there would have no book without the backing I received all along the line from Anthony Grahame, Editorial Director at Sussex Academic Press. From start to finish his personal encouragement and professional advice were irreplaceable. Thanks, Tony.

Third, were I to mention the names of all the friends and colleagues who gave me their advice and practical assistance at various stages of preparing the book, the list would be endless. So those whose names do not appear will forgive me if I convey my special thanks to the following: Judy Goldberg, who compiled the index; Yitzhak Dinur, who read the proofs; and Gershom Baskin, Najat Hirbawi and Ruth El-Raz. Needless to say, it is I and nobody else who bears responsibility for any blemishes which remain.

Finally, I would like to express deep appreciation to my family for their unfailing encouragement while I was working on the book. I could never have completed the project without their constant support.

DAN LEON
Jerusalem, March 2004

The Contributors and Their Topics

Be they from academia, journalism or the political world, the fifteen contributors to this collection are all experts in their subjects and are all declared leftists. In diverse ways, they offer radical alternatives to the most pressing social, economic and political problems of Israeli society today. Dan Leon notes that nowadays they are undoubtedly a minority group but quotes the words of British writer George Bernard Shaw: "All great truths start as blasphemies."

Dan Leon, who lives in Jerusalem, has been active for many years in Israeli leftist and peace movements. He is a former senior editor of New Outlook *and co-managing editor of the* Palestine–Israel Journal. *He is the author of* The Kibbutz, a new way of life.

"A land without a people . . ." by Uri Avnery

The early Zionists at the turn of the twentieth century believed in the slogan "A land without a people for a people without a land", though in reality "the Holy Land" had a population of half a million, nine-tenths of whom were Arabs. Even in the 1970s, Golda Meir refuted the existence of a Palestinian people. In tracing the course of the conflict over more than a century, the author expresses his conviction that the Holocaust motivated the Western powers to support the establishment of a Jewish state, regardless of the disastrous consequences for the Palestinians. Today, only a two-state solution is feasible.

Uri Avnery, a veteran journalist and peace activist, was editor of Ha'olam Hazeh *and a* Knesset *member. He is active in the* Gush Shalom, *the Peace Bloc. He and his wife Rahel were recipients of the Alternative Nobel Peace Prize in 2001.*

"The Palestinian Arab minority in Israel" by As'ad Ghanem

As "the state of the Jewish people", Israel can be classified as an ethnocracy rather than a democracy, since ethnicity and religion dominate all its decision-making. Numbering about a million, the Palestinian Israelis are both "incomplete Israelis" because they are discriminated against in all walks of life, and "incomplete Palestinians" because of their disconnection from the wider Arab and Palestinian world. The author discusses the prospects for this minority group within a two-state or a bi-national solution to the Palestinian–Israeli conflict.

Dr. Ghanem, who teaches political science at Haifa University, has conducted major research on many aspects of Arab–Jewish relations in Israel, and studies of legal, institutional and political conditions in ethnic states. His last book was The Palestinian Regime: a partial democracy *(Choice Outstanding Academic Title).*

"Israeli colonialism under the guise of the peace process, 1993–2000" by Amira Hass

In the decade of Oslo and Camp David, the number of Jewish settlements in the occupied Palestinian territories doubled, with a parallel growth in the number of settlers. The writer quotes experts who stress the difference between colonization and colonialism. After a detailed account of the settlement project during what is known as "the decade of the peace process", she concludes that the Israeli occupation since 1967 is colonialism par excellence.

Amira Hass, a prominent Israeli journalist, lives in Ramallah and covers the Occupied Territories for the daily Ha'aretz. *She is the author of* Drinking the Sea in Gaza: Days and nights in a land under siege.

"The end of Zionism?" by Avraham Burg

The Zionist revolution always rested on two pillars: a just path and an ethical leadership. The Israeli nation today rests on a scaffolding of corruption and on foundations of oppression and injustice. Seeing the possible end of the Zionist enterprise, the author urges that Diaspora Jews, for whom Israel is a central part of their identity, also speak out. He asks how if we see ourselves as "the only democracy in the Middle East" can we keep a Palestinian minority under the boot?

Avraham Burg, a Labor Knesset *member, is a former Chair of the Jewish Agency and was Speaker of the Knesset from 1999 to 2003. He was among the initiators of the Geneva Accords in 2003.*

"Religion, state and society" by David Newman

Various dimensions of the contemporary meaning of Jewish statehood are raised, including the internal secular–religious debate among Israelis; the dialogue between Israel and the Diaspora; the way in which religion affects the Israeli–Palestinian peace process; and the implications of post-Zionist thinking on Israel as "a state for all its citizens". The writer discusses how Jew and Arab can co-exist, and how Israelis from right and left, and Jews from Israel and the Diaspora, can find ways of living peacefully side by side.

David Newman is a professor of political geography at Ben-Gurion University. He is editor of the International Journal of Geopolitics *and has written widely on the territorial and geographical dimensions of the Israeli–Arab conflict.*

"The making and unmaking of the Israeli Jewish left" by Ilan Pappe

Political thinking in the 1950s and 1960s – in the struggle against military rule in Arab areas or the Wadi Salib riots – lacked a clear socio-economic vision. The author explains the significance of the Black Panthers in the early 1970s, and later of several more radical groupings, including feminists and the early IDF refuseniks. In view of its transformation since 1967 into a primarily "one-issue" movement against the occupation, the left now needs to reassess its goals and perspectives.

Dr. Pappe, a senior lecturer in Haifa University's political science department, chairs Haifa's Emile Touma Institute for Palestinian and Israeli studies. His most recent book was The Modern History of Palestine: One land, two peoples.

"Post-mortem for the Ashkenazi left" by Lev Grinberg

How can one explain the termination in 1977 of the long era of dominance by the (*Ashkenazi*) Socialist-Zionist movement known as the "left"? Founded on the historical concepts of settlement and military control, the writer analyzes how after 1948 the "left" failed to adapt to changing times (e.g. Golda Meir's "there are no Palestinians" or the "left's" eschewing overdue economic and democratic reforms). With Labor supporting settlement in the territories after 1967, it increasingly lacked a defined political identity and was rejected by the *Mizrahi* immigrants in 1977, putting an end to its long hegemony.

Dr. Lev Luis Grinberg is a senior lecturer in the Department of Behavioral Sciences at Ben-Gurion University and a former Director of the Humphrey Institute for Social Research there. A founder-member of Yesh Gvul, *he has written widely on the Israeli economy, society and politics.*

"Jewish national self-determination at the crossroads" by Hillel Schenker

It was liberal-left secular Zionism as a secular movement in *Eretz* Israel which pioneered the building of an autonomous Jewish community with a defense capacity, before and after 1948. While only after two decades of statehood did there arise a serious Palestine address for peace-oriented dialogue, the *New Outlook*, inspired by Prof. Martin Buber, was founded for this purpose in 1957. The writer sees the Geneva Accords of 2003 as a fulfillment of the dreams of the founders of this liberal-left Zionism.

Hillel Schenker is co-managing editor of the Palestine–Israel Journal. *He was a senior editor of* New Outlook *and is spokesperson for the Israeli branch of the International Physicians for the Prevention of a Nuclear War.*

"Left out: the ecological paradox of the Israeli left" by Alon Tal

By the end of the 1970s the pollution of the Israeli environment exceeded international standards, yet in the eyes of the country's leaders, both left and right, the environment subject to lip service and little else. Though the early Zionist pioneers were informed as much by Tolstoy as by Marx (for example, the legendary A. D. Gordon), economic development at all cost received priority, leaving concern for the environment not to parties but to devoted individuals. In environmental politics, the "left" was left out.

Dr. Tal is director of research at the Arava Institue for Environmental Studies. He teaches Environmental Law at Tel Aviv University and Environmental Politics at the Hebrew University of Jerusalem. He is the author of Pollution in a Promised land: An environmental history of Israel.

"The left needs two banners" by Victor Cygielman

Can someone who favors the rights of the Palestinian people to statehood yet ignores the glaring socio-economic gaps in Israeli society be considered a leftist? Or can someone else who demands socio-economic reform yet ignores the suffering of the Palestinian people under Israeli occupation be considered a leftist? In both cases, the answer is a resounding "No". In the complex Israeli reality, only by simultaneously raising the banner of peace and the banner of social justice can the left reassert its relevance.

Victor Cygielman, a veteran Israeli journalist, is co-founder of the Palestine–Israel Journal, *published in Jerusalem.*

"The roots of Israel's economic crisis" by Tamar Gozansky

Israel's post-1967 occupation policy and the conflict with the Palestinians accelerated the militarization of an Israeli economy characterized by the concentration of finance capital and increasing foreign, especially American, ownership. Israel's economic policies, maintaining 250,000 Jewish settlers in the West Bank and Gaza Strip and shattering the Palestinian economy, caused the systematic erosion of the welfare state in Israel, and growing socio-economic distress.

Tamar Gozansky, an economist and highly respected activist for peace, social justice and women's rights, represented the Communist-led Hadash *list in the* Knesset *from 1990 to 2003.*

"The dilemmas of Israeli education" by Shulamit Aloni

As a former Minister of Education in the Rabin government of the early 1990s, the writer surveys the history of Israeli education since 1948. Changes in education do not occur in a vacuum; therefore, in this period of occupation and religious intolerance, the values of democratic and pluralistic education, respecting both our own human rights and the rights of others, are bound to suffer erosion.

Shulamit Aloni was among the founders of the movements for civil rights and women's rights, and was a recipient of the Israel Prize for human rights. A founder of Ratz, *and later of* Meretz, *and a Knesset member from 1974 to 1996, she was Minister of Education and Sport in the Rabin government.*

"The Israeli woman and the feminist commitment" by Erella Shadmi

Within a society dominated by militarism, nationalism and religious fundamentalism, the Israeli woman occupies a traditionally inferior position. In spite of some progress on important women's issues, the general racial and gender structure of the state remains almost untouched. While in the writer's view, the achievements of Israeli feminism have been constrained by its largely elitist, *Ashkenazi* and middle-class character, she suggests that new trends in the movement can make a specific radical contribution to the Israeli left.

Dr. Shadmi, a feminist and peace activist, teaches feminist studies and the sociology of policing. A former Lieutenant-Colonel in the Israeli police, she has written books and articles on Ashkenazi identity, feminism, lesbianism and policing.

"The Mizrahim: challenging the ethos of the melting pot" by Henrietta Dahan-Kalev

Before and after 1948, the Euro-centered institutions of Zionism and Israel were discriminatory toward the *Mizrahim* (Eastern, Oriental, also called *Sephardi* Jews), as well as to non-Jewish "minorities", particularly the Palestinian Israelis (and non-Jewish immigrants from the former USSR). The writer refers to the mythical ethos of the "melting pot", to what she sees as a forced process of "Ashkenization", and to the demand for the legitimization of the *Mizrahi* narrative.

Dr. Dahan-Kalev is a sociologist who heads the Gender Study Program at Ben-Gurion University. She has written extensively on human rights, feminism and Mizrahi political culture.

"Jerusalem: constructive division or Spartaheid?" by Menahem Klein

For the writer, who was one of the initiators of the Geneva Accords, the question is not whether, but how, Jerusalem will be divided. Noting that since 1967 the Palestinians in a so-called "united Jerusalem" have been denied both sovereignty and equality, he proposes that the Israelis and the Palestinians agree on a two-state solution with their capitals in Jerusalem. Favoring President Clinton's principle that what is Arab is Palestinian and what is Jewish is Israeli, he warns that the final course of the separation fence ("enveloping Jerusalem") will decisively affect the future of the city.

Dr. Klein is a senior lecturer in the Department of Political Science at Bar-Ilan University and a senior research fellow at the Jerusalem Institute for Israel Studies. An international expert on Jerusalem, his last book was The Jerusalem Problem: the struggle for permanent status.

1

Introduction:
Radical Alternatives

DAN LEON

Any attempt to answer the question raised in the title of this book must tackle at least two questions: the first is *Who is left* in Israel in the sense that they were either born or came, and remained, here; the second question is *Who and what is the Israeli left* today, and what does it have to say for itself concerning its past and its future.

As regards the first question, Israel's population in 2003 numbers over six and a half million, about five and half million Israeli Jews and one and a quarter million Palestinian Israelis. Looking first at the Jewish population, it is part of a world Jewish population of 13 million, with which it retains strong contact. Over 200,000 Israeli Jews are holocaust survivors (in 1997 they accounted for 40 percent of Israelis over the age of 75).[1] They are among the three million immigrants who came to Israel from East and from West since it declared its independence in 1948. The Jewish population of Israel then stood at 650,000 but in its first two decades a million and a quarter newcomers arrived, doubling the population. The last decade of the twentieth century saw the immigration, among others, of nearly a million Jews from the former USSR. Today, 67 percent of Israeli Jews are Israel-born. Many Jews also left Israel: 760,000 ex-Israelis are today living abroad, including 160,000 children. Some 60 percent are in North America, 25 percent in Europe.[2] During the last decade, 270,000 Israelis left the country, including 68,000 (7 percent) of new immigrants from the former USSR.[3]

Israel's Palestinian population is composed of the 160,000 who remained in the country and their descendants, after the majority of their people, which had numbered 900,000, left or were forcibly expelled from the country before and during the 1948 war. This period is known in the Palestinian narrative as the *Nakba,* the collective tragedy of the Palestinian people.[4] Palestinians who were part of that exodus were not allowed to return to Israel after the war and became refugees. Of those who remained, As'ad Ghanem points out that the Palestinian Israelis constitute some 17 percent of the Israeli population and the same percentage of the Palestinian people, of which it is an indivisible part. Although the Palestinian Arab minority has Israeli citizenship, this was and is a minority suffering from widespread discrimination.

Radical alternatives

What, then, is the left today? The sub-title of the book provides an answer, since it speaks of "*radical* political alternatives for the future of Israel". A dictionary defines "radical" as "rapid and sweeping changes". But such a definition distances us from the terminology generally used in the Israel media about the political struggle between the "right", namely the *Likud* and its allies, and the "left" meaning the Labor party and its allies. Throughout his article, Lev Grinberg puts the word "left" in quotes, explaining how he sees the new socio-political agenda which the Israeli left must adopt if it is to constitute an authentic alternative to the present regime. He concludes by noting that "only when this *radical* change takes place . . . will we be able to speak not of the 'left' but of the left, without the quotes".

While it is fair enough to call Israelis "hawks" and "doves, the "doves" are not necessarily leftists. For example, in this writer's opinion however one evaluates the long political career of Labor leader Shimon Peres, he cannot be considered a leftist; here I would imagine that most of our writers would agree. However, knowing who is *not* left doesn't answer the question of who *is.* Almost all the contributors wrote their chapters specifically for this volume, but without coordination or consultation with each other. In general, be they from academia, journalism or the political world, I see them as having four things in common: they are experts in their subjects; they consider themselves as leftists; they are not writing brief off-the-cuff newspaper pieces but approach their subjects in depth; and in Israel as a whole, they unquestionably constitute a minority group

Even so, I am not sure that, though the writers share many common principles, a reading of the whole book will provide a complete and satisfactory answer to the question of who is left. There is no "party line" here, no overall uniformity, and there seems to be no agreed model to follow. For example, in so far as for years the kibbutz was frequently considered to be a model, at the beginning of the twenty-first century this is no longer so. However one evaluates the importance of its struggle for survival today, the kibbutz movement is rarely referred to by the contributors as an influential factor in the Israeli left. This in itself can provide much food for thought.

The fifteen chapters herein illustrate a high degree of diversity, providing guidelines, but nothing like a "party platform". One contributor has, I believe, spoken for the others when he wrote that he is dealing with ideological streams rather than with political parties. Without attempting to gloss over the difficulties, in their own way, (and the ways differ) the contributors strive to analyze their subjects – which cover the most pressing political, social and economic questions facing Israeli society today – and to map out *radical* responses. Whether the pluralistic approach is an advantage or disadvantage in the structure of the book is up to the reader to decide.

Patriots and traitors

The Israeli establishment has been arguing for decades that its policies are dictated by a "no alternative" situation in the region and at home for "security" reasons. They speak as if in the relations between Israel and the Palestinian people, 36 years of occupation and dispossession were inevitable; or as if there was no alternative to today's staggering socio-economic gaps in Israeli society. The chapters that follow set out to dismantle these claims and prove that alternatives existed in the past and exist today.

Super-patriots from the "my country right or wrong" school of thought (including, rather ironically, some Jews living abroad) will not be happy with "Who's *Left* in Israel?" and its expressions of dissent from the mainstream consensus. At the end of 2003, twenty-seven IDF Air Force pilots refused to carry out what they called the "illegal and immoral bombing of innocent civilians" in the territories since "the occupation is corrupting all of Israeli society and fatally harming the security of the State of Israel and its moral strength". They were accused of being "unpatriotic". Prior, in January 2002, a call not to fight beyond Israel's 1967 borders had been signed by 200 IDF soldiers and officers who called their movement "The Courage to Refuse". These refuseniks, like their predecessors in the *Yesh Gvul* ("there is a limit") movement, founded in 1982 during the Lebanon war, were also accused of being "unpatriotic". At the end of 2003 a national religious *Knesset* member publicly accused the initiators of the proposed Israeli–Palestinan peace agreement (the Geneva Accords) of treason (no less!) and demanded that they be tried and sentenced accordingly. Pondering over questions of dissent and patriotism, many may agree with what the great British writer George Bernard Shaw (who in today's terminology would surely be called a leftist!) wrote in 1919: *"All great truths begin as blasphemies."*

Reconciling two claims

Much of any leftist discourse inevitably deals with Israel–Arab conflict. As we note not all "doves" are leftists. One of the outstanding examples is Prof. Martin Buber (1876–1965), the world famous philosopher of dialogue. In a letter sent in February 1939 to the Indian leader Mahatma Gandhi, Buber, who had just come from Germany at the age of sixty to live in Palestine, replied to Gandhi's opinion that "Palestine belongs to the Arabs . . . why should the Jews not, like other peoples of the earth, make their homes where they were born and earn their livelihood"? Gandhi urged Jews "to claim Germany as their home" and follow the example of civil resistance.

Refuting this argumentation in his letter to Gandhi, whose voice he "knew and honored", Buber concentrated on expressing the basic world outlook of Jewish peace lovers. Jews and Arabs, he wrote, "must develop the land together without one imposing his will on the other. We consider it a fundamental point that in this case two vital claims are opposed to each other, two claims of a different nature and a different origin, which cannot be pitted one against the other and between which no objective decision can be made as to which is just and which is unjust. We consider it. our duty to understand and to honor the claim which is opposed to ours and to endeavor to reconcile both claims. We are convinced that it must be possible to find some form of agreement between this claim and the other; for we love this country and believe in its future; and seeing that such love and faith are surely present on the other side, a union in the common service of the land must be within the range of the possible".

I refer to Buber because, though this is not a history book, most of the chapters naturally emphasize the historical setting, without which one cannot focus on contemporary subjects and problems. Buber, in writing an introduction to a book about the Jewish–Arab conflict in 1970,[5] had this to say about past, present and future: *"History is written not to recall the past nor for the future, but essentially for the present, so that members of the present generation might learn its lessons"*.

It is in this spirit that we present this book, which is of the left but not only for the left. It is my sincere hope that the arguments and issues set out may contribute to a better understanding of the past, the present and the future of the Israeli left in the struggle for peace and justice.

Notes

1   *Yedioth Ahronoth*, June 3, 2000.
2   *Yedioth Ahronoth*, November 11, 2003. Figures from the Israel Ministry of Absorption.
3   Central Bureau of Statistics figures. See *Ha'aretz*, January 22, 2004.
4   See, for example "Narratives of Exile" by Salim Tamari in *Palestine–Israel Journal*, 9, 4 (2002).
5   Aharon Cohen, *Israel and the Arab World* (New York: Funk & Wagnalls, 1990).

Israel, Jews, Palestinians

2   A Land Without a People . . .

URI AVNERY

No one can shake off his shadow – as long as there is light. The more light, the darker the shadow. The shadow attached to the Zionist movement is the Palestinian resistance. It has been there – almost – from the very beginning. Almost – because at the earliest stage Theodor Herzl was not thinking about Palestine at all. His vision was not focused on any particular territory. It was an abstract idea, floating, as it were, in space, to be realized anywhere. Herzl did not worry about any specific population living in that country. If he favored any country at all, it was Argentina. At the time, he noted in his diary that the local population in the land chosen for the Jewish state would be induced to leave – but only after they had first eradicated all wild animals.

When in 1896 Herzl wrote his epoch-making work *Der Judenstaat* ("The state of the Jews"), which dealt with the future state in the minutest detail, such as the colors of the flag and the length of the working day, he referred to Palestine only once, in a short chapter entitled "Palestine or Argentina?" He did not mention the fact that Palestine was inhabited, but his line of thought can be divined from the statement that the Jewish state would constitute "a part of the rampart of Europe against Asia . . . We would serve as an outpost of culture against barbarism." Fateful sentences, that could have been written more recently.

Herzl and Palestine

Only when Herzl finally became convinced that there was no chance of realizing his ideas in any country but Palestine, because no other territory could possibly evoke the profound emotions necessary for mobilizing the Jewish masses, did he definitively focus his thought on this country. Before that, he could not possibly think about a "Palestinian problem". Even then, he did not pay any attention to the people living here. The word "Arabs" does not appear in the book at all.

There are two explanations for this oddity. First, Herzl visited Palestine for the first (and only) time long after he wrote the book and founded the Zionist movement. Even then he came only in order to meet the German Emperor, on whose support he pinned his hopes at the time. It is obvious from his writings that he did not like Palestine. It was much too hot for him – even in November, one of the mildest months of the year. Also, he detested Jerusalem, which seemed to him dirty and foul. He had no real contact with the Arab population.

The heyday of Imperialism

At the moment of its inception, when its "genetic code" was formed, the Zionist founders had never been in Palestine and had no idea about the country and its people. The 200 or so delegates who attended the first Zionist Congress in Basle in 1897 came from all over Europe – hardly any of them had ever set foot in the Holy Land. In their imagination, Palestine was the Land of the Bible, lying empty since the Jews were expelled by the Romans some 1800 years before. But if they had been familiar with the country and known about its inhabitants, would that really have made any difference? I don't think so.

The early Zionists were Europeans, children of the nineteenth century, the heyday of Imperialism, of the White Man's Burden. For them, culture was white, history was white. Non-white people – black, brown, red or yellow – did not really count. A country inhabited by such beings could be considered empty. The Second German Reich, which Herzl intensely admired, was then engaged in a genocidal war against the "natives" of German South-West Africa (today's Namibia). Cecil Rhodes, the archetypal imperialist, was engaged in setting up British Rhodesia on the ruins of African culture. Herzl admired him so much that he tried to arrange a meeting with him. Rhodes curtly refused.

The Zionists really believed in the slogan, "A land without a people for a people without a land". Without this belief, they could not have done what they did. The slogan was attributed to the Anglo-Jewish writer Israel Zangwill. An early supporter of Herzl, he left the Zionist movement and joined the "territorialists" (who believed in searching for a suitable territory for Jewish settlement, not necessarily Palestine).

The era of nationalism

What if Herzl had not been a Viennese journalist, completely assimilated in German culture, but, say, a Jewish merchant in Damascus or Cairo, familiar with Arab culture and aspirations. Things might conceivably have developed differently. But the Zionist idea in this particular form could only have been born only in Europe and only at that particular point in time. It was the child of its time and place.

According to the official Zionist myth, every generation of Jews had been longing to return to the Land of Israel and restore the Jewish state. But this has nothing to do with reality. Jerusalem was holy for the Jews just as Mecca is for Muslims, but there was no need to live there. The Jews were not a nation in the modern sense. The very idea of a "nation" still lay in the future.

In the nineteenth century all of Europe had become a hotbed of peoples striving for national liberation – Poles and Ukrainians, Slovaks and Estonians, Greeks and Lithuanians, all were dreaming of national states of their own, not to speak of the mighty German Reich or chauvinistic France. The nation-state had come to be considered as the only natural way of life.

All of these national movements had one thing in common: they were more or less anti-Semitic. Contrary to the new nationalistic creed, Jews did not belong to one single fatherland but were dispersed all over the world, living in different countries and speaking different languages, but intimately connected to each other. They were a strange, supra-national community that aroused deep-seated suspicions and hatreds everywhere. In Poland, anti-Semitism was the very foundation of the new nationalism. In Germany, the court-preacher of the Kaiser was an outspoken anti-Semite. In France, the motherland of Jewish emancipation, the infamous Dreyfus affair caused anti-Semitic riots on the streets of Paris.

In the Czarist Empire, pogroms had become an instrument of government policy. Even in Herzl's own beloved Vienna, a center of *fin-de-siècle* European culture and intellectual ferment, a politician by the name of Karl Lueger was elected mayor on a platform of straight anti-Semitism. For Jews, conditioned by centuries of oppression to look out for the slightest signs of approaching danger, alarm bells were ringing. Of course, no one could foresee anything like the Holocaust, the industrialized genocide that was still to come. But the pogroms in Czarist Russia and the spreading anti-Semitism everywhere were alarming enough. The "Jewish Question" was on the European agenda.

Zionism was basically one of the Jewish answers to this "question". The basic message of Herzlian Zionism was: if there is no place for us

Jews in the modern nations of Europe, we must constitute a nation of our own. It was one of the last national movements to be born in Europe. When Zionism became focused on Palestine, it borrowed the emotions of Jewish Messianism, history, traditions and symbols so as to provide an emotional and ideological basis for its aspirations. The Zionists just had to transfer their past, real or reinvented, onto the new nationalistic plane.

The Arab awakening

Many of the European nationalisms were also colonialist. Not only Great Britain and France, not only Spain, but also smaller states like Belgium, Holland, and Portugal, had extensive empires overseas. It was, therefore, not entirely unprecedented for the Zionist national movement to seek to establish its national home in an Asian country, empty of (European) inhabitants.

Unfortunately for the Zionist vision, Palestine was not empty at all. At the time it had a sizable population of half a million, nine-tenths Arabs and one-tenth Jewish. Palestine was a part of the Ottoman Empire. Like the other Arab provinces of the Empire – indeed, like most countries throughout Asia and Africa – it was feeling the first stirrings of a new national awakening. European nationalism, which had given such an impetus to Zionism, had begun to affect the Arab intelligentsia, too.

While young Jewish intellectuals gathered in feverish meetings all over Central and Eastern Europe to plan their adventurous new life in Palestine, Arab officers in the Turkish army and Arab intellectuals in Beirut and Damascus were holding clandestine meetings, plotting against their Turkish masters and looking for ways to achieve Arab independence. In 1868, thirty years before the publication of Herzl's book, the Arab poet Ibrahim Yazeji, at a secret meeting of the so-called Syrian Scientific Society, uttered the stirring cry, "Arise, ye Arabs, and awake!" In 1880 revolutionary posters appeared on the walls of Beirut demanding independence for Syria (including Palestine).

Compared to the complexities of Zionism, Arab nationalism was a simple idea. There was no question of moving a people, creating a new language, organizing a new society. The Arabs were living on their own land, tilling their own soil, even when oppressed by the governors and soldiers of a corrupt colonial empire. All they had to do was to rise against the Ottoman Empire, liberate their territory and create one great Arab state or a number of Arab states. The Arab population in Palestine was part of this awakening.

A conflict that has now lasted for five generations started with the simple – if unique – situation in which two great historic movements, both imbued with high-minded ideals, were planning to implement them in the same small territory, while being practically ignorant of each other. As we have seen, the early Zionists had very hazy ideas about Palestine, the "empty" land of their imagination. But an Arab officer of the Turkish garrison in Jerusalem, a landlord in Haifa or a merchant in Jaffa – what did he know of Zionism? How could he even imagine that an obscure gathering of 200 Jews in the Casino of Basle, a town he had probably never heard of, would adopt a resolution that would profoundly change his own life and the life of his family, his town, his country and his people? The Arabs and the Jews were heading for collision.

A pictorial description of the conflict was given by the historian Isaac Deutscher. As he tells it, a person living in a building that has caught fire jumps from an upper-floor window to save his life. He lands on a passer-by and grievously injures him. Between the two a mortal enmity develops. Like all analogies, this one has its limitations. The Palestinians were no casual passer-by; they lived in the country which the Zionists claimed as their own. Yet Deutscher's story does convey the essence of the tragedy. The Jews fleeing in desperation from burning Europe thought that right was on their side, while the Palestinians who saw themselves threatened by them were equally certain that justice was on their side. Looking back, the clash between Zionism and Arab nationalism was inevitable.

The first Jewish wave of immigration (the first *Aliya*, in Zionist terms) arrived in Palestine in the early '80s of the nineteenth century, some 15 years before the publication of Herzl's book. From then on settlements expanded constantly. Generally, the settlers' organization bought the land from absentee landlords, merchants who had purchased it from the Turkish government quite recently as an investment. The Arab tenants who actually tilled the soil were driven from the land at the request of the new owners, usually with *baksheesh* (bribery).

The Jews called it "redemption of the land". For the Arabs, these were acts of brutal dispossession, which sowed the seeds of opposition and resistance. One of the very few early Zionists who actually visited Palestine was the famous essayist Asher Ginsberg, called Ahad Ha'am ("One of the People"), who was revolted by what he saw. In his prophetic essay "Truth from *Eretz Israel*" (1891), he testified that, far from Palestine being empty, "throughout the land it is difficult to find fields that are not sowed," and described the harsh treatment meted out by the settlers to the local population.

The budding Arab nationalism gained strength with the revolution of the Young Turks in 1908-9. The winds of reform were blowing across the lands of "the Sick Man of the Bosporus". Turkish nationalism replaced the tolerant Islamic ideology of the Sultans. At first the Arabs expected positive changes and demanded the de-centralization of the Empire. Instead, the Young Turks oppressed them even more. Looking for allies, some Arab nationalists made tentative approaches to the Zionists, suggesting that they make common cause against foreign rule. The Jewish representatives in Palestine and Constantinople consulted their leaders in Europe. The moribund Turkish Empire, they said, was going to break up and disappear. The Arabs would remain. Shouldn't the Zionist movement build an alliance with them?

Fateful decision

This was met by total incomprehension. After the unexpected death of Herzl in 1904, the leadership passed to the German-Jewish writer Max Nordau. Earlier, it seems, he was upset when he discovered that there were Arabs living in Palestine. As recounted by Martin Buber, Nordau was deeply shocked and ran to Herzl, exclaiming: "I did not know that! We are committing an injustice!" However, he recovered from his shock handsomely. In his address to the seventh Zionist Congress in 1905, still before the Young Turks, he said: "The Turkish government may feel itself compelled to defend its reign in Palestine, in Syria, against its subjects by armed force . . . In such a position, Turkey may be convinced that it may be important for her to have, in Palestine and Syria, a strong and well organized people which, with all respect to the rights of the inhabitants living there, will resist any attack on the authority of the Sultan and defend this authority with all its might." In other words, Nordau offered to fight for the Turkish Empire against the Arab population. It was a declaration of war against the rising Arab national movement. Hardly noticed at the time, it was a fateful decision – the fore-runner of many such decisions in days to come.

Herzl had sought an alliance with the German Kaiser, an ally of the Turks. Nordau offered his services to the Turkish Sultan. One of his successors, Chaim Weizmann, tried hard to achieve an alliance with the mighty British Empire. The underlying logic of all these efforts, which led in the 1950s to the Zionist alliances with France (and the Sinai Campaign of 1956) and still later to the alliance with the United States, was quite elementary: We are going to take over Palestine; the Arabs are bound to resist. In order to win, we need the assistance of at least one great imperial power. Such assistance will only be given by a power which views the Arab national movement as an obstacle to its own imperial interests.

This logic was confirmed when Great Britain forged an alliance with

Zionism with the publication in 1917 of the Balfour Declaration, which promised the Jews a "national home in Palestine". With the occupation of Palestine by the British army near the end of World War I, the lines of the conflict were drawn. Vladimir (Ze'ev) Jabotinsky, the most extreme Zionist leader, saw the situation most clearly. In, 1923, in his frequently quoted article "The Iron Wall", he set out the following line of thought: We are Western settlers taking over a land from its local population. The Palestinian Arabs are inevitably going to resist, as would any other native people threatened by the influx of white settlers. We cannot bribe them. Therefore, we need an iron wall to defend ourselves against the Palestinian Arabs. This must be a military force. Jabotinsky argued that this force must be a part of the British occupation army. Later he and his adherents created their own military underground army, the *Irgun*.

The Balfour Declaration, the disintegration of the Ottoman Empire and the subsequent upheavals in the region brought with them a historical development: the birth of a distinctive Palestinian national movement. Until then, the separate national identity of the Arab population of Palestine was not clearly defined. When the Muslim Arabs conquered Palestine thirteen centuries ago, they created two "*junds*" (military districts): Filastin (Palestine) and Urdun (Jordan), dividing the country on both sides of the Jordan River from east to west (instead of from north to south, as now). But in Arab consciousness, Palestine was a part of Syria, and the inhabitants of Palestine considered themselves Southern Syrians.

The British gave the country a new identity. It was now officially called "Palestine" in English, "Filastin" in Arabic and "Palestina" in Hebrew (EIY = *Eretz Israel*). Also, the fact that the Arabs in Palestine alone were directly threatened by the Zionist aspirations distinguished them from Arabs elsewhere. Therefore, perhaps for the first time in their history the Palestinians saw themselves as a distinct national entity, albeit within the greater Arab community, as a people with their own destiny. A distinctive Palestinian flag – black, white and green, with a red triangle – started to appear at anti-Zionist demonstrations.

Jews, and later Israelis, could not accept the idea that a Palestinian people did actually exist. Until recently, they denied it fervently. "There is no such thing as a Palestinian people!" Golda Meir insisted as recently as the 1970s. Why? If a Palestinian people existed, then Palestine could not have been a "land without a people", as claimed by the founders of Zionism. It would mean that Zionism had displaced another people, that it was based on a historical injustice. This was quite intolerable. Therefore, denial became a center of Zionist self-consciousness, an act of faith, a near-religious dogma. It had to shake off the ghost of the "Palestinian problem" that shadowed it relentlessly.

A growing gap

Zionism demanded from its early pioneers a level of self-sacrifice that could be inspired only by an unquestioning faith. Spoiled youngsters went to Palestinem and there worked twelve back-breaking hours a day in the burning sun on hunger rations, speaking a new language, giving up all privacy in a kibbutz. Like monks and nuns in a monastery, they needed an intense belief in the absolute justice of their cause. They could not *see* Arabs, they could not *perceive* their cause, they had to *deny* their very existence.

This explains the growing gap between the perceptions of the two peoples, which made any understanding between them impossible. For example, Zionist idealism demanded the creation of a new society, built on labor. In Europe, Jews had been merchants, money-lenders and speculators. In their old-new country, they would be workers and peasants. The upside-down social pyramid would be righted, a people of "parasites" would become productive again. In its fanatical negation of Jewish existence in Europe, Zionism had obviously unconsciously absorbed many of the anti-Semitic notions of the European nationalists.

To make this revolution possible, places of work had to be found. For this worthy end, Arabs were evicted from the orange groves now owned by Jews, often by force. The slogan "Hebrew Labor" became a national and social dogma. Jews employing Arabs were considered traitors and sometimes punished. The more "socialist" a Zionist was, the more he believed in Hebrew Labor. The trade union organization, the *Histadrut*, later a powerful national body, did not admit Arabs. It was officially called "The General Organization of the Hebrew Workers in *Eretz Israel*" and considered itself a central instrument for the realization of Zionism.

To the Arabs, of course, things looked quite different. The Zionists were intent on creating an exclusively Jewish economy; they drove the Arabs from their places of work and deprived them of their livelihood, expelling them from the land they had tilled for generations. What for the Zionists was a struggle for an ideal society appeared to the Arabs as discrimination and oppression by foreign invaders. The same was true for all other aspects of life in British-governed Palestine between the two world wars, when a fast-growing Jewish community was faced with an Arab population that resisted with growing violence.

In all these struggles, the Zionist left was generally more nationalistic than the right. Capitalists and orange grove owners, looking for cheap and efficient workers, generally preferred Arabs and were less strident nationalists. The left was far more extreme. The kibbutzim, a unique Zionist experiment based on the dream of a perfect social order, were acclaimed the world over as the very embodiment of social idealism. But the kibbutzim saw themselves first of all as national bulwarks and military outposts; no Arab was ever admitted to a kibbutz, even when he married a kibbutz member. The first *Aliyah* at the end of the nineteenth century, composed of private Yiddish-speaking colonists, was less nationalistic than the socialist, Hebrew-speaking "pioneers" of the second *Aliyah* at the beginning of the twentieth century.

Phases of conflict

The clash between the two great movements can be described as the meeting of an irresistible force with an immovable object. The "genetic code" of Zionism drives it, consciously or unconsciously, toward the goal of establishing a Jewish state in all of historic *Eretz Yisrael*, at least up to the Jordan river, leaving as few non-Jews as possible there. The "genetic code" of the Palestinian national movement commands it to resist and achieve national independence in all of Palestine or, at least, in as large a part as possible.

Since the very beginning, this struggle has never ceased, but it has undergone changes and can be divided into several distinct phases. Roughly the following phases can be identified:

1 The first stirrings of the conflict, before World War I.
2 The beginning of the armed conflict, between the two world wars, when growing Arab resistance found its expression in sporadic violent outbreaks, while the Jews built up a solid state-within-a-state (called in Hebrew "the-state-on-its-way") with all the structures of a real state.
3 The 1947 United Nations partition resolution and the ensuing war of 1948, during which the State of Israel came into being.
4 The creation of a solid political, economic, military and demographic base for Israel as a Jewish state.
5 The 1967 war and the occupation of all of Palestine by Israel, the setting up of settlements and the outbreak of the first *Intifada* (1987).
6 The Oslo agreement (1993), the so-called peace process and the outbreak of the second *Intifada*.

Throughout the struggle, the Zionist drive to use any opportunity for the acquisition of land has gathered momentum and is today stronger than ever, as is the Palestinian resolution to resist this drive by any available means.

One event of historic magnitude has had an overwhelming impact on this struggle: the Holocaust. Before it, Zionism was a dynamic movement of minor proportions; after it, it became the dominant force among the Jews. The Western world, moved by remorse and guilt, supported the establishment of the State of Israel, in total disregard of the disastrous effect on the Palestinians, most of whom became refugees in the Israeli–Palestinian war of 1948.

If the Palestinians had had to confront any other people but the Jews, they probably would have attracted world-wide sympathy, like the blacks of South Africa struggling against racism. On the other hand, because one of the protagonists of this conflict was the Jewish people, whose every move aroused centuries-old memories and emotions throughout the Christian world, the fact that their enemies were Jews made it easier for the Palestinians to keep their struggle in the center of the world agenda.

The role of the Israeli left, as it is called, must be judged in this context. Apart from a small minority, it defines itself as the "Zionist left" and is an integral part of the historical Zionist enterprise. There were exceptions, Zionists like Martin Buber and Hashomer Hatzair who strove for Jewish-Arab co-operation and a bi-national state. Such voices went largely unheard. The "mainstream" left was in control of the Zionist movement and the State of Israel up to 1977 (and on and off since then), has led most of Israel's wars, and when in power was more active than the Zionist right in the acquisition of land and the creation of settlements. Between the two world wars, the "practical Zionism" of the left ridiculed the more "political" Zionism of the right as empty talk.

Confronting the truth

The Israeli–Palestinian conflict is unique. Its uniqueness stems from the quite extraordinary circumstances that brought it about. Therefore, it is futile and even dangerous to identify it with other conflicts, because such analogies induce misleading conclusions. It has similarities with colonial regimes, but it is far more than just another colonial enterprise. Some of its aspects resemble the apartheid regime in South Africa, but these similarities are superficial, owing to the vastly different origins of the conflict.

Both Israelis and Palestinians seeking to analyze this conflict in the search for a solution must confront it on its own merits, see its underlying causes and the unique chain of events that led up to it. Without a clear understanding of the past, beyond myths and propaganda, all attempts at a solution will fail, as they have all failed up to now. A major step toward a solution is to seek such an understanding.

Is there a way out of this seemingly intractable conflict? Even in theory, the number of possible solutions is limited. A list of them might look like this:

1   Ethnic cleansing: Israel drives the Palestinians into the desert or the Palestinians throw the Jewish Israelis into the sea.
2   Apartheid: One people takes control of the whole country between the Jordan and the Mediterranean and subjugates the other one. For the foreseeable future, this could only mean Jewish domination.
3   A bi-national state: The two peoples live together in one state embracing the whole country.
4   The two-state solution: the sovereign state of Palestine will come into being alongside the State of Israel, with Jerusalem as a shared capital.

The first solution is both immoral and impossible. In any imaginable future, the huge advantage of Israel in almost all fields – economic, technological, military, etc. – would make a Palestinian dream of "throwing the Jews into the sea" unrealizable. In Israel, there are politicians and even political parties openly advocating the expulsion of all Palestinians from Palestine (code-name transfer), completing what was begun in 1948. Small-scale ethnic cleansing is already going on all the time. However, the obstacles to a wholesale expulsion, both political and psychological, are immense. In any case, it would not put an end to the conflict. It would just change the battlefield and intensify the battle. The presence of eight million Palestinian refugees in the region, a number that doubles with natural increase every 18 years, would cause a revolution in the Arab world, with unforeseeable and possibly catastrophic consequences.

The apartheid "solution" is more practical. Actually, it is already being practiced to some extent in the occupied Palestinian territories. Ariel Sharon has indicated that his aim is the creation of a number of Palestinian enclaves on some fifty percent of the West Bank, each one surrounded by Israeli settlers and military forces and cut off from the neighboring enclaves. The building of the so-called "separation fence" (more correctly "wall") is a most dangerous step in that direction. Sharon is even ready to call this caricature a Palestinian state. This, of course, is no solution at all. It is a continuation of the occupation by other means. It will intensify the conflict, rather then putting an end to it. It has no more chance of survival than the original Bantustan in South Africa.

The bi-national solution has lately gained support in some small circles of the extreme Israeli left. It means that the Israelis dismantle the State of

Israel and that the Palestinians give up their hope of founding a state of their own. Instead, Israelis and Palestinians will live side by side in one common state, adopt a joint constitution, obey the same laws, pay the same taxes, serve in the same army, man the same police force.

After a conflict that has been going on for 120 years, into which a fifth generation has already been born, a situation of total hostility would have to turn overnight into a state of total reconciliation. It needs an act of faith to believe that this is possible in the present or next generation. The bi-national project is not only an idealistic dream, completely detached from reality – it is also dangerous. By presenting the situation created by the occupation as "irreversible", the advocates of bi-nationalism (unwittingly) fortify the settlements, justify the ongoing immense investment in them and sabotage any movement for their evacuation. They also tell the Israeli public that peace is possible only if they agree to the destruction of their state. It will push 99 percent of Israelis (and Jews generally) into the arms of the settlers and other extreme rightists.

In the past decades, many multi-national and bi-national states have broken apart (The Soviet Union, Yugoslavia, Czechoslovakia, Cyprus, to mention a few). States harboring different populations for centuries (Belgium, Canada) live in unease, constantly faced with the danger of break-up. Switzerland, which has maintained its bi-national nature, is a special case, its structure having evolved over centuries.

Around the two-state solution a world-wide consensus has formed. It is the solution adopted by the Quartet of the UN, the United States, Europe and Russia. This is quite astonishing, considering that 50 years ago, when a few Israelis and Palestinians (including myself) raised this flag, only a handful of people in Israel and around the world saluted. This solution takes into account that among Jewish Israelis, there is absolutely no inclination to abolish their state. After the Holocaust, the vision of a state where Jews will be secure and be masters of their own destiny has become overwhelming. There are no signs that this urge has been weakened, rather the opposite. If they had to choose between peace and the existence of Israel, peace would lose. Fortunately, peace and the existence of Israel are not incompatible.

On the Palestinian side, the overwhelming desire is for a national state of their own, like all other states. During the late 1960s there was some talk of a "democratic non-sectarian state, where Muslims, Christians and Jews will live together" (note the purely religious definition), but it was widely accepted that this was but a euphemism for dismantling the hated Israeli state. Except for Islamic fundamentalists and, perhaps, some intellectual leftist circles, the decisive majority in Arab Palestine wants the same as the decisive majority in Israel: a state of their own.

This does not mean that the negative deeds of Zionism and Israel should be excused or condoned, nor that the acts of violence by both sides should be forgotten. But it does mean that in a situation of peace, the narratives of both sides can be seen in a new, more objective light and that a true dialogue about the past can develop. Two independent states living side by side in a small country will necessarily create joint structures. Like Germany and France after centuries of wars and conflict, they will, hopefully, find ways to cooperate within the framework of new economic and political structures. The European Union does not compel the dissolution of its member-states, or do away with their national flags. It is a free association of nation-states, moving toward growing integration. The two-state solution, which should receive the full support of the Israeli left, can perhaps be followed later by the creation of a regional union. This may not be an ideal vision. But it is the only realistic one and its great advantage is that it can be achieved in the foreseeable future.

The Palestinian Arab Minority in Israel

AS'AD GHANEM

A growing feeling that we are approaching a decisive watershed grips all those involved in the Israeli–Palestinian conflict. This is a period that is apt to witness far-reaching changes in the structure and distribution of power in the Middle East. Some four decades after the reorganization of the Palestinian national movement in the form of the PLO, it expects to achieve a state in the West Bank and Gaza Strip, although the boundaries and territorial scope of this solution remain unclear.

Among the many questions we face are the following. Do we truly stand on the threshold of a fair and lasting solution? Or will there be a continuation of the Israeli domination of the Palestinians in the West Bank and Gaza Strip by means of Palestinian collaborators? Can such a solution cope with the Palestinian problem in its totality, as it developed after the expulsion of the Palestinians in the 1948 war, or only with the outcome of the 1967 war? Will the refugee problems be resolved in this solution? What will be the fate of Jerusalem and what is the future of the settlers and settlements in the West Bank and Gaza Strip? Is the ascendant Israeli right-wing prepared to tackle such fundamental problems?

Intertwined with these issues is the future of the Palestinians in Israel. This is a minority group twice over – about 17 percent of the Palestinian people on the one hand and the same proportion of the population of Israel, on the other. Its problems, though part and parcel of the broader Palestinian–Israeli conflict, have been neglected because of the urgency of grave policy questions relating to the occupation of the West Bank and Gaza Strip and other facets of the conflict. Neither of the two main parties to the conflict, the Palestinian national movement and Israel, has placed the issue of the Palestinian minority in Israel at the top of its concerns. In trying to deal on its own with the innate contradiction of its situation, this group has managed in a number of issues to make some progress but in many others has failed to make headway.

The general sense among its members is one of neglect, omission from the regional agenda, and its own failure to score major achievements in the minds of Israelis, the Palestinians in general, and the world at large. The major rise in the politicization of the Palestinians in Israel during the last three decades has not been translated into effective operating methods or significant accomplishments.

Minority and majority

The case of the Palestinian Arab minority in Israel is that of a non-dominant national minority group in an ethnic state with an ethnocratic regime; that is, a state that offers a national home to one ethnic group among those that compose its society and systematically discriminates against the other groups. In such a regime, the majority uses its control of the various systems of the state to deprive the minority of individual and group equality.

The literature offers many examples of minorities in ethnocracies that offered "partial democracy" to the minority while preserving the supremacy of the majority group. In Northern Ireland there was a confrontation from 1922 until the start of "The Troubles" in 1970 between the dominant Protestant majority, and the Catholic minority, under the auspices of the autonomous Northern Ireland government. The Catholics waged a parliamentary and extra-parliamentary struggle for their individual and group equality, which eventually overflowed into violence. A counter-reaction by the Protestant majority put an end to the political system that existed until 1970. Currently a dialogue is being conducted between the parties, with the support of the governments of the United Kingdom and the Irish Republic, and under the auspices of the United States, in the hope of restoring order and solving the intergroup problem there.

In Canada, the Anglos dominated the Francophones ever since the British merged the provinces of Canada into a single federal state in 1867. Aspiring for equality through independence or self-rule within Canada, the French Canadians have conducted a protracted struggle, parliamentary and extra parliamentary, which sometimes became violent. The recent relaxation of tensions engendered a debate between independence for French-speaking Québec, and remaining in Canada with substantial autonomy and individual and group equality for the French *vis-à-vis* the Anglo majority. Similar ethnocratic regimes can be found today in Estonia, Latvia, Lithuania, Romania, Turkey, Malaysia, and elsewhere.

Under ethnocratic regimes, minorities can, in principle, experience gradual or quicker change processes, usually not for the collective but for individuals: better education, the striving for westernization and for a higher standard of living, etc. All in all, individuals may be satisfied with their progress, but as a collective they cannot shape events or win a reasonable degree of self-rule.

Lacking a recognized collective national status, the minority in an ethnocratic state is powerless to influence decision-making at the country-wide level or to penetrate the political center as an equal partner. Thus it is unable to organize as a collective that can legally operate distinctive and autonomous institutions aimed at achieving its aspirations or defending its rights.

The Israeli system: ethnocracy and democracy in a context of control

In democratic regimes there are provisions for civil liberties and equality before the law, aiming at guaranteeing that a minority can campaign for its right to equality. Do arrangements or conditions permitting such guarantees for the Palestinian Arab minority exist in Israel? Or does the state's Jewish-Zionist commitment interfere with the realization of these demands?

From the perspective of its combination of democracy and ethnicity, Israel can be classified not as a democracy but as an ethnocracy. The minority is granted partial equality and a limited integration as individuals into its political and economic life. At the same time, a long-term and unchanging policy of control and surveillance guarantees the continuation of the majority's dominance and the minority's marginality. An ethnocratic regime is guided by the following principles:

- A dominant ethnic group seizes control of the mechanisms of the state.
- Ethnicity (and religion), rather than citizenship, become the key to the distribution of resources and power.
- Politics undergoes a gradual process of ethnicization, according to ethnic-based classes.
- There is a chronic lack of stability.

This is the logic shaping immigration policy since the Law of Return applies only to Jews. Land policy is founded on the "Judaization of the Galilee" and "redemption of lands" for Jews only. A petition to the High Court of Justice is needed for an Arab to live on such national land. A central role is granted to the Jewish religion. Capital and development resources flow almost exclusively to Jewish communities. Hebrew culture dominates the entire public space (the *Knesset*, courts, and media). All of these undermine the very existence of the state as a modern institution that seeks to include all its citizens.

In principle, Palestinian citizens enjoy their basic rights, such as suffrage, the right to be elected, freedom of expression, movement, and association. Israel boasts of a democratic system of government as shown by regular elections and other democratic norms. However, it lacks an essential feature of democracy, because as a state it is identified with a single and superior ethnic/national group – the Jews.

In the current demographic and political situation, the prospects for a change in the Arabs' condition are negligible. This in turn catalyzes the Arabs' rapid descent to a crisis situation or to a quest for revolutionary solutions to remedy their status. Hence the lack of stability. It is the ethnic logic that is the key tool for analyzing the Israeli regime, not the logic of civil democracy or of equality and citizenship.

Is important to remember the ethnocratic regimes can be democratized, as can be seen in Canada, Belgium, and Spain. It is a difficult and uneven process but inevitable if the goal is stability and prosperity.

The social and economic condition of the Palestinian minority in Israel

Israel exploits Basic Laws (the state has no constitution) to rule out any possibility of equality for the minority, maximizing the ethnic and limiting the democratic component. The latter, while limited, nevertheless creates a sense of normal development that deceives and confuses even members of the minority group. This results in a severe existential crisis around the questions of how the Palestinian minority relates both to the state and to the Palestinian people as a whole. Below I shall relate only to the internal dimension – the development of the Palestinian Arab minority in Israel.

Demographic expansion accompanied by economic distress: The demographic expansion of the Arab population in Israel is a crucial issue. In 2002, there were about one million Palestinians in Israel, or 18 percent of the country's population. Population growth has created large Arab communities, including fair-sized towns. Of the 112 localities in Israel with at least 5,000 residents, 41 are Arab; 15 of these have more than 10,000 inhabitants. In a number of places there is a solid bloc of Arab communities. There are even areas where the Arabs constitute an over-whelming majority (around Nazareth, in the western Galilee, around Sakhnin, in Wadi Ara, around Majd al-Kurum). There are also many Arabs living in the mixed cities.

These demographic developments have not been accompanied by adequate economic development, particularly grave in the lack of indus-trial development. Some 60 percent of Arab citizens live below the poverty line, about double the proportion in the Jewish sector. They suffer as the result of government policy from a severe and growing housing problem. Arab localities occupy the bottom rungs on Israel's socio-economic ladder and many are still not recognized by the authorities and lack basic services such as running water and electricity. The Palestinian Bedouin in the Negev, who constitute about 10 percent of all the Arabs in Israel, are subject to continual harassment by the authorities. The law does not recognize their title to their lands, and the state is attempting to concen-trate them in settlements especially designated for them, whereas Jews in the Negev can freely choose where and how to live.

Incomplete Israeli and Palestinian identity: The essence of the problem of the Arab citizens of Israel lies in the fact that they are simultaneously incomplete Israelis and incomplete Palestinians; that is, they have incom-plete Israeli and Palestinian identities. This epitomizes the problem of their collective identity.

While the Arabs of Israel are officially defined as citizens of the state, the essence of group identity lies in a sense of psychological belonging and emotional sympathy. Israel retains its Jewish-Zionist character as the state of the Jewish people, exacerbated by the amendment to the Basic Law: the *Knesset*, passed in July 1985. This states that "a list of candidates shall not participate in elections to the *Knesset* if its object or actions, expressly or by implication, include . . . negation of the existence of the State of Israel as the state of the Jewish people". This prevents the creation by the state of a liberal Israeli identity that would include the Arabs within it, like the French, English or American identities. Israeli identity includes significant elements of Judaism and the Jewish heritage, which only Jews can adopt fully and become Israelis, as did most of the Jews who immi-grated to the country since its birth. On the other hand, the Arabs cannot be Israelis in the full sense of the word.

As for the Palestinian component of their identity, until 1948 the Palestinians in Israel developed as part of the Palestinian Arab national movement. The separation from the Arab world forced on them by the results of the 1948 war created a situation which the Arabs in Israel had to develop in isolation, unable to draw directly from the vital life-cycle of the Arab world and the Palestinian national movement. The continuing hostilities and security situation worsened this separation. There are as yet no signs of change in this situation because even in the wake of Israel's peace agreements with some of the Arab states and an arrangement with the PLO, the disconnection from wider Arab and Palestinian circles is perpetuated. The Palestinian component of the identity of the Palestinians in Israel cannot be complete when the Palestinian national movement is in the process of establishing the Palestinian homeland somewhere else. The problem is not in the contradiction between two complete identities, Israeli and Palestinian, but in the incompleteness of both.

The absence of a clear concept of the Arabs' future in Israel: None of the leaders of the Israeli Arab community have ever formulated, even in general terms, a demand for recognition of the group distinctiveness of the Arabs in Israel as a national minority with its own ethnic, linguistic, cultural and ethical traditions. The practical meaning of recognition of the Palestinian Israelis as a national minority remains vague.

Problems of social structure: The clan as a primitive and traditional institution retains its power and remains the basis of the social structure among the Arabs in Israel, in spite of the key economic role of the nuclear family today. This clan structure denies the individual the space for normal development and impedes the progress of the Arab community in Israel, questioning its ability to adapt to democratic norms and behavior.

The most salient manifestation of this is the condition of Arab women as individuals subject to massive pressure; in practice they constitute a minority within the Arab minority, with weak and deficient status both in the absolute sense and relative to Jewish women in Israel.

The failure to internalize the principles of democracy: These processes of partial democratization, growth, change and discrimination have caused the Arabs in Israel to adopt an imperfectly democratic lifestyle, thinking and behavior. This has created major contradictions. Here are some of them.

Active participation in Israeli politics at the country-wide level but a limited ability to affect decision-making; a struggle for equality and integration into the Israeli system, alongside the establishment of separate Palestinian Arab national organizations; a rise in the number of "violent" incidents perpetrated by Arabs during the *Intifada*, alongside the emergence of a consensus that they must wage their struggle within the confines of Israeli law; the inability to elect an effective country-wide Arab leadership, alongside the ostensible functioning as such of the Supreme Monitoring Committe; voting in national elections on national and ideological lines, while voting in local elections on a clan basis; and participation in *Knesset* elections despite the awareness that the Arabs lack influence on the major issues on the agenda.

These contradictions attest to the practical difficulty of internalizing democracy and transforming it into an integral part of the Arabs' lives. Living in two worlds, the contradiction between the democratic and the traditional–undemocratic factors weighs heavily on the Arabs and impedes their development as a democratic group.

Cultural crisis: The acute identity crisis is associated with an intensifying crisis of cultural and social values, at least among the Israeli Palestinian elite. The 1948 war involuntarily isolated the Palestinian minority in Israel from Palestinian culture and the Arab world. Their urban centers were liquidated and the middle class and cultural elite, that would have continued to nurture Palestinian Arab culture, were uprooted. No infrastructure remained for creating and cultivating Arab culture, and channels linking it to the Arab mother culture were blocked. The first window to the Arab world was opened in 1967, with others following peace treaties with Egypt and Jordan. But the Arab world itself is beset by an existential cultural crisis. Israel, on the other hand, offers vibrant cultural institutions and a developed cultural life, but is dominated by Jewish and Zionist values. Thus, lacking contact with their own authentic roots, the Arabs can only adopt the external sheen of Israeli and Western culture.

The above difficulties (as well as many others that cannot be examined here) could even devolve into a total crisis that would encumber the Arabs of Israel in their relations both with the Jewish majority and with the Palestinian national movement. Without changes on both the Palestinian and Israeli levels, this twofold crisis could transcend its own sphere and influence developments throughout the region. The Arabs must at the same time be assured of belonging, theoretically and practically, to both worlds, the national and the civic. This can happen only in an egalitarian and binational state.

The Palestinian leadership in Israel: generations of opportunism and hypocrisy

Whereas in the 1950s and 1960s, primarily because of the military government, the Palestinians in Israel were unable to develop a strong leadership, the abolition of the military government in 1966 gradually allowed the consolidation of a collective leadership for the first time. The Committee of the Heads of Arab Local Councils, established in 1974, and the Supreme Monitoring Committee in 1982, have led the Arabs' struggle, which peaked in the late eighties with two general strikes, the Equality

Day strike of June 1987 and Peace Day in December 1987. Since then there has been a slow deterioration in the status of the Supreme Monitoring Committee. In the eyes of the public at large and even of its own members, for the past decade it has not generally served as a source of authority – to say nothing of the paralysis resulting within it from internal power struggles.

A political pluralism emerged among the Palestinians in Israel during the 1980s, with the appearance and entrenchment of the Islamic Movement, the founding of the Progressive List for Peace and the Democratic Arab Party, and other country-wide and local organizations. But instead of buttressing the stature of this more representative leadership, this pluralism caused the leadership to disintegrate through internal squabbling and bickering. Since the early 1990s, the weakened Committee has ceased to play a significant role, both for the Arabs and for the Israeli authorities.

At the same time the Arabs' participation in *Knesset* elections and the election of *Knesset* members to represent them nurtured among the Arabs themselves, among Israelis, in the Palestinian people and in the entire world, a common delusion: that the Arabs in Israel have an effective collective country-wide leadership, elected in *Knesset* elections. Since the founding of Israel, three patterns of leadership have crystallized in face of the Jewish majority and the discriminatory Jewish state.

1 The first category consists of leaders who collaborated with the Jewish Zionist enterprise. These include overt collaborators in the 1950s, 1960s and 1970s, notably the Arab *Knesset* members representing the *Mapai* satellite lists; and since the 1970s, *Knesset* members mainly in Jewish parties, who base their status on cooperation with the Jewish establishment and their ability to attract Arab voters. These leaders, who receive personal benefits as a reward for their collaboration, have occasionally achieved some limited objectives. But their dependence on the Jewish establishment excludes any autonomous agenda essentially different from that of the Jewish mother party.

2 The second category has consisted since 1948, and particularly in the 1960s and 1970s, of leaders who opposed the Jewish-Zionist enterprise and the official expressions of discrimination against the Arabs. Challenging both Israel and the Palestinian national movement, they expressed, each in their own way, a point of view about the distinctiveness of the Palestinians in Israel. This category includes the leaders of the Communist Party, the al-Ard movement of the 1960s, and the Sons of the Village, the Progressive List, and some heads of the Islamic Movement in later years.

3 The third category, consisting of pragmatic leaders of the Palestinian Israelis, first appeared when MK Abdulwahab Darawshe quit the Labor Party to found the Democratic Arab Party in 1988. Since then came an entire generation of leaders who seized control of the lives of the Palestinians in Israel and imposed their agenda, through complex and often contradictory policies. They are marked by a number of key traits.

Generally more modern, better educated and more sophisticated than the former leadership, they are better able to penetrate the Israeli system, develop personality cults and promote their own and group interests. However, they are at odds with each other and are quite unable to work together: the three Arab lists elected to the fifteenth *Knesset* had fissioned into six separate parties by the end of its term at the beginning of 2003! Next, they are unable to mobilize the public at large, or even their own supporters, for protest actions or significant political campaigns. In 2000, when the Arab *Knesset* members claimed to have played a role in mobilizing the population to protest against the activities of the Israeli government in the West Bank and Gaza Strip, they were crowning themselves with stolen laurels. No Arab party that has appeared in the last decade and none of their leaders can bring out tens of thousands for political protests.

Moreover, these leaders bear different messages for different publics. While they put to the Israelis their demand for equality in a "state of all its citizens", as members of the Israeli parliament they and their parties are funded by the Israeli *Knesset* and Israeli resources. Even the nonprofit organizations they have established are funded by international Jewish and Zionist foundations. Yet they portray themselves in the Arab world as advocates of pan-Arab principles and as representatives of independent Palestinian Israeli political bodies. They misrepresent themselves as fighters against the occupation, rather than as members of the *Knesset* who are paid by and enjoy the benefits of Israeli democracy. Also, they have played the role of mediators between the two sides in the conflict (Israel and the Palestinian Authority, Israel and Syria) despite their declared unwillingness to do so.

Finally, these leaders have enjoyed wide Israeli support, particularly in their almost daily exposure in the Israeli media, which immediately acquires high visibility in the Arab media. How can a member of the Israeli *Knesset* allow himself to preach pan-Arabism?[1] Yet this type of younger leadership, the first of whom was former MK Darawshe, appears as the exclusive representatives of the Palestinians in Israel, supplanting the other two types mentioned.

The Palestinian leadership failed to shape the collective vision of the

Arab population of Israel or to develop appropriate methods to conduct a struggle for change. This was illustrated for me as an Arab by the fact that, during the events of October 2000, when 13 Arabs and one Jew were killed, there was no organized political protest. The unrest was disorganized, lacked a vision of the future, and occasionally deteriorated into acts of vandalism. Had the leaders taken prior steps to organize the Arab population to turn out for significant demonstrations that would disturb the peace in Tel Aviv, it would have effectively combined protracted militant and conventional levels of struggle. The total failure to rally the general public to protest replaced the former successes in this area of the Communist Party, and later the Islamic Movement.

Though the struggle of the Palestinians in Israel has failed to take off because they have no collective leadership, this is not to say that the leaders bear sole responsibility for this. The decisive factor is the discriminatory Israeli policy. Nevertheless, promoting the Arabs' struggle depends on their own leaders. The chief concern of the current leaders is to be re-elected. The Arabs in Israel today lack even to a minimum degree that collective civic protest found in democracies. Recently an open discussion on this matter has begun to gather momentum, including the demand for the election, on a country-wide and general basis, of a supreme Arab organization to represent the Palestinians in Israel to the state, to the Jewish majority, to the Palestinian national movement, to other centers of the Palestinian people, and to interested international organizations.

On politics: The limits of political influence

Elections are a procedure that permit citizens to participate in shaping the present and future of the society and the state. It is plausible that if the Arabs in Israel did not have the suffrage their struggle would have to focus on attaining this right. But because the Arabs can vote, staying away from the polls on voting day does not detract from their citizenship. Voting is only one small component of citizenship. It should be a tool for influencing decision-making and for fundamentally changing the regime, as well as for determining the nature of the country-wide Arab political leadership.

To what extent has Arab participation in *Knesset* elections helped the Arabs promote their interests? To what extent have electing Arab representatives, and participating in parliamentary politics, really influenced the Israeli agenda? First, let us enumerate several basic characteristics of Arab voting in Israeli elections:

1   The deepening of the divisions. In this decade we have seen a system in which factionalism has reached the point where most Arab *Knesset* members have their own individual party and wield their mandate from day to day in total disconnection from the public mood.

2   The "no alternative" situation. The system of direct election of the prime minister, which has now been repealed, offered the Arabs in Israel a historic opportunity to compel the Israeli left to conduct a dialogue with them as equals. In both the 1996 and 1999 elections, settling for a choice between the candidates of the left and the right placed the Arabs in the situation of no alternative. For example, the Arabs did not want Shimon Peres but voted for him against Benjamin Netanyahu, did not want Barak but again voted for him by default. In 2001, the Arabs chose to stay away from the polls. Here they had a golden opportunity to run an Arab candidate for prime minister, but political factionalism and infighting destroyed their ability to do so.

3   Permanent opposition: The day after elections, the Arabs in Israel always find themselves in the parliamentary opposition. Non-Jews are strategically ruled out for participation in the senior executive echelons of the Jewish state and the Jewish sector opposes any prime minister who might take the step of including Arab parties in his coalition. Nevertheless, as we have seen, the Arabs' participation in elections supports the illusion that Israel is a democracy.

The question is whether the Arabs, though ineffective in the political system, will continue to vote, even when many elected Arab *Knesset* members are incapable of promoting Arab interests. Or should they boycott the elections, thus giving up in advance any chance of participating in an anti-rightist block to fight for a less inflexible policy *vis-à-vis* the Palestinian citizens of Israel, the Palestinian Authority, and the Palestinians in the occupied territories?

The future: binationalism as an option for Palestinians and Jews

As a native group whose identity is distinct from that of the majority, the Palestinians in Israel aspire to group equality and not merely individual parity. This is their collective mentality, which is the ethical component of their struggle. I believe the Arabs in Israel must wield, brandish, and display at every opportunity and in every place that they belong here as a group entitled to equal rights.

A number of general solutions have been proposed to resolve the question of the status of the Palestinians in Israel. Of course all the Jewish parties in Israel are satisfied with the status quo which, perhaps with cosmetic changes, guarantees Jewish hegemony. Israeli Jewish scholars have proposed improving the status of the Palestinians in Israel, including the option of *institutional autonomy* – a "privilege" granted to the minority so as to perpetuate the Jewish-Zionist character of the state (or as compensation for its continuation).[2] This idea has garnered significant attention and has even been adopted by some Palestinians in Israel as a possible solution for their collective status.

The *"state of all its citizens."* is the public name for the liberal option proposed in the 1990s that founds group relations on the development of a civic super-identity. This becomes the chief identity, while the ethnic and national identities become secondary. This concept was first proposed by leftist members of classic colonialist movements seeking a comfortable solution that would assuage their consciences through finding a common language with the natives. They sought to persuade them to create a new basis of identity as an alternative to their ethnic and national identity. In Australia, the United States, Canada and South American states, this option was proposed on the assumption that the native minority will agree to subordinate their original ethnic or national identity to the new civic identity, in exchange for the colonialist majority's willingness to entertain the idea of universal equality.

In Israel, the concept of creating a state of its citizens arose among Israeli leftists, both Zionist and non-Zionist (along with one or two Palestinians) when there was a widespread notion in the early 1980s that the Palestinian–Israeli conflict was now on the way to its ultimate solution. This option posits a willingness by the Palestinians in Israel to accept their own Israelization in exchange for a change in the nature of the state – in the civic direction at the expense of its Jewish-Zionist and ethnic character. Naturally, this option was acceptable to a majority in neither the Jewish nor the Palestinians sectors in Israel. The fact remains, after all, that in Israel there are two nations, one of which has realized its right to self-determination while the other is still fighting for recognition as a national movement (or part of such a movement) with its own right to self-determination, even in the context of a shared state with the Jews.

From its founding, the Sons of the Village (along with Palestinian organizations in the West Bank, the Gaza Strip, and the Palestinian Diaspora) promoted the concept of the *secular democratic state* while political Islam propose a *pan-Islamic* solution. Such ideas are not realistic, considering the balance of power between Jews and Palestinians.

They ignore the collective identity that has coalesced among Israeli Jews since the founding of Israel. I will not deal here with the Jewish right-wing proposals for *"transfer"* or *revoking the citizenship* of Palestinians in Israel.

As long as no revolutionary changes take place in Israel or in the Israeli–Arab and Jewish–Palestinian conflict, a number of fundamental characteristics dictate the boundaries of the discussion.

1 Today the Palestinians in Israel have no clearly defined status. The Palestinians in Israel have accepted their minority status and the fact that their future will be separate from that of other Palestinians. They overwhelmingly accept Israel as a political entity and an incontrovertible fact. They want to continue to be its citizens without renouncing their right to self-determination. Most of them reject the Jewish-Zionist character of the state and want to be recognized as a Palestinian national minority. Most Jews accept the presence of an Arab minority in Israel but sees the rejection of its recognition as a national minority as an existential requirement for the Jewish-Zionist character of the state. Thus both sides fundamentally accept coexistence between Jews and Palestinians in the state, but each side wants a different format for this coexistence.

2 The Palestinians in Israel are divided along a number of axes: religiously, with 80 percent Muslims, 10 percent Christians, and 10 percent Druze; geographically, with 60 percent living in the Galilee, 20 percent in the Triangle, 10 percent in the Negev, and 10 percent in the large cities along the Mediterranean coast; and by other social, political and economic divisions. Nevertheless, a majority of them, in addition to accepting their minority status, have developed a complex identity with Palestinian-national and Israeli-civic elements, which distinguishes them from the other citizens of Israel on the one hand, and from the majority of the Palestinian people on the other. They are a non-assimilated minority differing in its culture, language, social customs, and in many other aspects, from the Jewish majority. Hence there is no real possibility of their total Israelization and surrender of their national distinctiveness, while their Palestinian identity is unique within the Palestinian national movement.

3 Israel is a centralized country in which all power is wielded by institutions or bodies elected on a country-wide basis, including the *Knesset* and the government. It is through these institutions that any future decision on the Palestinian status in Israel must pass. They must rely on changing the attitudes of a critical mass of Jews, since the Palestinians in Israel are a powerless minority.

4 Because the Palestinians in Israel are opposed to the Jewish-Zionist character of the state and its fundamental objectives, and because of the history of the Jewish-Arab conflict, the Jews view them as hostile and as part of "the enemy". Any attempt by the Palestinians in Israel to modify their current status without coordination with a significant sector of the Jews will only reinforce this perception. In an era when the Zionist movement and its representatives have recognized the Palestinian national movement and the Palestinians' right to self-determination, there is room for normalizing Jewish–Arab coexistence within the Green Line (1967 borders).

A possible settlement must be based on recognition of the Palestinian Arab citizens of Israel as a national minority with collective rights and on recognition of the individual members of this collective as equal and first-class citizens. In practice, this would constitute the start of a binational Jewish–Palestinian polity within the Green Line. Ending the crisis of the Palestinian Israelis *vis-à-vis* the rest of the Palestinian people would also depend on an arrangement in which all Palestinians, including those in Israel, are represented in the institutions that represent the whole Palestinian people.

All of this depends, I believe, on the existence of an independent Palestinian state alongside Israel and the success of peace accords between Israel and the PLO. A failure on this front would reopen the possibility of other future scenarios affecting the status of the Palestinians in Israel. It could lead to a rethinking among the Palestinians in general and among the Palestinian citizens of Israel in the direction of a binational option in the entire territory of Palestine/*Eretz Israel*. In such a settlement the Palestinians in Israel would be equal citizens and be part of the Palestinian national group that would crystallize as part of the binational option in the entire territory.[3]

Conclusion

Three main political major events have occurred during 2003 that influence the Palestinian minority. The first is the detention of the leaders of the Islamic movement, the second is the Or Commission report on the tragic events of the year 2000, and the third is the municipal elections as a means for choosing the leaders of the local community. It is clear that the Palestinian minority is handicapped and unable to crystallize a proper reaction, both at the public and at the leadership level, to such events.

For the Palestinian minority in Israel, politics must be a tool to advance its interests both at home and in the international community, including those that protect human rights in general and minority rights in particular. Yet there is no substitute for the organization of the Palestinians in Israel as a national group with unified objectives and employing moderate means to achieve them, while preserving pluralism and open internal debate. The organization of Palestinian society is currently the only important task of the political leadership, whose past record leaves so much to be desired. Only when the minority is politically organized – and not merely in nonprofit organizations and voluntary associations that are controlled by interest groups and extend preference to their founders and directors – will it be possible to begin progress on the long road toward achieving normalcy for the native group in its homeland.

The first step must be to elect a supreme representative body, chosen directly by the Palestinians in Israel, and not indirectly through local government or *Knesset* elections. Such a body, composed of a small number of members (no more than 15 and perhaps fewer), would be an appropriate forum to help shape a clear perspective on the future status it wants to achieve, and on mobilizing the Palestinian public for such a campaign.

Major modifications are imperative in the internal structure of Arab society. Such a "quiet revolution" must involve changes in the status of women, the economy, education, local government and culture, where the present level of performance is inappropriate for a group in the twenty-first century. This stands in stark contrast to the achievements of Jewish society, the reference group for the Palestinians in Israel.

In addition to being discriminated against by the establishment, in many aspects of Palestinian society internal factors like the disgraceful administration of local government, prevent change and progress. We must stop arguing that the Israeli establishment is the sole impediment to such changes. Palestinian Arabs must also look in the mirror and have the courage to face up to the reality and deal with the inadequacies that exist within our own society.

Notes

1 A significant number of the representatives of the Israeli and Arab media, with representatives in Jerusalem or Ramallah, complain bitterly about the number of calls they receive from leaders of this type to interview them, or not to interview other spokespeople of the Palestinians in Israel.

2 See, Sarah Ozacky-Lazar, As'ad Ghanem and Ilan Pappe (eds.), *Theoretical Options for the Future of the Arabs in Israel* (Givat Haviva, The Institute for Peace Research, 1999 [Hebrew]).

3 See, "The Bi-national Idea in Palestine and Israel: Historical Roots and Contemporary Debate 2002" by As'ad Ghanem in *The Holy Land Studies Journal* 1/1.

4

Israeli Colonialism under the Guise of a Peace Process, 1993–2000

AMIRA HASS

There are many who regarded the 1990s as the decade of the Israeli–Palestinian "peace process". This period witnessed the Madrid conference of 1991, the Oslo "Declaration of Principles" of 1993, and the Oslo-related negotiations and accords between 1994 amd 2000. But at the same time, as many (even on the right) were speaking of a "Palestinian state" as "the solution to the conflict", the physical area available for the proposed state was being consistently whittled down. The policy of accelerated Jewish settlement and expansion resulted both in a reduction of the available area on the ground and in its fragmentation into enclaves separated from each other. Thus the main achievement of the Jewish colonization project in the Palestinian territories conquered in 1967 occurred precisely when many people assumed that there would be a complete halt to building settlements as a prelude to their evacuation.

In this decade of the "peace process", the number of settlers in the West Bank, including East Jerusalem, and in the Gaza Strip, increased by over 50 percent, reaching about 380,000.[1] Moreover, in the "Oslo period" (1993–2000) both the Rabin government and its successors built a network of bypass roads, specifically aimed at connecting Israel proper to all, even the very smallest, settlements. These roads were constructed on land confiscated from Palestinian villages, leaving them cut off from each other and from their agricultural lands. Settlements, both large and small, were expanded and "thickened" by unauthorized outposts,[2] while new industrial areas were built in and near the settlements.

How Israel maintained control

On the eve of the *al-Aqsa Intifada*, some seven years after the signing of the Declaration of Principles and six years after civil responsibilities were handed over to the Palestinian Authority, the IDF continued to exercise supreme sovereignty (according to the Oslo Accords), in the Palestinian territories. Israel maintained its absolute rule, civil–administrative as well as security, over 60 percent of the West Bank (area C as defined in the second Oslo agreement), and over 20 percent of the Gaza Strip. Throughout these extensive areas, Israel retained direct authority for all building and development and for all initiatives for destruction, dispossession and discrimination.

The remaining areas – 40 percent of the West Bank and 80 percent of the Gaza Strip – were dispersed like islands marooned between the areas under direct Israeli rule. Here too during the Oslo period, Israel could and did dictate the parameters of all Palestinian development – urban, industrial and agricultural – as well as social and personal. This was implemented through various measures: absolute Israeli control over Palestinian freedom of movement, forcing their dependence on bureaucratic Israeli permits; the network of settlements and roads that physically fragmented the area under Palestinian responsibility; and the fact that the main Palestinian lands were located in area C.

As the sovereign military power, Israel retained the absolute right to determine, for example, the size of the water pipes (which had to pass through area C), which the PA tried to install in villages that were not connected to the main pipeline. Similarly, Israel retained the right to prevent the construction of schools in villages if available and suitable land for this purpose was in area C. It also continued its policy of refusing building permits to Palestinians, whilst issuing villagers with demolition orders or orders to stop building unlicensed houses. In addition Israel sometimes uprooted Palestinian trees, including ancient ones, claiming that they "encroached on state land".

In the area annexed in 1967 to Jerusalem, the process of transforming Palestinian neighborhoods and villages into slums was accelerated. Compared to areas inhabited by Jews, these densely populated Palestinian parts of Jerusalem experienced persistent discrimination in the provision of municipal services, expropriation of land for use by Jewish "neighborhoods" (settlements), and in being denied public housing and mortgage benefits.

A lost opportunity

Thus in a decade of political negotiations, the State of Israel lost a golden opportunity to demonstrate that it was able and intended to curb its colonialist characteristics, habits and impulses. For years Israelis had believed that having secured the ultimate goal of establishing the state, the next goal would be to achieve *de jure* recognition, normalization and peaceful relations in the region. However, an essential prerequisite for such normalization – ending Israeli colonialism – was not implemented.

This lost opportunity was not, however, a random event. How can one interpret this interplay in which the mother state uses its military strength and its material, economic and political superiority (with or without Divine promises) to impose its rule over a conquered territory, over a people that has lived in this land for generations? How can one explain a state that settles its own people on a piece of land, which it exploits and develops for its own benefit, while constantly dispossessing the original population, thus creating a reality of legalized discrimination based on ethnicity?

There is no need to rely on "radical" researchers for an answer. Ran Aaronsohn, of the Hebrew University of Jerusalem's Geography Department, participated in a discussion on whether Zionist settlement before 1948 can be categorized as colonialism.[3] Noting the distinction between "colonialism" and "colonization", he outlined the main features of colonialism. According to Aaronsohn:

> Not only did the outstanding characteristics of colonialism (conquest, economic exploitation and control over the centers of power) not exist at all at the beginning of the Zionist activity in the country, there were very few characteristics of an exploiting-settlement. Such exploiting-settlement rests upon privileges granted by the authorities, and at the center of the settlers' actions and their supporters' is the exploitation of human and nature resources for financial profit . . . To my mind, the kernel of colonialism is the use of force and the element of exploitation, generally European (but also Japanese . . .) where a state, or sometimes its institutions, takes over external resource, both territories and people, by force, and exploits them for political, strategic and economic purposes. (Jacoby, 1999)

A colonialist act

If one applies Aaronsohn's model of colonialism to the Israeli occupation of the Palestinian territories since 1967, it is revealed as a colonialist act *par excellence*. There are those who oppose defining Zionism as a colonialist movement[4] and "interpret" or "understand" the process of Jewish settlement from 1967 to 1993 as resulting from "security and political needs". The onus is precisely upon them to explain why the colonialist project was not stopped in the decade of "peace". Alternatively, they have to explain how this project is compatible with the universal principle of the equality of all human beings.

Although this is not the place to resolve the debate on the period preceding 1948, it is clear that settlement expansion in the Oslo period is rooted in a legacy of more recent, as well as older, colonizing traditions. Some of these methods are uniquely Israeli; others are almost replicas of other colonialist endeavors. The anthropologist John Comaroff argues that classical colonialist projects are based on four main aims. First, the conquest of the land – generally justified in religious terms as "redemption" or in secular terms as "modernization". Second, the exploitation of local resources. Third, the rationalization of the administration and bureaucratic institutions in order to govern. Fourth, pacifying the local residents (the "natives") and preventing a possible uprising by creating and reproducing ethnic divisions (Comaroff, 1998). All these aims are clearly evident in the Israeli process of settlement in the Palestinian territories since 1967 in general, and in the Oslo years in particular.

1 Conquest of the land, exploitation of its resources and justification of the settlement process

Following the occupation in 1967 Israel began expropriating for its own benefit the Palestinian territories' main natural resources: land, water and quarries. It started establishing settlements (according to the Alon plan), which it justified on the grounds of "security" and with a range of legal arguments. Israel claimed that it was not dealing with a conquered territory according to international law, but with an "administered" territory, since the West Bank and the Gaza Strip had not constituted part of a sovereign state. Simultaneously, the secular and religious protagonists of a "greater Israel" added to these claims their own Messianic justification for settlement. This process of planned exploitation of land and water resources had a number of characteristics:

a) Legalistic sophistry

Israeli governments, helped by the *Gush Emunim* movement in different guises, employed a range of legal arguments and subterfuge. For example, confiscating Palestinian lands for the use of Israeli citizens was defined as confiscation for "security" purposes; a work camp for young people or

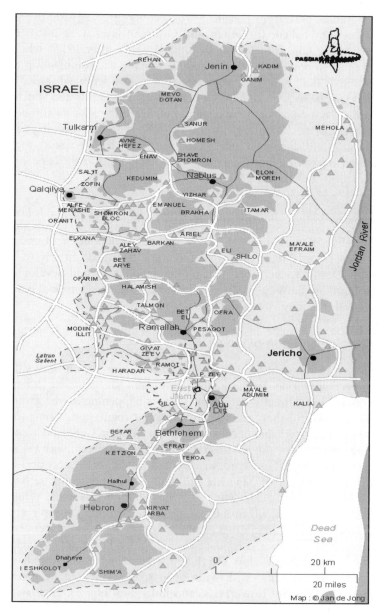

Distribution of Israeli settlements in the occupied West Bank.
Courtesy of *Passia*, Palestinian Academic Society for the Study of
International Affairs, 2001.

an archaeological site was transformed into a settlement with the help of hastily granted permits or permits retrospectively granted after the settlement was established; Jordanian and Ottoman laws were distorted to convert public land into Jewish land, particularly after 1977 (when the *Likud* came to power). In similar vein, after 1993 the colonization agencies routinely built new "neighborhoods" at a considerable distance from the settlements, to get around their commitment to the United States that they would not construct new settlements. Security roads swallowed up vast tracts of Palestinian agricultural land. So there was nothing new in the recent establishment of about 120 "outposts" by West Bank settlers, portrayed as having been carried out without the knowledge or the encouragement of the government.[5]

b) The complete identification of public land with "Jewish land"

The Israeli colonization agencies drew on the considerable experience they had gained since 1948, in denying the rights of Palestinian citizens of Israel (usually referred to as "Israeli Arabs") to land, space and development. "State land" in the West Bank and the Gaza Strip, like "national land" in Israel itself (the majority of the land), is for Jews only.

c) Planning and non-planning

In contrast to the meticulous planning of Jewish areas, on both sides of the green line, one finds a deliberate lack of planning wherever Palestinians live. Directly witnessing what is happening on the ground is far more powerful than reading any order or regulation. Compare the Palestinian Israeli villages of Mashhad or Ein Mahil in Galilee, whose land was expropriated for the Jewish town of Upper Nazareth, with the small town of Abu Dis, whose land, private and public, was expropriated to build the settlement of Ma'aleh Adumim. Or compare the settlement Neveh Dekalim with Khan Yunis on whose land it was built. Wherever Palestinians live, you will find the same overcrowding, the same greyish hotchpotch jumble of buildings, and piles of construction materials – all crammed into a restricted residential area that is constantly decreasing, and has no room to develop. On the other hand, wherever Jews live one sees generous planning, with wide open spaces enriched by greenery, squares with colorful flowerbeds, and individual houses, each with its own garden.

2 The employment or non-employment of Palestinians as a function of politics and colonization

When the Israeli labor market was opened up at the end of the 1960s to Palestinian workers, this served the capitalist interests of the Israeli economy very well. The influx of very cheap, unprotected labor helped the then failing Israeli economy to emerge from a recession. This open market did indeed improve the personal economic situation of tens of thousands of Palestinian families. However, Israel prevented any collective economic improvement for the benefit of the Palestinians within the territories it had conquered, making only minimal investment there in the infrastructure and strictly limiting industrial and agricultural development. Money paid by the Palestinians in taxes and customs was transferred to the Israeli Treasury, not invested for them as a collective in their own territory (The World Bank, 1993; Sadan, 1991).

Working in Israel (and working abroad, a trend equally encouraged by the authorities) became almost the only route for Palestinians to make a living. The result was Palestinian economic dependence on Israel. The Labor government assumed that improving the welfare of individual Palestinians would defuse popular national aspirations, whilst collective non-development would prevent the establishment of a substantial infrastructure for an independent state.

Since 1991, a new policy was introduced: closure. Palestinian unemployment and economic collapse was the inevitable outcome. Fearing a violent backlash because of the declining economic conditions, Israel did allow Palestinians in the occupied territories to develop alternative sources of income by starting new businesses where they lived. However Israeli supervision and control restricted such initiatives.

3 The civil administration

In 1981 the Israeli government established the civil administration (CA) as a separate arm of Israeli military occupation. Using Comaroff's model, this equates with the administrative "rationalization" characteristic of colonialism. The CA's self-proclaimed goal was to serve the civilian Palestinian population. In practice it helped Israel achieve two objectives: control over an occupied population in order to subjugate it; and control of its land. The CA's close ties with collaborators and with the *Shabak* (General Security Services), combined with the Palestinian people's complete dependency on the CA for all aspects of daily life (from a telephone line to medical treatment), gave it intimate and powerful knowledge about the population and its needs. The very CA officials and planning bodies that are responsible for coordinating the expansion of the settlements with the government, also examine and decide on Palestinian applications for building permits. These officials send observers and helicopters to locate every "illegal" Palestinian building and then carry out demolition orders. Moreover, many settlers are employed as officials in the CA. The CA was not dismantled after the Oslo Accords were signed.

4 Controlling freedom of movement in order to consolidate demographic separation

This involves surveillance and control, and curbing and suppressing potential or actual opposition and resistance. As already noted, Israel established the closure in January 1991, thereby subjecting all Palestinian residents of the West Bank and the Gaza Strip to a pass system, similar to the Apartheid system in South Africa.[6] There is no truth in the claim that the closure policy was introduced as a response to suicide bombings. The phenomenon of Palestinian suicide bombers in the occupied territories started in 1993 and in Israel in April 1994 (after the Hebron massacre carried out by Baruch Goldstein).

The context for the closure policy was the *cul-de-sac* of the first *Intifada* and of its suppression in 1991. The Palestinians were unable to sustain the popular uprising against the occupation and the settlements, or to convert this into an ongoing guerilla war. Israel had no intention of responding to the PLO's demand to fully withdraw from the occupied territories in order to establish a state alongside Israel and correctly assumed that the uprising would not die down. However, as the occupying force, Israel was also mindful that it was constrained by international law, and that it was responsible for the well-being of the residents under its rule. Israel thus could not allow itself to develop more extreme methods of repression in the event of the Palestinians widening the scope of their armed resistance. So it resorted to bureaucratic tactics in the form of the closure. This provided a way of calming down a possible uprising, as Comaroff put it.

Freedom of movement is both a human right and a primary "means of production" for every individual and community. It is a resource no less vital than land and water. Israel forbade the entire Palestinian population freedom of movement (between the West Bank and Gaza Strip and into Israel, and subsequently within the West Bank and the Gaza Strip). Israeli military officials both devised the categories and controlled all decisions about travel permits that were issued for specific circumstances. Over the years the closure policy was streamlined. During the Oslo negotiations closure became a way of exerting pressure on the Palestinian Authority, resulting in a kind of political and economic war of attrition. Under the closure policy, Israel alone determined the number of workers permitted into Israel, and all movement of goods, services and raw materials. Closure served as the primary tool for supervising and controlling individual movement. It also functioned as a bureaucratic technique by which the demographic separation of Jews and Palestinians living in the same territorial unit could be assured.

The system of travel restrictions culminated in the years 2002–2003 in three separate stages: First, the large cities and hundreds of Palestinian villages were cut off from each other and from the main arteries through mounds of earth, concrete slabs and military checkpoints. Soldiers manned these areas backed by tanks, patrols and the ever-greater presence of a military infrastructure. The closer the Palestinian population was to a Jewish settlement, the more tightly the roads were blocked and the more difficult it became for Palestinians to be granted permits. The movement of Palestinians on the main roads of the West Bank and the Gaza Strip was stopped or restricted to an absolute minimum. These roads were ultimately made into roads for Jews only. Israeli drivers were even forbidden to take Palestinian passengers. In other words, internal closure was intended to ensure Israel's colonialist enterprise.

In the second stage, beginning in the spring of 2002, the West Bank was divided into eight separate regions geographically separated from each other by area C. Entry to and exit from these regions is allowed only by means of special travel permits, granted to a few select applicants. The process of acquiring these permits involves a series of time-consuming bureaucratic hassles with Israeli officials in the civil administration.

The third stage involves the conception and development of the "separation fence" whose construction began in mid-2002. This so-called "security barrier" involves a system of fortifications cutting into Palestinian areas where the Israeli military has licence to shoot to prevent any Palestinian presence near the fence. (In Gaza such licence to shoot near settlements has caused the death of many Palestinians, both armed men and non armed civilians.) Between the Green line and the fence, now winding deeply into the Palestinian West Bank, a new "closed military zone" has been created. Tens of thousands of Palestinians now find themselves and their lands locked into this area, legally closed off to them but not to Jews. Recent military orders have created a new status of "permanent resident" for the vast Palestinian population living in this area (often referred to as the "seam zone"). The new orders grant the civil administration and the army, including quite a few officers from the settlements, the authority to deny certain people the right to live on their land, and to demand that they relocate on the other side of the fence. Similar measures and fences are imposed on Palestinians in Gaza, whose lands have also been invaded through the years by Israeli settlements.

The "separation fence" is therefore a tangible extension of the pass system policy. There is no real difference between the fence built beyond the Green line deep into Palestinian territory, and the fences built around the settlements proper. These are not fences separating Israel from the West Bank and the Gaza Strip. Rather, they separate Jews from Palestinians and Palestinians from each other. In this way Israel perfected the process of imprisoning Palestinians into smaller and smaller enclaves alongside prosperous Jewish settlements linked up with Israel proper. The barriers in the West Bank dividing villages from cities are gradually being replaced by a system of barbed wire fences and deep trenches, and sometimes by concrete walls. The settlers determine the route of the fence, which involves the destruction of high quality Palestinian agricultural land and water resources, and the division of tens of thousands of Palestinians from their cultivated land and from their nearby urban centers.

So it ensues that the internal closure imposed while Israel sought to suppress the second *Intifada*, as well as the "separation fence", constitute a substantial toughening of a system adopted in 1991 and upgraded from 1994 – including what we refer to as the economic "war of attrition". This is a quantitative, not a qualitative, change in the search for bureaucratic and military "solutions" to Palestinian resistance. These measures provide us with the evidence that there is no intention of changing the status quo of occupation, control and colonization.

5 Demographic manipulations

In 1948 approximately 750,000 Palestinians were expelled from Israel and prohibited from returning to their homes, while those who remained were granted citizenship. In contrast, the post-1967 occupation policies allowed the population to remain without yet granting it citizenship. Israel therefore refrained from the *de jure* annexation of most of the territory it conquered, emphasizing bureaucratic regulations and orders instead. Since 1967, these regulations have denied residency to thousands of Palestinians born in the West Bank and the Gaza Strip who happened to be out of the country in 1967. In the decade of the "peace process" Israeli occupation authorities pursued an aggressive policy of pushing out Palestinians living in area C into PA controlled areas. This was justified by the continual expropriation of land for "security" needs, by the expansion of settlements and by the paving of bypass roads.

Furthermore, in 1996 the Ministry of the Interior under Haim Ramon (Labor) instituted a policy of denying Jerusalem residency to thousands of Palestinians who had moved to the West Bank as a result of a housing shortage deliberately created by Israel. According to the Oslo Accords, Israel continued to control population registration in the PA areas restricting and preventing the return of Palestinians uprooted in 1967.

6 Ethnic and demographic separation

The contradiction between not granting citizenship and actual (but not legal) annexation of the land for the sake of exclusive Jewish settlement was solved by transforming the settlements into legal Israeli territorial enclaves. Every Israeli citizen living in a settlement was subject only to Israeli law. Law and practice have made sure that such "Israeli citizens" not be Muslim or Christian Palestinians. Only those born Jews, or, for example, Christian "new immigrants" from Russia, or converts to Judaism from Peru, could be citizens. All this was buttressed by active Israeli legislation, confirmed by the legal authorities and the Supreme Court. Two legal systems in the same area therefore emerged: a superior one for Israeli citizens and an inferior one for Palestinians. For Israelis this became accepted fact, just as for generations of South African whites racial segregation was both legal and natural.

7 Legalization

The State of Israel was established in 1948 in accordance with a United Nations resolution. This international recognition was necessary and expected given the inseparable role played by Europe in the Nazi German industry of mass murder. The prior settlement process within the 1948 borders was endorsed by the recognition of the 1949 armistice lines, followed by the UN Security Council resolution demanding that Israel withdraw from the territories conquered in 1967 (the United Nations General Assembly also demanded the return of the Palestinian refugees).[7]

Between 1967 and 1993, Israeli governments and the agencies of colonization had to rely on highly legalistic interpretations by Israeli jurists in order to explain how Jewish settlement in the Occupied Territories did not violate international law. The protagonists of colonization relied just as heavily on non-legalistic factors: on Divine promises, Israel's ever closer alliance with the United States, and on the diplomatic lull that brought about the peace agreement with Egypt.

In 1993 Israel and the PLO signed the two-party agreement known as the Oslo Accords. It was the direct result of a protracted process in which the Palestinians made clear that they would never accept subjugation within a "greater Israel". At the same time, however, the agreement that Arafat hastily signed – and which went on to become an internationally valid document – downplayed the illegality of the settlements under international law. The Oslo Accords never specifically demanded the freezing of settlement construction. Oslo II stated only that each party would refrain from taking steps that would change the status of the West Bank and the Gaza Strip "pending the outcome of the permanent status negotiations".[8]

The agreements neither specified the goal of a Palestinian state nor defined the size of that state. At the same time, however, they mentioned that the question of settlements would be discussed in the final status negotiations. In this manner the status quo was ratified, permitting Israel to devise ways to justify further settlement construction and encourage more and more Jews to go and live there.[9]

Israel maintained the status quo until 2000, taking advantage of its own military and economic superiority and neglecting to redeploy its forces according to defined schedules. Even if Israel had followed the schedules, however, the agreements failed to designate the areas to be evacuated before the final status negotiations.

The Palestinian expectation of a "retreat from 92 percent of the area on the eve of a final settlement" had no chance of succeeding owing to the huge disparity in military strength. As for the Israelis, most, including opponents of the settlements, interpreted the status quo differently. An erroneous perception of the reality was created by the closure policy, which made the Palestinian territories and their population less visible than at any time since 1967. The establishment of the Palestinian Authority under the Oslo Accords combined to reinforce this distortion. There was a widespread belief that the Israeli occupation was effectively over, if only because the PA had become responsible for civil affairs in the Palestinian-populated areas. With the outbreak of the *al-Aqsa Intifada*, the dominant misconception was that there were two almost symmetrical sovereignties: Israel and the PA. This misconception enabled the army to launch its prolonged and bloody military attacks against the civilian Palestinian population as if the latter were not Israel's responsibility as the occupying power, but rather an aggressive, politically independent entity.

In December 1999, with Ehud Barak prime minister of Israel, the Palestinian Authority attempted to suspend the final status negotiations because of the continued building of settlements.[10] Under American pressure, Barak halted the publication of tenders for settlement building for two and a half months, or until March 2000, the date when he hoped that the "framework agreement" for the final settlement would be signed. In a press conference that included then US Secretary of State Madeline Allbright, Barak was asked a question that implied his "surrender" to Palestinian pressure. He angrily replied, "[This] is our approach [which] strengthens our hold over *Eretz Yisrael* . . . and our position in the negotiations . . . (while) the position of those who say that 'now we must continue by force [with] tenders' is one which weakens the State of Israel in the struggle for control over *Eretz Yisrael*" (Hass 1999). Indeed in 2000 an eight-year record high was set in the registration of new building in the territories (Maor and Basok 2003).

In other words what lay behind the decision of a Labor prime minister to freeze building tenders for a short time was not peace, not the Palestinian rights, not international resolutions and political agreements, and not Palestinian hopes for a viable state. Rather, it was "our hold over *Eretz Yisrael*". This declaration was made in the language of the religious *Gush Emunim* settlers or in that of the secular supporters of a "greater Israel" like Yitzhak Tabenkin and the *Kibbutz Meuchad*, to which Yigal Alon, of the "Alon plan" also belonged. Yet the statement went unnoticed. Within a few days the United States compelled Arafat to resume negotiations on a final status agreement.

Thus after 1993, as the clock of a "peace" agreement" with the Palestinians ticked on, the overriding principles guiding the Israeli colonizing agencies acting on behalf of the mother country, were identical to those of the Zionist and Israeli establishment in the pre-1948 and post-1967 periods. This guiding principle was that it is the location and strength of Jewish settlement that will determine the state's final borders.

8 The sense of superiority

We have described the interplay of physical, material and legal factors in policies of Israeli development, and Palestinian dispossession, in which the Palestinian people does indeed remain in the occupied territories but with diminishing land resources. But there is an additional dimension to this physical and material supremacy: the strengthening and enhancing of feelings of "Jewish superiority" justified on religious, historical, cultural, ideological, economic and security grounds. Consciously or unconsciously, this superiority "explains" both legally and in practice, why it is "correct", "natural" and "just" to apply a clearly discriminatory policy of planned inequality. This policy is perpetuated through direct Israeli control of as much land as possible with as few Palestinians as possible, and achieved through indirect control of enclaves whose residents are forced into a third world existence. This is a self-fulfilling variant of the false slogan about "a people without a land for a land without a people". It goes without saying that a sense of ethnic superiority is an important component in the creation of colonialist societies and of their self-perception.

Notes

This essay was first written in October 2003 and published in Hebrew in *Theory and Criticism*, Vol. 24 Spring 2004.

1   Without the settlements in East Jerusalem, the number of settlements in the West Bank and the Gaza Strip was doubled: in 1991 there were 91,400 settlers, in 1993, 116,300; in 1995, 137,400; in 2000, 198,300 (from data provided by the Peace Now Movement). The figures for the settlements in East Jerusalem are as follows: 1992, 141,000; 1993, 146,800; 1995, 155,000; 2000, 173,000 (*B'Tselem, The Land Plunder: Settlement Policy in the West Bank*). While Israelis, and even members of the peace camp, accept the annexation of East Jerusalem and the construction of Jewish settlements ("neighborhoods") there, this essay does not distinguish between occupied Jerusalem and the rest of the territories occupied by Israel in 1967.

2   The false terminology in Israel about "illegal outposts" differentiates between outposts on the one hand, and on the other hand neighborhoods or settlements which received governmental confirmation either in advance or after the event. This misleading language corresponds with the spirit in which the settlements are legalized and with the policy of what is in effect annexation. However, according to international law, the occupying population cannot be settled on conquered territory.

3   For the whole discussion in book form, see Jacoby, *One land, two peoples.*

4   The following are some of the claims made by various Israeli sociologists and historians as proof that Zionism cannot be included among colonialist phenomena: the European context of anti-Semitism and the persecution of Jews, as an explanation for the growth of Zionism; the development of Zionism as a national movement striving for national liberation, the 2,000 year-old Jewish connection to *Eretz Yisrael*; the lack of a settler–colonial mother country, the fact that *Eretz Yisrael* was not a source of profit for the settlers, but rather the opposite; the fact that the settlers acquired land by agreement, the claim that the Palestinians gained from the development process and that many Arabs emigrated to the country as a result of the Zionist settlement and the claim that the settlers' breaking away from European culture negates the thesis of a "white" superiority complex. See Friling, *An answer to a Post-Zionist Colleague* and Jacoby, *One land, two peoples.*

5   In fact in many cases the location of the outposts was coordinated with the

Prime Minister's Office and the date of their establishment was coordinated with the army. See Harel, "The ties that bind".

6   The policy of closure and travel permits is reminiscent of the period of the military government in Arab areas of Israel which lasted until 1966.

7   This is a factual description of the course of events, which neither passes judgment nor justifies nor opposes. I am convinced that without the Nazi anti-Semitism, the Zionist solution would not have been transformed from a minority movement into one adopted by a majority of the Jewish people in the Diaspora. In other words, without Nazism there would not have accrued the critical mass of immigrants which pressed for the creation of the state. There would not have been the financing (reparation money) and the international support, all of which facilitated the establishment of the state and the expropriation of the people living there. Moreover all this took place in a period of anti-colonialist struggles for national liberation.

8   The Interim Agreement on the West Bank and the Gaza Strip.

9   In the opinion of the legal advisor to the Foreign Ministry, Alan Baker, the agreements improved the legal situation of the settlers, "The central claim was that they are living in the area contrary to international law which precludes the transfer of a civilian population to a conquered area. Now they are living there by agreement – by right of an international agreement which lays down that their status will be determined in the permanent settlement (Gorli, "Existing and Not Existing")".

10 In 2002 41.9 percent of the area of the West Bank, including Jerusalem, was already within the jurisdiction of the settlements and under their judicial sway. This included built-up areas, undeveloped municipal areas and land reserves outside the municipal boundaries, a total of 2,345,900 dunam out of 5,608,000 dunam of the West Bank area. (See B'Tselem, *The land grab: Settlement Policy in the West Bank.*)

References

Hebrew

Basok, Motti and Maor, Ziv 2003: "NIS 11 billion on homes". *Ha'aretz, Rosh Hashanah supplement*, September 26, 2003.

B'tselem 2003: *The land grab: Settlement Policy in the West Bank*, Jerusalem.

Friling, Tuviah (ed.) 2003: "As Answer to a Post-Zionist Colleague". *Yedioth Ahronoth.*

Goreli, Moshe 2003: "They aren't observed but they exist". *Ha'aretz*, September 11, 2003.

Harel, Amos 2003: "The ties that bind". *Rosh Hashanah supplement, Ha'aretz*, September 26, 2003.

Hass, Amira 1999: "The State of Israel against *Eretz Yisrael*". *Ha'aretz*, December 22, 1999.

Jacoby, Danny (ed.) 1999: *One Land, Two Peoples*. The Magnus Press.

English

Comaroff, John L. 1998: "Reflections on the Colonial State in South Africa and Elsewhere: Factions, Fragments, Facts, Fictions", *Social Identities* Vol. 4/3.

Sedan, Ezra 1991: A Policy for Immediate Economic-Industrial Development in the Gaza Strip (unpublished report).

The Interim Agreement on the West Bank and the Gaza Strip (Oslo 2). 28 September 1985, Chapter 5.

The World Bank 1993: "Developing the Territories and Investment in Peace". Washington, D.C.: The World Bank.

5 The End of Zionism?

AVRAHAM BURG

The Zionist revolution has always rested on two pillars: a just path and an ethical leadership. Neither of these is operative any longer. The Israeli nation today rests on a scaffolding of corruption and on foundations of oppression and injustice. As such, the end of the Zionist enterprise is already on our doorstep. There is a real chance that ours will be the last Zionist generation. There may yet be a Jewish state here, but it will be a different sort, strange and ugly.

There is time to change course, but not much. What is needed is a new vision of a just society and the political will to implement it. Nor is this merely an internal Israeli affair. Diaspora Jews for whom Israel is a central pillar of their identity must pay heed and speak out. If the pillar collapses, the upper floors will come crashing down.

A state of settlements, run by an amoral clique

The opposition does not exist and the coalition, with Arik Sharon at its head, claims the right to remain silent. In a nation of chatterboxes, everyone has suddenly fallen dumb, because there's nothing left to say. We live in a thunderously failed reality. Yes, we have revived the Hebrew language, created a marvelous theatre and strong national currency. Our Jewish minds are as sharp as ever. We are traded on the Nasdaq. But is this why we created a state? The Jewish people did not survive for two millennia in order to pioneer new weaponry, computer security programs or anti-missile missiles. We were supposed to be a light unto the nations. In this we have failed.

It turns out that the 2,000 year-old struggle for Jewish survival comes down to a state of settlements, run by an amoral clique of corrupt lawbreakers who are deaf both to their own citizens and to their enemies. A state lacking justice cannot survive. More and more Israelis are coming to understand this as they ask their children where they expect to live in 25 years. Children who are honest admit, to their parents' shock, that they do not know. The countdown to the end of Israeli society has begun.

It is very comfortable to be a Zionist in a West Bank settlement such as Beit-El or Ofra. The biblical landscape is charming. From the window you can gaze through the geraniums and bougainvilleas and not see the occupation. Traveling on the fast highway that takes you from Ramot on Jerusalem's northern edge to Giloh on the southern edge, a 12-minute trip that skirts barely half a mile west of the Palestinian roadblocks, it is hard to comprehend the humiliating experience of the despised Arab who must creep for hours along the pockmarked blockaded roads assigned to him. One road for the occupier, one road for the occupied.

This cannot work. Even if the Arabs lower their heads and swallow their shame and anger forever, it won't work. A structure built on human callousness will inevitably collapse on itself. Note this moment well: Zionism's superstructure is already collapsing like a cheap Jerusalem wedding hall. Only madmen continue dancing on the top floor while the pillars below are collapsing.

We have grown accustomed to ignoring the suffering of the women at the roadblocks. No wonder we don't hear the cries of the abused woman living next door or the single mother struggling to support her children in dignity. We don't even bother to count the women murdered by their husbands.

Israel, having ceased to care about the children of the Palestinians, should not be surprised when they come washed in hate and blow themselves up in the centers of Israeli escapism. They consign themselves to Allah in our places of recreation because their own lives are torture. They spill their own blood in our restaurants in order to ruin our appetites, because they have children and parents at home who are hungry and humiliated.

We could kill a thousand ringleaders and engineers a day and nothing will be solved, because the leaders come up from below from the wells of hated and anger, from their "infrastructure" of injustice and moral corruption.

If this were inevitable, divinely ordained and immutable, I would be silent. But things could be different, and so crying out is a moral imperative.

There is no middle path

Here is what the prime minister should say to the people: The time for illusions is over. The time for decisions has arrived. We love the entire land of our forefathers and in some other time we would have wanted to live here alone. But this will not happen. The Arabs, too, have dreams and needs.

Between the Jordan and the Mediterranean there is no longer a clear Jewish majority. And so, fellow citizens, it is not possible to keep the whole thing without paying a price. We cannot keep a Palestinian majority under an Israeli boot and at the same time think about ourselves as the only democracy in the Middle East. There cannot be democracy without equal rights for all who live here, Arab as well as Jew. We cannot keep the territories and preserve a Jewish majority in the world's only Jewish state, not by means that are humane and moral and Jewish.

Do you want the Greater Land of Israel? No problem. Abandon democracy. Let's institute an efficient system of racial separation here, with prison camps and detention villages. Qalqilya Ghetto and *Gulag* Jenin.

Do you want a Jewish majority? No problem. Either put the Arabs on railway cars, buses, camels and donkeys and expel them en masse or separate ourselves from them absolutely, without tricks and gimmicks. There is no middle path. We must remove all the settlements, all of them, and draw an internationally recognized border between the Jewish national home and the Palestinian national home. The Jewish Law of Return will apply only within our national home, and their Right of Return will only apply within the borders of the Palestinian state.

Do you want democracy? No problem. Either abandon the Greater Land of Israel, to the last settlement and outpost, or give full citizenship and voting rights to everyone, including Arabs. The result, of course, will be that those who did not want a Palestinian state alongside us will have one in our midst, via the ballot box.

That's what the prime minister should say to the people. He should present the choices forthrightly: Jewish racialism or democracy. Settlements or hope for both peoples. False visions of barbed wire, roadblocks and suicide bombers, or a recognized international border between two states and a shared capital in Jerusalem.

But there is no prime minister in Jerusalem. The disease eating away at the body of Zionism has already attacked the head. David Ben-Gurion sometimes erred, but he remained straight as an arrow. When Menahem Begin was wrong, nobody impugned his motives. No longer. Recent polls published showed that a majority of Israelis don't believe in the personal integrity of the prime minister yet they trust his political leadership. In other words, Israel's current prime minister personally embodies both halves of the curse: suspect personal morals and open disregard for the law combined with the brutality of occupation and the trampling of any chance for peace. This is our nation, these its leaders. The inescapable conclusion is that the Zionist revolution is dead.

Why then is the opposition so quiet? Perhaps because its summer, or because they are tired, or because some would like to join the government at any price, even the price of participating in the sickness. But while they dither, the forces of good lose hope.

This is the time for clear alternatives. Anyone who declines to present a clear-cut position, black or white, is in effect collaborating in the decline. It is not a matter of Labor versus *Likud* or right versus left, but of right versus wrong, acceptable versus unacceptable, the law-abiding versus the lawbreakers. What's needed is not a political replacement for the Sharon government but a vision of hope, an alternative to the destruction of Zionism and its values by the deaf, dumb and callous.

Israel's friends abroad, Jewish and non-Jewish alike, presidents and prime ministers, rabbis and lay people should choose as well. They must reach out and help Israel to navigate the road map toward our national destiny as a light unto the nations and a society of peace, justice and equality.

Note

This chapter originally appeared in the Hebrew paper *Yedioth Ahronoth* and is reprinted with the author's permission. This English version, translated by J. J. Goldberg, appeared in the *International Herald Tribune*, 6 September 2003.

6

Religion, State and Society

DAVID NEWMAN

The relationship between religion, state and society in Israel has been deeply controversial ever since the establishment of the state and even before then. Even the moderate definition of a state within which Jewish values determine the nature of state practices, gives rise to quite different interpretations. They range from a strictly religious orthodox definition of Jewish values, to that of a modern cultural renaissance of a "new" Hebrew people, freeing itself from the shackles of religious rituals and restrictions. Zionism, as a political ideology, was a secular movement, with minimal religious involvement in its early phases. For some ultra-orthodox groups, Zionism was even seen as an antithesis to "authentic" religious Jewish beliefs.

During the over fifty years of statehood, there has been constant tension between religious and secular interests, exacerbated during the past twenty years as national–religious and ultra-orthodox political parties have played a more active part in government and the decision-making processes. This has caused growing opposition by the wider Israeli public, culminating in a secular backlash in the January 2003 elections in what some have described, perhaps with a degree of exaggeration, as the beginning of a "secular revolution".

This chapter examines three dimensions of the contemporary meaning of Jewish statehood, touching upon the internal debate between Israelis, the dialogue between Israel and the Diaspora, and the way in which religion affects the implementation of a peace process between Israel and the Palestinians.

The Jewish state: the religious and cultural dimension

The dilemma of defining just what constitutes a "Jewish" state has in recent years become even more problematic than in the past with the emergence of post-Zionism, the notion of an alternative definition of the polity as a "state of all of its citizens", and the idea of bi-nationalism as an alternative to a two-state solution to the Israel–Palestine conflict. Though restricted to intellectual circles, these concepts raise critical questions concerning the definition and *raison d'être* of the state.[1]

For secular Israel, a Jewish state is one where Jews live and constitute a majority of the population, and in which Jewish cultural and historical values, and the Hebrew language, form a major part of their national identity. Jewish traditions are to be valued but in their broadest sense, in the understanding that one does not have to be religious or orthodox to be Jewish, nor to conform to ritual practices. Secular, Reform and Conservative streams are all legitimate expressions of Jewishness.

For orthodox Jews, the Jewish state is a state which is run according to strict ritual practices. The state does follow this definition in many areas of daily activities, like the observance of the Shabbat and Jewish festivals as holidays, the maintenance of strict religious dietary standards in all public institutions like the army, government offices and universities, and – of greatest significance – the exclusive control of all issues relating to personal status (birth, marriage and death) by the orthodox clerical establishment.

This set of arrangements became erroneously known as the "*status quo*" in the early days of statehood and was vigorously defended by the major political parties of government during Israel's first three decades.[2] The first public acknowledgment of cracks in this religion–state arrangement began to appear following the elections of 1977 when, for the first time in the country's history, ultra-religious parties became part of the ruling coalition. As such they of course attempted on a number of occasions to introduce religious legislation which would have intruded even further upon the public space of the country's citizens, including the vast majority who are secular. During the past two decades, the disproportionate power wielded by relatively small religious political parties, and their (largely unsuccessful) attempts to impose new religious legislation, tended to foster in a largely apathetic public an animosity to all things religious.

The large Russian immigration of the 1990s was generally anti-clerical and views attempts to impose any forms of religious restrictions on their lives as unacceptable. Neither were they commited to the *status quo*, in which they had no part. They, like the ultra-religious groups, were largely segregated in their own neighborhoods, within which there were no traces whatsoever of religious lifestyles and practices, even in the public domain.

In reality, during the past two decades Israel has become more religious and more secular at one and the same time, but in highly separate and segregated spaces. Religious and secular politicians continually bemoan the increase in the influence of the "other" who, they argue, are trying to impose their alien way of life on the whole of society. But these are no more than socially constructed myths on the part of political leaders who manipulate the growing secular–religious tensions for political ends. In reality one is not threatening the other but the discourse of exclusivity – "either my lifestyle or yours" – prevents the two from reaching a modus vivendi of co-existence, albeit in parallel and separate spaces.

These religious–secular tensions came to a head in the January 2003 elections, when the *Shinui* party ran on a militant anti-religious platform and succeeded in obtaining fifteen seats in the *Knesset*, becoming the major coalition partner in the new government. With the National Religious Party (down to only six mandates) in the government, the two ultra-orthodox parties (16 mandates) were excluded from it, while the new *Shinui* ministers promised the legalization of commerce and public transportation on the Shabbat, civil marriage and burial as an alternative to the exclusive orthodox practices, and a major cut in the allocation of resources to religious educational and cultural institutions.[3]

The Reform and Conservative movements have been the major victim of growing secular–religious polarization. For orthodox Israel, these movements are non-religious. The orthodox establishment went out of its way to try and deny them any form of representation on religious councils. Reform and Conservative clerics are not recognized by the Minister of Interior for the performance of marriages and other state-defined religious ritual, while they are denied resources for their religious and educational institutions.

Ironically, however, for some secular Israelis alienated by orthodox politics, the Reform and Conservative movements are labeled as "religious" and have not necessarily received the expected political support from the major secular political parties. Without representation in the *Knesset* they find themselves in a weak position in terms of Israeli power politics and decision-making. Their situation has somewhat improved in recent years as some local authorities have recognized their rights to public sector resources, and as their supporters in the Diaspora have began to fund them directly rather than rely on the non-democratic and unequal allocations of resources practiced by the government and the Jewish Agency. However, there is still a perception of Reform Judaism as being imported from America. Within the polarization of the religious–secular discourse in Israel, movements professing alternative forms of religious self-definition have not succeeded in seriously challenging the monopoly of the religious establishment, or in playing any major role in redefining the Jewish character of the state.

The Jewish state: the demographic dimension

Opinion polls amongst the Israeli Jewish public show time after time that the single concern common to the largest majority of the Jewish population is their desire to retain a clear Jewish demographic majority in the State of Israel. This explains why even politicians on the moderate right of the political map support the ultimate creation of a Palestinian state, even when they have doubts on the security aspect. Without partitioning the country, there is widespread fear lest the continued occupation of the West Bank and Gaza Strip with its three million, and rapidly growing, Palestinian population, will eventually bring about the creation of a single bi-national state in which Jews would be transformed into a minority.

As regards the demographic implications of bi-nationalism to both post-Zionism and to the radical rightist neo-Zionism,[4] they see each other as constituting the major existential threat facing the State of Israel. Neo-Zionists believe that post-Zionists are endangering Israel by withdrawing from territories perceived as constituting a historical and strategic asset, as well as their being bereft of any form of Jewish identity which is the *raison d'être* of the state. For their part, post-Zionists see neo-Zionists as committing the state to endless conflict by refusing to exchange land for peace and accuse them of selling the future of their children for a set of symbolic and unachieveable myths. While a small minority on the far left of Israeli society is prepared to accept a single bi-national state, such a scenario is anathema to both the neo-Zionists and most of the post-Zionists, both of whom see a Jewish majority and sovereignty as a dominant ideological and national value.

By refusing at one and the same time to accept both the single bi-national state scenario or to withdraw from any of the occupied territories, neo-Zionism has created a structural dilemma for itself which it is unable to resolve. This brings the more extreme elements amongst the neo-Zionists to propose more radical solutions, such as the "transfer" of the Palestinian population to other Arab countries of the region. Alternatively, they envisage the creation of a two-tiered apartheid state in which Arab Palestinian residents are denied any political rights or access to power and resources. This is of course wholly unacceptable to the vast majority of Israelis as being morally abhorrent and politically suicidal, even if the supporters of "transfer" see themselves as remaining true to their "Zionist convictions".

Given the present demographic realities and the Jewish fear of being "swamped" by an Arab–Palestinian majority, it is not surprising that the Jewish State traditionally appreciated "large families", formally defined as any family with four or more children. Such families have been entitled to increased family benefits and generous child allowances. This policy benefits specific population groups, such as the ultra-religious, the West Bank settlers and, paradoxically, the Arab and Bedouin sectors, all of whom have large families for a variety of traditional and religious reasons.[5]

Demographic fears are therefore twofold. One addresses the fear that the overall Jewish majority in the state will eventually become a minority,[6] the other that the rapid growth of the religious and orthodox Jewish populations will assure even greater religious power at the expense of the secular majority. The two demographic "threats" are closely linked with each other in the public discourse. The generous child-allowance benefits to "large" families has been criticized by the secular parties for promoting continued poverty amongst families who should undertake family planning and limit the number of children to those that can be supported by gainful employment. The economic policy of Finance Minister Benjamin Netanyahu, supported by the anti-clericalist, secular *Shinui* party, in spring 2003 significantly reduced the level of child benefits as part of a broader *laissez faire*, privatization-oriented economic policy. Religious leaders attacked this policy as being "anti-religious" and as an obstacle to waging the demographic war against the rapid growth of the Arab and Palestinian populations.

Neither does any perspective of continued Jewish immigration to Israel resolve this problem. With the mass immigration from the former Soviet Union, the vision of the Jewish State as constituting a safe haven for Jews from countries of economic or political hardship has largely been realized. *Aliya* figures are declining. The remaining large Jewish populations are mainly to be found in western democracies where they are part of the wealthy and middle classes. With few exceptions, these populations are not interested in relocating to Israel though they support it, encourage Jews to visit it and have traditionally been prepared to raise funds and lobby politicians on behalf of Israel. But this stops short of uprooting their families and coming to live in Israel.

The Jewish state and the Diaspora

The relationship between Israel and the Jewish Diaspora has undergone major changes during the past decade. What used to be seen as an unquestioning and unanimous support of all Diaspora communities for Israel can no longer be taken for granted. Paradoxically, the more questioning and critical attitude in the Diaspora toward Israel is itself a victim of the state's military and economic success. The continued occupation of the West Bank and Gaza Strip, the obvious military superiority enjoyed by Israel over all of her regional neighbors, and the middle-class lifestyles enjoyed by so many of Israel's citizens – these are now facts of life, not to speak of what is seen as a wasteful and often irresponsible management of public resources on the part of successive Israeli governments. Consequently Diaspora communities are far less open to appeals to their conscience to make donations to a "poor and beleaguered" Israel. This is exacerbated in periods of global economic recession when the available resources for charitable donations have dwindled significantly and when every request for assistance is examined with far greater scrutiny and questioning than in the past.

The nature of Diaspora support for Israel has also changed in another way, with the increasing sectoralization of the pro-Israel lobby, particularly as regards the United States Administration. Pro-settlement or pro-peace lobbies have flourished, often bypassing the official Israel organs of representation like the consular officials and diplomats. The American pro-settlement lobby has been particularly active, opposing the Oslo peace process at every possible opportunity and moving into Washington strongly following the election of President George Bush and his right-wing allies. The decline, some would call it the collapse, of the peace movements in Israel[7] has largely been mirrored by a weakening of these same organizations in the United States, thus leaving the field open to rightist and religious forces who, in turn, have created an unholy alliance with the right-wing Christian evangelist groups which exert significant pressure on the Bush administration.[8]

Within the social and cultural fields, support for Israel has also fallen away, as major Diaspora groups have become increasingly frustrated with the way in which they see their rights of representation being ignored by the Israeli body politic. This is particularly the case with respect to the large Reform and Conservative movements in North America, whose counterparts have been almost totally disenfranchised in Israel itself. Groups which were traditionally amongst the major donors to public causes in Israel have either stopped giving altogether, or have insisted on donating directly to causes and institutions inside Israel with whom they directly affiliate. They are no longer ready to allow their resources to be distributed by a central organization (the government or the Jewish Agency) based on political and sectoral interests contrary to those of the donors.[9]

In the mid-1990s the then deputy Foreign Minister Dr. Yossi Beilin went so far as to suggest that Jews in the Diaspora cease making donations to the Jewish Agency, arguing that the era of a "poor and beleaguered" Israel was behind us and that such terminology was no longer of any relevance. Beilin's view was rejected after being attacked both from the right and the left. However, the strongest opposition came from some of the Jewish organizations and bureaucracies in the Diaspora, stemming from their fear that were Beilin's policies to be adopted they would lose their own standing within the Diaspora community.

If at least since 1967 Israel lacked a successful "advertising message" within the wider global community, it has become even worse during the past decade. In the first place, the world has become increasingly frustrated with Israel's continued occupation of the West Bank and Gaza Strip. Media views from this troubled region, particularly of Israeli tanks in West Bank towns, or checkpoints harassing unemployed and poverty stricken Palestinian families, can only serve to weaken Israel's cause in the world, including parts of the Jewish community. Though counter images of the carnage and destruction visited upon innocent Israeli civilians by suicide bombers and terrorists partially soften the negative impact, the longer-term impact of the protracted occupation has generated an increasingly critical and divided Jewish Diaspora.[10]

Clearly, Israel's position as the heart of the global Jewish community is now contested territory. This is buttressed by the fact that hundreds of thousands of Israeli citizens have chosen to leave Israel and move permanently to the Western world. These groups have either disassociated themselves from the wider Jewish community altogether or, if involved, have largely adopted extreme right-wing positions on the Israel–Palestine conflict, infuriating much of the Diaspora community.

At the same time, and more significantly, the bulk of the religious and orthodox community in North America and Western Europe has thrown in its lot with the most extreme right-wing supporters of Israel. They are in the forefront of the anti-peace publicity campaigns, raising funds for West Bank settlements, using their synagogues as public platforms for right-wing politicians and settler leaders from Israel, berating the Israeli left for being "traitors", and for "selling out their homeland".

Thus the Diaspora has become as polarized about Israel as their Israeli counterparts. Observing Israeli society, Jewish organizations and institutions abroad feel themselves threatened as they become less relevant to the concerns of a contemporary globalized middle-class Israel. They fear finding themselves even less relevant in an era of peace, when ex-territorial lobbyists in Washington, London or Brussels might be superfluous. Some ultra-orthodox groups continue to demonstrate against Israel because of what they see as its increasing secularism. But it is far more important to note how liberal groups have tuned down their unquestioning support of Israeli government policies because of their opposition to the lack of progress on the peace front, and to the lack of religious pluralism in the Jewish State. These polarizations have been strengthened by the irresponsible behavior of many Israeli politicians and other public figures who use their frequent flying visits to Diaspora communities to whip up support for their own sectoral causes.

Religion and the Arab–Israel conflict: is anyone left?

The notion of a "Jewish State" is not only a cultural discourse. It is closely linked in with the ongoing Israel–Palestine conflict and the way in which different groups in Israel and in the Diaspora interpret the political, demographic and territorial implications of peace or conflict. For most, this is not just a conflict about the existence of a state, but is tied up with alternative understandings of what should constitute a Jewish State. The reference is to issues which occupy people of liberal and leftist tendencies like the rights of the Arab minority population in Israel, the continuation of occupation, and the constructed sanctity of borders and territory.

Throughout the Middle East, religion has been used as a means of adding fuel to the flames of conflict, rather than as a means of promoting peace and reconciliation. It is the nationalist and exclusive messages of Judaism which have gained prominence, with religion used to justify the policy of a Greater Israel (the Promised Land) and the preference of Jewish rights (the Chosen People). Religious leaders have been in the forefront of the West Bank settler movement and in making public pronouncements to the effect that it is "forbidden" to relinquish even one centimeter of "liberated" territory in the Land of Israel to foreign (Palestinian) control. Retaining control of the land is seen as a religious and Divine imperative, not to be overturned by any human decision, even, in the most extreme version, by that of a democratically elected government.

There have been some attempts to put forward an alternative pro-peace message in the name of religion. During the 1970s, the *Oz V'Shalom* movement was established by a group of religious academics who objected to the narrow, nationalistic messages promoted by the right-wing national–religious group, *Gush Emunim*.[11] During the Lebanon War in

1982, another group of younger religious soldiers established the *Netivot Shalom* movement, drawing on religious and scriptural sources for their pro-peace, anti-occupation, message. These two movements eventually amalgamated but neither had much long-term success in combating the exclusive nationalist message of the mainstream religious political groups.[12] The *Meimad* party was formed as a dovish alternative to the National Religious Party, but never succeeded in getting elected to the *Knesset* in its own right, eventually being subsumed as part of the Labor Party.

Another pro-peace religious group is the Rabbis for Human Rights, formed by a group of Orthodox, Conservative and Reform Rabbis in the early 1990s with the aim of promoting the cause of peace in the name of religion. This group won a high public profile for its activism, along with other peace-oriented and leftist groups, in defending Palestinian human rights and its role in protesting the demolition of Palestinian houses and in assisting in the construction of new homes.[13]

Nevertheless, the religious peace groups were to meet a similar fate to that of the Conservative and Reform movements. As far as the religious mainstream was concerned, the pro-peace groups speaking in the name of religion were either misguided or were tainted by universal and global values, such as equality and human rights. They thus dared to refute the exclusive national message of "the Jewish people returning to its ancient homeland after two thousand years of Exile". In the case of Rabbis for Human Rights, the fact that so many of the activists were not orthodox Rabbis strengthened the religious mainstream's dismissal of their cause, even if the source material used in promoting the pro-peace message were from the same authentic scriptural sources as those used by the right-wing nationalists. Religious pro-peace activists were not allowed platforms in the synagogues and, largely prevented from reaching those populations to whom their message was aimed, they remained somewhat peripheral.

As far as the country's secular pro-peace population was concerned, there was a feeling that religion and peace simply did not mix. The National Religious Party was perceived as "the settlers' party". The ultra-orthodox population emerged time after time in public surveys, as holding extreme right-wing, even racist, anti-Arab beliefs.[14] If there was a time when some ultra-religious *Sephardi* leaders were prepared to withdraw from parts of the occupied territories if it would bring about an end to the loss of Jewish life, the same voices were now heard expressing extremist religious–political messages.

Orthodox Jewry viewed the religious peace movements merely as a small maverick group of well-intentioned individuals, whose universalistic language had no place in Judaism. Many religious Jews were active, for instance, in Peace Now, but religious peace movements as such never succeeded in reaching either the religious or secular populations on any scale which could significantly change public opinion amongst large sectors of the population. Thus, just as the Jewish identity of the state was hijacked by the exclusive orthodox definitions of what it means to be Jewish, so too in the religious domain has the issue of peace remained in the hands of those who preach nationalism, territorial maximalism and the exclusive Jewish right to the Land of Israel.

Concluding comment

This chapter has described the changing understandings of what it means to be a Jewish citizen, or a member of a Jewish community in the Diaspora, in relation to the Jewish State of Israel. It has also raised questions concerning the nature of religion as a source of Jewish identity and the way in which this feeds into the adoption of political positions concerning the Israel–Palestine conflict. The glue which cemented the Israeli–Diaspora relationship for the best part of fifty years has on the one hand began to become unstuck. On the other hand, internal competing intellectual discourses of post- and neo-Zionism could fragment Jewish Israel from within.

It is possible that many of these dilemmas could have been avoided had the power elites in Israel enabled a more democratic and pluralistic definition of Jewish statehood. Instead, they continually attempted to enforce a narrow and rigid definition on large non-orthodox population groups, both traditional and secular, for whom such definitions do not reflect their life practices or beliefs. The language and semantics of religious and national affiliation which were relevant to the state's founder generation are not relevant to a global, universal and high-tech generation of teenagers and young adults. Neither is the narrative of an isolated and beleaguered state relevant to a younger generation which lives with the continued conflict and serves in a powerful army, much of whose time and resources are devoted to controlling and occupying another people – a people which has taken the place of the Jewish people as the disenfranchised and impoverished.

For a society to successfully obtain the loyalty and support of its own citizenry and its Diaspora partners, it has to continually undergo a process of internal questioning and re-evaluation, in order to bring its self-definitions into line with the realities of the times, both inside and outside Israel. This is a major challenge facing Israel if it aspires to go forward in this process of re-thinking so as to enable both right and left wing, religious and secular, Israeli and Diaspora Jews, Jews and Arabs, to find a way of living side by side. For all those concerned, this demands accepting the legitimacy of the narrative professed by the "other", instead of competing over a zero-sum game in which one side is always the victor and the other is vanquished and delegitimized.

Notes

1 Many of these trends are discussed in A. Kemp, D. Newman, U. Ram and O. Yiftachel (eds.), *Israelis in Conflict: Hegemonies, Identities and Challenges* (Brighton & Portland: Sussex Academic Press, 2004). See also: L. Silberstein, *The Postzionism Debates: Knowledge and Power in Israeli Culture* (Routledge, 1999).

2 For a discussion of the status quo, see: C. Liebman and E. Don-Yehiye, *Religion and Politics in Israel* (Indiana University Press, 1984). Also, C. Liebman, *Religion, Democracy and Israeli Society* (Harwood Academic Publishers, 1997).

3 Following *Shinui*'s accession to government, the anti-religious rhetoric was toned down. Some policies were pursued, most notably the dismantlement of the Religious Affairs Ministry, while other – more contentious issues, such as civil marriage have, for the moment, remained untouched.

4 The use of the term neo-Zionism as a counterweight to the post-Zionism terminology has been posited by sociologist Uri Ram. See "Between post-Zionism and neo-Zionism", *Gesher*, 42 (1996 [Hebrew]), and his chapter "The State of the Nation: Contemporary Challenges to Zionism in Israel", in A. Kemp, D. Newman, U. Ram and O. Yiftachel (eds), *Israelis in Conflict: Hegemonies, Identities and Challenges*.

5 D. Newman, "Population as Security: the Arab–Israeli Struggle for Demographic Hegemony", in *Redefining Security: Population Movements and National Security* (Praeger, 1998), pp. 163–86.

6 A doomsday prophet in this area has been Haifa University geographer/demographer Arnon Sofer whose public lectures are replete with "demographic swamping" terminology.

7 D. Newman, "How Israel's Peace Movement Fell Apart", the *New York Times*, August 30, 2002.

8 See A. Eldar, "An Unholy Alliance with the Christian Right", *Ha'aretz*, July 4, 2003. Also, D. Newman, "Unhealthy Partners", *Jerusalem Post*, March 12, 2003.

9 See for instance, D. Ostrich, "How to Support Reform Judaism in Israel", http://www.uahc.orgOcongs/fl/fl006/bhhow.htm.

10 This is not helped by the fact that there is no longer any balanced English language reporting of the conflict coming out of Israel itself. *Ha'aretz* adopts a left of center position in most of its articles, while the *Jerusalem Post* has become representative of the most extreme right wing political positions, even criticizing the present Sharon government for not being hard line enough and for being prepared to negotiate new avenues to peace.

11 See E. Sprinzak, "Gush Emunim: the Iceberg Model of Political Extremism", *Jerusalem Quarterly*, 1984; D. Newman, "Gush Emunim between Fundamentalism and Pragmatism", *Jerusalem Quarterly*, 1986; M. Feige, "Two Maps to the Land: Gush Emunim and Peace Now" (Magnes Press, 2002, [Hebrew]).

12 T. Hermann and D. Newman, "The Dove and the Skullcap: Secular and Religious Divergence in the Israeli Peace Camp", in C. Liebman (ed.), *Religious and Secular: Conflict and Accommodation between Jews in Israel* (Keter: Jerusalem), pp. 151–72.

13 See Rabbis for Human Rights at: http://www.rhr-na.org.

14 These, and other public attitudes, can be found in the monthly Peace Index produced by the Steinmetz Center for Peace Research at Tel Aviv University. See: http://spirit.tau.ac.il/socant/peace/.

Who's Left?

7

The Making and Unmaking of the Israeli Jewish Left

ILAN PAPPE

Ever since 1948, individuals and groups have been adopting largely ad hoc positions on the three major cleavages tearing Israeli society from within since the inception of the state: the Palestinian question, the rift between *Mizrahi* (Eastern) and *Ashkenazi* (European) Jews, and the religious-secular *kulturcampf*. Fifty years later, in the 1990s, the left was articulated in a more coherent ideological formulation as a stream in contemporary Israeli political thought. This chapter deals not with leftist political parties, but rather with ideological streams. Some were translated into political policies, others, while failing to do so, are worthy of mention because of the intellectual challenge they presented to mainstream thinking.

The first "hawks", the first "doves"

Among the many issues crowding the early political agenda of the young state, one stood out overshadowing all the others: the military rule imposed on the Palestinian Arabs within the state. The basic positions adopted toward this issue would in due course mark the dividing line between those seeing themselves as on the left and right, "hawks"and "doves", on the Israeli political scene.

The status of those Palestinian citizens (called "Israeli Arabs" by Israelis) who were left within Israel after most of their compatriots were expelled, acted like a magnet drawing in everyone concerned with the nature of the new state. The debate raised the question of the compatibility of having both a Jewish nation-state and a democracy. The political elite was divided on this issue in the 1950s and 1960s into more liberal-minded and more security-minded politicians. Both groups operated within the Zionist consensus and not against it, led by the dominant *Mapai*, now the Labor party. They differed on tactical questions of national priorities and on how Zionism should interpret the Israeli–Palestinian conflict in terms of actual solutions.

Within this debate, therefore, the harsh measures meted out to the Palestinian Arab minority were not basically questioned.[1] But in its margins one could trace the beginning of a different kind of leftism – associated with Communism or universalism. Some groups offered a principled challenge to the policies pursued, others even offered alternatives to the hegemonic orientations of the state. But these were marginal; on center stage Zionism was not challenged.

The liberals were troubled by the use of the Mandatory emergency regulations against the Palestinian citizens. On these regulations Menahem Begin, from the extreme right, had said in 1946: "Even in Nazi Germany there was no such rule".[2] The Socialist-Zionist *Mapam* party (now a part of the leftist Zionist *Meretz*) tried in vain ever since 1951 to ensure its abolition. But the security minded politicians, aided by Ben-Gurion's experts on Arab affairs, won the day. The systematic abuse of the minority's human and civil rights continued under the military rule until 1966 (even after the evils of this regime were exposed in full in the 1956 Kafar Qassam massacre, when 49 Arabs were shot dead for "breaking" a curfew they didn't know of).

After the military rule was finally abolished, its discrimination continued to operate in indirect channels, particularly through the vast expropriation of Palestinian land in the Galilee in the 1960s. It was on the barricades of opposition to this arbitrary land confiscation that the possibility was formulated of a non-Zionist left as the best means of confronting the issue of Palestinian existence within the Jewish state. The way was shown by the Palestinian Israeli politicians of the day who were backed by a few Jews on the left (and supported by the ageing Professor Martin Buber, in his last political statement). One exceptional response was that of Uri Davis, a peace activist who in the 1960s drew the public's attention to land expropriation and the attempts at the "Judaization" of the Galilee.[3]

Davis left the country in 1972, a year when the issue of civil rights appeared for the first time on the political agenda in Israel. The Association for Civil Rights in Israel (ACRI) was established in 1972 as a non-partisan body for the promotion of human and civil rights in Israel and in the occupied territories. Ever since then, ACRI's principles and manifestoes have been impressive, with its court actions particularly commendable. But all in all it lacked a political edge, which prevented it from deviating from the Zionist consensus; thus, with all its importance in the field of civil rights, it left little impact on the political scene. Its significance lay elsewhere. It acted as an agent for a new discourse that can serve in the future for a more thorough leftist liberal movement that would boldly challenge those intrinsic features of Zionism, if not all of them, that contradict the very basic universal principles of humanity and civil rights represented by ACRI.

Civil rights was in Western terms a liberal and not a socialist agenda. Its status, along with the Palestinian issue, at the center stage of what was seen as the left in Israel, demonstrated the absence of a "social" left with a clear socio-economic vision, despite the conditions that should have enabled such a force to emerge.

The unmaking of a "social left"

Israel in its early decades was wrought with social protest that was crying out to be incorporated into political activity of a socialist hue. The important landmarks of this movement of unrest were the seamen's strike of 1951, which was brutally crushed by the authorities in cooperation with the official Labor movement (*Histadrut*); and the Wadi Salib riots of 1959, where unemployed *Mizrahi* Jews from a Haifa slum, demonstrating against poverty and discrimination, were dispersed with violence by the police, with their leader jailed. These social movements did not immediately produce any new political thought. Twenty years later such a new stream did emerge but it was less class orientated and much more ethnically based.

It began in the early 1970s with a relatively naive and moderate call for the assertion of a *Mizrahi* identity within the Jewish state by the Black Panther movement: a group of young *Mizrahi* activists emulating the movement and goals of African Americans. The movement demanded a fairer distribution of the state's economic and social resources, and a larger share in the definition of the country's cultural identity. Theirs was an incomplete radicalism and it did not seek to exit from within the Zionist consensus.[4] It was therefore easy for the powers that be to delegitimize the Panthers as anti-patriotic and to silence or coopt them.

With the failure of the Black Panther movement to undertake any protracted political activity, or to create an ethnic party, the politics of identity reverted ironically to the *Likud* party, representing the right in Israeli politics (a mixture of expansionist ideology and liberal economics).

This party was engaged in shaping a colonialist ideology that would justify the "redemption" of the 1967 occupied territories. However,. it was also flexible enough to absorb the ethnic protest and win over its *Mizrahi* voters. The opportune moment came in 1977, when the Jewish electorate lost confidence in the longstanding Labor rule, due to the trauma of the *Yom Kippur* war in 1973 and the exposure of high-level corruption in the government.

As for consolidating a social left, its aspirants lost whatever chance existed by their failure to tie into the radical energy that was generated by the social and geographical *Mizrachi* margins in the 1980s. New NGOs led renovation and restoration projects in slums and protest movement arose in development towns. This was followed by the emergence of a radical *Mizrahi* intellectual thought, which had been so badly needed on the political scene. Among other things it stressed the relevance of questions of multiculturalism, which dominated the social agenda elsewhere in the world. It also helped to refresh the rather dogmatic Marxist thought in Israel and re-orientate it on neo-Marxist lines. This was achieved through an impressive group of university people, working mainly in Haifa University between 1978 and 1984, when the university dissolved it (by terminating the career of its leading members). It had its own publication, *Mahbarot Le-Mehkar ve le-Bikoret*, where ethnicity, colonialism and nationalism were discussed through updated versions of the Marxist paradigm.[5]

Some of the radicalization, whose potential has yet to be realized, even went as far as a fundamental questioning of Zionism. At the center of this intellectual activity stood Ella Shohat, who only now is being recognized in Israeli scholarly circles, particularly for her introduction of post-colonial thought into the local discourse.[6] A colleague of Shohat, Sami Shalom Shitrit, joined forces for a while with one of the leading figures in the *Mahbarot* group, Shlomo Svirsky, in an intriguing exercise to try and formulate a *Mizrahi* educational stream, called *Kedma* ("Going East" in ancient Hebrew). Despite its eventual failure to take off, its significance lay in the way it stimulated new thinking on issues of cultural and ethnic identity in Israeli education and politics. While the mainstream educational system acted as if on questions of identity there was a national consensus, the new thought indicated that there were people and groups who had been symbolically and practically victimized by the accepted hegemonic ethnic-social views.

As an academic, Shohat represented the possible, but as yet unfulfilled, bridge between the ethnic, class and gender issues. This triangle, which is at the heart of some of the more updated global left movements, is totally missing from the Israeli political theme. Gender issues as a political platform were introduced in the early 1970s with the appearance of the first women activists. By the 1980s the various organizations and activists impacted legislation and governmental attitudes to women's safety, well-being and equality. By the 1990s the achievements of the feminist left were still a mixed bag – success in improving the level of political representation, and failure in the continued disparity in salaries.

Feminism as a theory and as practice was mainly *Ashkenazi*-based and oriented and could not speak effectively for *Mizrahi* or Palestinian women. In the 1990s, therefore, *Mizrachi* and Palestinian women established their own movements with a special agenda. Recently, a revived bi-national feminism appeared, in the wake of the paralysis of the male dominated peace movements during the second *Intifada*. Among its more recent manifestations is a very vocal organization like New Profile – a feminist movement based on a pacifist paradigm that opposes occupation and military service and calls for the demilitarization of Israeli society. Significant activity was carried out by a more veteran and cautious organization – *Bat-Shalom,* working with a parallel Palestinian organization, and enjoying a larger membership and public profile.

The feminist scene today is full of different voices. *Al-Fanar* (the Israeli–Palestinian feminist organization); *Bat Shalom*; New Profile; various women's peace centers; *Claf* (the lesbian feminist organization); *Isha le-Isha* (women to women) and *Yadid* (Friend) to mention only a few. The many other feminist organizations today may testify to a diversity but seem nonetheless to be moving toward a clear agenda that combines peace, ecology, and human rights with a feminist perspective. This common ideological basis may provide feminism with a chance to play a more meaningful role in the Israel left. But before this could come about, the Israeli left had to find an agenda beyond what has been, since 1967, its major and dominant theme – the struggle to end the occupation of the West Bank and the Gaza Strip.

The issue of occupation: the making of a new left?

Immediately after the end of the June 1967 war, the fate of the occupied territories became the criterion for left and right in Israel, pushing aside all other economic, social or cultural policy lines. The debate over continuing or ending the occupation raged more outside than inside the official political realm, for both Labor and *Likud* supported the occupation. Even so, it was always a main issue in almost all election campaigns.

The opening gambit was made by those who demanded an immediate end to the occupation. At its center stood people who had been directly involved in the 1948 expulsion (ethnic cleansing) of the Arabs, but were now terrified by the idea of imposing Jewish control over such large number of Palestinians. Thus the new Israeli "left" was born: an uneasy alliance centered solely on the demand to leave the occupied areas, consisting of communists, socialists, liberals, capitalists, Jews and Arabs, all sharing the vision that had been pronounced clearly for the first time in the Israeli polity by the Communist party: two states for two peoples.

There was, however, a difference, for the Communist party was also commited to a fully sovereign Palestinian state and a principled Israeli recognition of the Palestinian Right of Return. The Zionist-led peace camp offered the territories (which constituted only 22 percent of Mandatory Palestine, in which there had been an Arab majority before 1948) to the Palestinians without supporting full sovereignty as the final act of reconciliation. When in the course of time the leaders and gurus of this camp were to find out, at various junctures in discussions on a final peace settlement, that for most Palestinians this offer could not constitute an end to the conflict, they felt "insulted"and "betrayed". But they did build and maintain an activist movement that clearly voiced Jewish-Israeli opposition to the occupation. This movement succeeded in influencing the policies of the parties of the center and left of center. For a while (1992–6) it was even a dominant voice directing the peace policy of the Labor party and the government. But if in 2004 we look back, we see that the opponents of occupation lost the battle to its supporters, not only in the *Likud*, but also in the Labor party.

Distancing itself from the official political arena, a very different ideological perspective on the occupation and its relation to Zionism was developed by *Matzpen* (Compass). This movement started in 1962 as a small intellectual drawing-room discussion group, composed mainly of disappointed Communists who sought a more updated Marxist agenda. It was a bi-national group, with a paper and few hundreds members and supporters, which remained on the political periphery. Despite their meager numbers it is an important factor in understanding the genealogy of critique in Israel. Its emphasis on social, economic and political critique of Zionism contexualized the objection to the occupation in a very different way from that of the Zionist left. Maybe this is why they succeeded in impressing the security services as being a meaningful movement that could sway the young into questioning not only the legitimacy of the occupation but also that of Zionism altogether.

After 1967 they were among those recording and reporting to the Jewish society on what it did not want to know on the brutality of the occupation from its first day, on house demolitions, expulsions and mass arrests as the daily experience of the Palestinians. Most of *Matzpen's* leading activists gave up the struggle from within in the early 1970s and emigrated, leaving a lull not easily filled. The anti-occupation movement had philosophical articulators such as Yeshayahu Leibowitz, a Hebrew University professor, who drew his fiery call for a unilateral and unconditional withdrawal from his reading in both humanism and Judaism. The movement had its heroes such as the first "refuseniks" who objected to military service in the occupied territories and paved the way to a more significant movement of refusal later on.

The anti-occupation movement was institutionalized when Peace Now came into being in 1978. It first emerged as a lobby for peace with Egypt – a kind of an old boys' club which included only officers who were serving or had served in elite or combat units. It diversified and grew in significance when it opposed – after initial hesitations – the Israeli invasion of Lebanon in 1982. Supported by the dovish wing in Labor and by *Meretz*, under its banner the most massive ever anti-war demonstration ("the 400,000 demonstration" in Tel Aviv) took place in the wake of the Sabra and Shatila massacres of 1982. It remained active throughout the *Intifada* (1987–93), but when Labor was in power it became inactive and it was virtually silent during the period of the Rabin-led government (1993–5). Whether it can now revive its fortunes in the Sharon era remains to be seen.

Peace Now's reaction to the Lebanon war and later to the *Intifada* did not deviate from Zionist perceptions. More specifically, its criticism was and still is directed only toward the post-1967 Israeli policy, and its main concern is the effect that this policy can exert on the moral character of Israeli society. Though many academics were associated with the movement, their affiliation did not cause any change in the mainstream scholarly works on political issues.

During the Lebanon war Peace Now, which opposed refusing army service, was challenged by more radical offshoots, such as *Yesh Gvul* ("There is a Limit") and the "Four Mothers" movements. Unlike the mainstream peace movement, these did not hesitate to follow Yeshayahu Leibowitz's call to refuse to serve in occupied Lebanon. All peace movements were united in their call on Israel to unilaterally and unconditionally withdraw from Lebanese territories. Those whom I will later on define as post-Zionist scholars were quick to define the refusal movement, though it involved only about one thousand people, as the most significant challenge to one of Zionism's most sacred cows – service in the IDF. So far this reading has not as yet been vindicated by events on the ground. Seeing themselves as Zionists, the refuse-niks like the "Courage to refuse" movement in 2002, or the 27 pilots who refused to bomb civilian population centers in September 2003 because it was "illegal and immoral", restricted their protest to one issue. They perhaps lacked an overall ideological–political perception or framework enabling them to see their refusal to serve as part of a broader and more comprehensive picture. Be this as it may, theirs remained a significant act of protest against the occupation, with vital potential for the future.

An impressive commitment against the occupation was demonstrated by the bodies that emerged as a response both to the growing callousness of the military occupation or to the inadequacies of the mainstream peace movement. Such was the Israeli Information Center for Human Rights in the Occupied Territories, *B'Tselem*, founded in 1989 by academics, attorneys, journalists and *Knesset* members, and taking its name from Genesis 1: 27, "And God created human beings in his image (*Tselem)*. In the image of God He did create him". Since its establishment it has scrupulously documented every aspect of the daily mechanism of the occupation, together with journalists like Gideon Levy and Amira Hass, cutting through the wall of silence and denial in the Israeli media and society. In its Charter, it vowed to change Israeli policy in the occupied territories; while it did not yet succeed in doing so, the importance of its providing authoritative information to the public at home and abroad on the real meaning of the Occupation cannot be exaggerated.

Roughly at the same time and also using the Jewish sources as its inspiration, the "Rabbis for Human Rights" organization was created. It was even more focused on reporting to the world, and to the Jewish world in particular, the "serious abuses of human rights by the Israeli military authorities in the suppression of the *Intifada*". Unlike *B'Tselem* it did not feel the need to balance its report on the Israeli conduct with the abuses of rights on the Palestinian side. Even more active was the "Committee Against House Demolition" and similar bodies helping in practice to alleviate the hardship of life under occupation such as *Ta'yush* (Living together) and *Machsom* Watch, which protected Palestinian rights at IDF checkpoints in the territories. In the worst year of the occupation, 2002, *Ta'yush* was particularly active, with a growing membership of Israeli Jews and Palestinians.

One of the most dynamic movements in this respect was founded by the veteran peace activist, Uri Avnery, *Gush Shalom* (The Peace Bloc). It came on the scene a little later than the organizations described above, striving to unite the peace camp in 1993 behind a clear platform, differentiated from the consensual ambitions of Peace Now. Its boldest declaration was that it proposed to recognize the Palestinian Right of Return and in the late 1990s it suggested that as part of this recognition half a million refugees should return to Israel. Its broad and systematic list of activities included an examination of the boundaries of the Israeli law, reporting officers and soldiers of the occupation as war criminals to relevant global judiciary institutions, and the boycott campaign against products coming from the occupied territories. After some hesitation it also endorsed the refuseniks.

I have not included in this survey any of the joint Israeli–Palestinian ventures as I am trying to view the history of ideas from within the Jewish society. Clearly, *Gush Shalom* was the nearest to the ideas and perceptions put forward by those Israelis, who in the tradition of *Matzpen* saw their role as political activists very much as Whites saw theirs within the struggle to end Apartheid in South Africa. This was a chapter in political thought that avoided the discourse of co-existence so favored by the Zionist left, seeing as its objective first and foremost to assure the sovereign existence of the Palestinian people, which was a pre-condition for reconciliation on the ground. Another such organizations was the Alternative Information Center that publishes *News From Within*. This publication also represents the Palestinian secular left and its struggle against both the occupation and the Oslo Accords (until their demise) and regards the Palestinian Right of Return as an essential component of any future solution. The *Palestine–Israel Journal*, another publication which represents more mainstream Palestinian political thought together with left Zionist and non-Zionist contributors, has also enriched discourse within the Israeli left.

A veteran and consistent player on this scene was *Hadash*, the Democratic Front for Peace and Equality, including the Israel Communist party. With a history going back to pre-state years, its fortunes were not improved by the connection with Moscow and rigid Marxism. However, it became a solid stage on which alternative opinions could be voiced in view of its consistent fight against military rule in Arab areas in the 1950s, its struggle against the confiscation of Arab lands in Galilee in the 1960s, and its clear position against the occupation since 1967. One of its problems is that most of its support comes from the Arab sector rather than from the Jewish public. Azmi Bishara originated in *Hadash* before moving on to more national lines with the *Balad* party. As a professor of philosophy, his philosophical background contributed to the introduction into the political discourse on the left clearer notions of civil society. Particularly important was the concept of Israel as "a state for all its citizens", rather than as a "Jewish State". The significance of this combination of new thinking and political activism can be expected to persist in the years ahead.

The ideological triangle of the 1990s: Zionism, post-Zionism and neo-Zionism

In the world of political thought in Israel in the 1990s, the world where we continue to live today, there was a clash between three ideological streams within Zionism, which were sharpened by the Oslo Accords and their demise. Historically, the leading stream of *traditional Zionism*, to which both Labor and *Likud* belong, has underlayed the plans and policies of all Israeli governments since the creation of the state. The two other streams emerged as a challenge to this mainstream: from the left *post-Zionism* and from right *neo-Zionism*.

All definitions of traditional Zionism, also called Labor or mainstream Zionism, refer to the hegemonic stream in Zionism from the pre-state period until the fall of the Labor party from power in 1977. So in 1977, Labor Zionism was successfully challenged by the Revisionists (formerly *Herut*, now *Likud*), an alternative more ethnocentric and chauvinistic variant of Zionism, with Labor only briefly returning to power in 1992 and in in 1999. Yet the two Sharon governments of 2001 and 2003 basically represent the same mainstrream Zionist policies. This was epitomized by the governments of "national unity" of 1984–90 and 2000–1, where the two parties shared power. Traditional Zionism has therefore remained the principal prism through which the political center and the professional elites in Israel view the Israel/Palestine conflict. Indeed, this was the ideological basis on which the architects of Oslo constructed their peace settlement and it is still, in our post-Oslo period, the bedrock underpinning the present Israeli posture toward the final stages of any Israeli–Palestinian settlement.

From the left, traditional Zionism has been challenged by post-Zionism. Toward the end of the 1980s a number of Israeli scholars, both inside and outside the country, wrote studies on aspects of both the past and the present which contradicted the conventional Zionist, and the official Israeli, historical narrative. These works debunked the most sacred "historical truths" of Zionism and questioned their validity for the present generation. Moreover, these scholars criticized the role played by Israeli academic institutions in shaping the Zionist self-image, and its portrayal of the Palestine reality. Directly and indirectly, they debunked the works of those who had dominated Israeli academic writing on contemporary Jewish society and Palestinian history. Because of their prominence in the public consciousness they constituted a veritable cultural phenomenon in Israel.

The post-Zionist scholars also adopted the causes of deprived groups, and, with the help of historical or sociological research, represented them as valid in scientific terms. Meanwhile, an attempt was made to tie together three of the major underprivileged groups in Israel – the Palestinians Arabs, *Mizrahi* Jews and women – and to create a joint political front between them. While this proved to be a total political failure, it remained a popular vision for the more optimistic members of the academic protest movement.

During the seven years in which the Oslo Accords rose and fell, post-Zionism therefore had an impact on the cultural public arena in Israel and on constructing a non-Zionist interpretation of past and present events. For example, the work in 1988 of one historian, Benny Morris, threw an entirely new light on the birth in 1947 to 1949 of the Palestinian refugee problem. While the critique varied in its intensity, and in the courage with which it was expressed, it was voiced by some who identified themselves as Zionists, while others declared themselves to be anti-Zionists. The most useful way of describing this movement of critique was to call it "post-Zionism".

The post-Zionist discourse did not attract anyone beyond what might be called the chatterboxes and the scribblers. Though it was an elitist exercise, it may have had wider implications for the society as a whole. Meanwhile, any hope for an alliance with the Palestinian minority in Israel, or with other under-privileged groups, failed to materialize or had not yet become realistic. Accordingly, one cannot talk about post-Zionism as a political challenge. (Incidentally, Morris himself was later to claim that his work was misinterpreted.)

In the 1980s, both the post-Zionist potential, and powerful traditional Zionism, were confronted by a new regrouping of the political forces on the right which can be termed as neo-Zionism, whose thinking has penetrated all the rightist and religious parties. The new right, which has shared power with traditional Zionism since 2000, is an alliance between the settlers in the occupied territories and deprived and marginalized sections of Jewish society in Israel. It is an uneasy union between expansionist nationalists, orthodox and ultra-orthodox rabbis, and ethnic-spiritual leaders of the *Mizrahi* Jews. All presented themselves as champions of the underprivileged Oriental Jewish communities. Until recently, the *Mizrahi* Jews as an electorate still supported this alliance, but the complex and sophisticated problems involved here prevent us from defining the location of the *Mizrahim* on this ideological map we are describing. Quite probably, it is divided, very much like the rest of the Jewish community in Israel, between the three ideological streams. The neo-Zionists have the advantage of two important power centers, the settlers and the traditional national–religious establishment.

Lacking any distinctive social agenda, the left remained at the end of twentieth century a movement of one issue – peace with the Palestinians. With the start of the second *Intifada* in September 2000, even that mission proved to be too much for the Israeli left.

The demise of the Israeli left, 2000–2003

Even a very imaginative and determined visitor would find it difficult in 2004 to reveal any trace of post-Zionism since the outbreak of the second *Intifada*. It would be equally hard to find very many people who still declare themselves to be on the left. A large portion of those who in the past identified themselves as such publicly and privately confessed in the immediate aftermath of the second *Intifada* how wrong they had been "to trust the Palestinians". Many voted without hesitation for Sharon in the 2001 and 2003 elections. The chief "gurus" and leaders of this group also expressed their "disappointment" with Israel's Palestinian citizens – with whom, so they claimed, they had concluded a "historic alliance". The Israeli Palestinians' loss of 13 casualties in clashes with the authorities in October 2000, and the boycott of the February 2001 elections, came as the last straw that broke the back of that "historical pact"; and the re-participation of the Palestinians in the 2003 elections was not enough to mend the fences.

The "dehydration" of the Israeli intellectual, academic and cultural scene came with the disappearance of a political moral voice that accepts at least the Palestinian right to independence and equality, if not their Right of Return. These were processes that occurred at an amazing speed. One would have expected, especially in more learned and intellectual circles, that long processes of reflection would precede such a fundamental change of views. But it seems that what took place instead was a frantic rush, accompanied by loud sighs of relief at the chance to shed the few thin layers of democracy, morality and pluralism that had overlaid Zionist ideology and praxis throughout the years. The swift disintegration of the institutions that advocated policies of peace and compromise, the hasty removal of peaceful and moral terminology from the public discourse, and the disappearance of any alternative views to the overall Zionist consensus on the Palestine question – all testify to the shallowness of the Israeli peace camp and peace discourse before the recent *Intifada*.

Israeli analysts attribute this phenomena to genuine trauma over a shock caused by three factors: Arafat's insistence on the Right of Return, the Palestinian Authority's rejection of Barak's "generous proposals" at Camp David, and the violent uprising in 2000. However, these explanations cannot stand the test of any objective enquiry. For example, Arafat never relinquished the Right of Return – indeed, he could not have done so even had he wished to do so. He openly and constantly talked about it from Oslo onward. As for the fable of the generous offers made at Camp David, people who were involved like Shlomo Ben-Ami and Yossi Beilin have meanwhile admitted that such offers were made only at Taba – and then tongue in cheek, since everyone concerned already knew that Barak was a lame duck and lacked the power to execute them. As for Barak, he has said that in the negotiations he only wanted to prove that Arafat is not a partner for peace. It is a fact that he now accepts Sharon's boycott of the Palestinian leader. Moreover, many Israeli "leftists" read in *Ha'aretz* the American reports from Camp David and knew that Arafat was presented there with a dictate he could not accept under any circumstances. Did he really disappoint them by failing to resist the popular anger in the occupied territories at the dead end into which both sides had been pushed, and which for the Palestinians meant the perpetuation of the occupation? Therefore, did the second *Intifada* come as such a surprise?

The manifestations of disappointment and disintegration in the Israeli left indicate that the Oslo process did not cause any significant change in the basic Israeli interpretations (from the self-styled "left" and from the right) of the past, present and future in Israel/Palestine. In their view, most of Palestine belonged to Israel, the Palestinians would have to make "concessions" even on the 28 percent of the territory available, and there was no Palestinian Right of Return. For the Jews, the only hope of survival was within a Zionist state, in as much of Palestine as possible, with as few Palestinians as feasible in it. If there was any argument on these assumptions, it was about tactics, not goals.

The "moderate" tactics of the left, and their agenda for peace which was all they had to offer at the beginning of the twenty-first century, were not accepted by the Palestinians in the occupied territories or within Israel. The bubble was burst. In a situation demanding an alternative approach, the very narrow limits of a genuine Jewish peace camp were exposed. Now the time has come for the Israeli left to attempt a sober and realistic reassessment of how the forces struggling for true peace within Jewish society can regroup and reassert themselves. This is the lesson of the past and their obligation for the future.

Postscript

In the summer of 2003 the left in Israel was revitalized to some extent by the "Ayalon-Nusseibeh principles", a short joint statement aiming to mobilize support for a feasible Israeli–Palestinian treaty; and by the

"Geneva Accords", a highly detailed model for a future agreement on all outstanding issues between the parties, along the lines of a two-state solution. These appeared to provide an alternative agenda to the Sharon government's policies of occupation and stagnation.

The initiatives had one thing in common: they believed that a Palestinian renunciation of the Right of Return would pave the way for a consensus in Jewish public opinion in support of total evacuation of the occupied territories and the creation of an independent Palestinian state.

This writer happens to disagree with this approach, as I regard Israeli recognition for the principle of the Right of Return as a pre-condition for peace. There is, however, no denying that in the wake of these initiatives and other positive developments on the political scene, some movement is apparent in the peace camp in the country, Whether and how this could have an impact on the broader political scene in Israel remains to be seen.

Notes

1 Ilan Pappe, "Uneasy Co-existence: Arabs and Jews in the First Decade of Statehood" in Ilan Trone and Noah Lucas (eds.), *Israel: the First Decade of Independence* (New York: State University Press, 1995).

2 The Minutes of the *Knesset* Meetings, Volume 33, June 30, 1962.

3 Danny Rabinowitz, "Uri Davis", in Adi Offir (ed.), *Fifty to Fifty-Eight* (Jerusalem: Van Leer Institute, 1999 [Hebrew]).

4 This is a point made by Sami Shalom Shitrit in a new film on the Black Panthers.

5 Uri Ram, *The Israeli Society: Critical Aspects* (Tel Aviv: Breirot [Hebrew]).

6 Ella Shohat, *Israeli Cinema: East/West and the Politics of Representation* (Austin: University of Texas Press, 1989).

8

Post-Mortem for the *Ashkenazi* Left

LEV GRINBERG

The central political force which defined Zionism and led it to the estab-lishment of the State of Israel was Socialist-Zionism. In time, and with the decline of the appeal of Socialism, this came in short to be called the "left".[1] It was Socialist-Zionism which established the political, economic and cultural institutions that paved the way for the establishment of the State of Israel and shaped the national community which was dominant within it. Similarly, it established the central institutions of the State of Israel itself: the army, the governmental structure and its dominant systems – legal and legislative, educational, economic and financial, and welfare.

Socialist-Zionism, a dynamic and creative movement with gifted lead-ership, was historically capable of leading a national movement and of reaching impressive achievements in realizing the goals it set for itself. As against this, the "left" finds itself today at its lowest ebb, incapable of fresh or critical thinking and unable to generate a leadership which could provide answers to the political and economic crises facing Israel. This failure has recently been expressed in the party's increasing decline in recent elections. It stood out even more in the election in 2003 of Shimon Peres as temporary Chair of the party in order to "revitalize" it, notwith-standing that he himself had led the party during its stagnation period between 1977 and 1990. This loss of vitality of the "left" reflects the unreadiness to face up to the problems and contradictions which had already became evident in the 1960s, when the Labor movement enjoyed hegemony on the Israeli political scene. It was the Labor movement itself which established the policies in which Israel's present crises originated, and which buried the movement beneath them. What follows is an attempt to place in historical perspective the question of why and how the wheel turned full circle, from the heyday of Socialist-Zionism to the unhappy situation of the Zionist "left" today.

Ever since the political forces called the "left" lost power for the first time since 1948 to the "right" in 1977, they were unable to redefine their political role. The Labor party twice joined governments led by the *Likud*, which were called "National Unity governments", in the periods 1984–90 and 2001–3, while twice they won power for short periods which ended in political disgrace and electoral defeat – the Rabin–Peres period from 1992 to 1996 and the Barak government of 1999–2000. Smaller parties on the Zionist "left" outside the Labor party joined together to form *Meretz*, which won an impressive 12 mandates in the 1992 elections (with Labor itself then achieving 44 mandates – 56 altogether for the "left"). With the five mandates of factions supported mainly by Palestinian Israelis, there could have arisen a body of 61 mandates (out of 120) to block a *Likud*-led coalition. This was not to be for the "left" preferred a coalition with the "right". The failure of the comeback of the Zionist "left" in the 1990s led to a decline in the joint strength of Labor and *Meretz* to 24 mandates in 2003, a process which we will analyze later in this chapter.

The "left" as nation-builders and rulers

The theory and practice of Socialist-Zionism

Socialist-Zionism grew in Eastern Europe in the beginning of the twentieth century on the background of the rise of the Socialist movements on the one hand, and increasing anti-Semitism on the other. Small groups of petty-bourgeois Jewish youth preferred immigrating to Palestine, and establishing a new Jewish national community there, to emigrating to the West or assimilating.

The common denominator in all the groups, organizations, parties and movements included in the category of Socialist-Zionism was their aspiration to immigrate (to make *aliya* – "ascend" in ideological language) to Palestine, to settle there and build a new life for the persecuted Jews of Eastern Europe. They developed a contemptuous attitude toward the "Diaspora Jew", striving instead to create a "new Jew" who would work the land, be muscular and fighting. These characteristics corresponded with the needs of settlement, in view of the presence of the Arab population in Palestine which had been working its land for generations. As in every European settlement project, the central issue facing the young immigrants was how to push the local residents out from their land and how subsequently to maintain control over it.

Facing these first challenges, the young immigrants adopted solutions characterized first by collective settlement, subordinating aspirations to individual freedom and transferring the ownership of the land to national institutions; second, by displacing the Arab population from land acquired by the Jews and establishing cooperative and communal frameworks (kibbutzim and moshavim) which would prevent the employment of Arab labor. This strategy of settlement was called "Hebrew labor". The third element, military control, was essential in view of Arab hostility and the limitations of the settlement strategies, which until the British left Palestine in 1948 had managed to acquire only 10 percent of the land in the country. It was the Zionist labor movement which established military organizations from among the second generation of the European settlers. In an era of war and violent confrontation, these forerunners of today's Israel Defense Force (IDF), were a focus of identification for Socialist-Zionist youth in building the nation. Here, I will call this type of nationalism "a nation in conflict".[2]

Various streams competed within the Socialist-Zionist camp, reaching full unity only after the 1967 war, but enjoying a consensus around the three elements noted above. The actual realization of Socialism was never on their agenda. In the eyes of the centrist wing of the movement (*Poalei Zion, Hapoel Hatzair, Achdut Avodah* and *Mapai*) Socialism was merely an instrument for mobilizing public support for the national effort. As for the Marxist groups (*Hashomer Hatzair,* left *Poalei Tsion* and *Mapam*), they always delayed the Socialist revolution until some later stage which would come only after the realization of Zionism.[3]

Maintaining dominance over the land and the Jewish population in pre-state Israel necessitated centralized political control, preventing the growth of an autonomous Jewish civil society. The institutions of the Labor movement dealt with economic activities – agriculture, construction, industry, transportation, marketing, banking, insurance, etc. – and controlled a whole series of social services, from health and education to housing, pensions and sport. The centralized political control over most areas of life created a dependence of the Jewish immigrants on the institutions handling their absorption, mainly the *Histadrut* and *Mapai*.[4] Through this dependence, the institutions of the Labor movement were able to concentrate tremendous power in their hands, particularly over control of land, production and services. Thus, a small idealistic minority of committed pioneering settlers dictated to the majority of the Jewish community the meaning of the national project. This was the concept of a "a nation in conflict".

Along with this dependence of the immigrants on Socialist-Zionist institutions, the strength of the Labor political parties was consolidated. They were elected according to the system of proportional representation used in the Zionist movement where, once the mandates were allocated, the parties agreed on the sharing of power. This generated a democracy which was mainly formal. Within this system, Zionist Socialism was in power from 1933 to 1977.[5] In the attempt to transform different groups of mainly Eastern European Jews into a nation and establish an exclusive Jewish state, one can see two sides to the same coin. One was the lack both of democratic contestation between parties and of the dynamic influence of a civil society; the other was the permanent national confrontation with the Arab population.

My argument is that the fundamental failure of Socialist-Zionism after the establishment of the State of Israel was the result of its inability to break away both from the undemocratic patterns of domination and discourse, and from the practices of the "nation in conflict". The movement became trapped by the very institutions and practices which it had itself created before 1948. The required changes after the establishment of the State of Israel in 1948 would have necessitated a new division of power based on concrete principles of democracy, and not only in the formality of periodic elections. This should have been applied on two levels: to relations between the Jews and the Palestinian Arabs, and within the Jewish population toward various groups not belonging to the dominant Eastern European immigrants.

In other words, the failure of the "left" lay in its parties and organizations being too strong, too undemocratic and representative only of one social group – secular *Ashkenazi* (Eastern European) Jews – which in the course of time became a minority. Having achieved its goal with the establishment of the state, the Labor movement entered a crisis caused by the attempt to establish a formally democratic state on the ruins of war, the expulsion of most of the Arab population and the transformation of those who remained into a peripheral and oppressed minority. The formal democracy did not create a legitimate political space for the Palestinian citizens. Moreover, in the long run this deficiency turned out for the "left" to be an even graver error: it failed to cater for the new Jewish immigrants coming from the Arab countries, who had no common culture with the dominant Eastern European groups. Given the formal democratic rules in the newly established state there was a potential for the strengthening of the civil society and new political identities and organizations. When this opportunity was missed, the maintenance of the Zionist Labor's centralized rule was challenged.

A secular–Ashkenazi *nation and a politically centralized-state*

The Zionist vision was based on the millions of Jews in Eastern Europe and the concept of a European style of modern secular state in the new homeland. From its inception, the Zionist movement did not really relate to the Jews of the Arab countries as part of the nation. Before World War II, the *Ashkenazi* Jews constituted the great majority of the world Jewish population; they had a common language (Yiddish), joint communal, political and religious and cultural activities and institutions. Subject to anti-Semitic persecution and seeking their survival, the Zionist interpretation was that all that was lacking for *Ashkenazi* Jews in order to be a nation was a territory and army of their own. Thus the conquest of the land and army service became the most salient virtues of the "nation in conflict". Only after the recognition of the disastrous consequences of the Holocaust and the extermination of the European Jews did the Zionist movement start to to mobilize the Jews from Arab countries to immigrate to Israel, and incorporated them as an integral part of the nation.

After 1948 the new state was defined as the state of the Jewish people, namely a state that belongs to the whole Jewish people wherever it may be, and not only to its citizens – certainly not to its Arab citizens who had remained within its borders (160,000 out of the 900,000 from before the 1948 war). Although these Palestinian citizens were attributed civil and political rights, they were subject to military rule and perceived as part of the "Palestinian enemy". From 1948 this is how the public good in the State of Israel was defined by the "nation in conflict": the Arabs, who were part of the enemy, and ultra-orthodox Jews, who were not part of the secular Zionist project, were freed from army service. The state did not even pretend to make equal citizens of these two communities. However, in order to incorporate the Jews from the Arab countries as part of the "nation in conflict", they were enlisted into the army and sent to settle on the lands and property formerly owned by the Palestinians. The soldier and the settler remained the main components of the "nation in conflict".

After 1948 vast resources were concentrated in the hands of state institutions. The state expropriated the property of the Palestinian refugees; it received contributions from American and European Jews and grants and loans from the US government, and later from the German government as reparations. *Mapai*, the ruling party, directly controlled the senior echelons of the army. It also controlled the *Histadrut*, which continued its pre-state role as roof-organization for all the labor-owned economic activities and welfare services (such as health, employment agencies and pension funds). After ten years, when full employment was reached, the fundamental contradiction in the maintenance in a formally democratic state of the same undemocratic institutions and organizations established during the British colonial period, came to light.[6]

Full employment first of all caused the breakdown of the military government's rule over Palestinian citizens because they had to be mobile in order to meet the demand for working hands in the industrialized central areas.[7] In addition, the situation of rank-and-file workers was strengthened, their dependence on the *Histadrut* apparatus and the ruling party was weakened, and they dared to undertake independent action to protect their interests. The middle class and private employers also began to see signs of weakness in the government and sought ways to organize independently in the political area. The crisis of full employment started in 1959 in the revolt of unemployed immigrants from North Africa (the Wadi Salib riots) and ended after the 1965 elections, when the government announced a policy of recession.

The recession policy in the years 1965–7 was another sign of the problems facing Socialist-Zionism with the establishment of the State of Israel. The power of the *Mapai* leadership was founded on the conditions of the political economy prior to the establishment of the Jewish State. The dominant factors were first the weakness of Jewish middle classes due to the dependence of the immigrants on state services provided exclusively by the Labor Zionist movement; and second, the weakness of the Jewish worker in competition with the Palestinan worker, which strengthened the former's dependence on the *Histadrut* for work and livelihood. The new situation with statehood constituted a threat to the undemocratic institutional structure of the labor movement. Surprisingly, rather than the political institutions undergoing reform and adapting themselves to the new conditions of a formally democratic tate, the opposite took place. In the Six Day War the dependence of civil society on political institutions was reestablished, only to prolong the rule of the Labor movement's institutions for ten years (1967–77), but it was to end with a crash from which it would be hard to recover.

Military conquest, settlement and the permanent status of the "nation in conflict"

The decisive question concerning 1967 is not why the war broke out, but how did it happen that the Labor movement, which strove to establish an exclusively Jewish state, created with its own hands a bi-national state. My research indicates that the Labor movement saved its institutions from complete collapse with the help of the results of the war.[8] First, the waning control over rebellious workers was restored through competition with unorganized Palestinian workers. Second, large *Histadrut* economic companies threatened with collapse in the recession period were saved by the heavy subsidization of *Histadrut* industries. These took the form of unlinked loans and direct subsidies to security-oriented companies and military industries under *Histadrut* and cooperative ownership.

Therefore, in the wake of the 1967 war, blind to the dangers ahead both for the state and the movement itself, the leadership of the Labor Movement saw only the glory of victory in war, and organizational and financial profits for its institutions. In the political arena this lack of fore-sight was best expressed by Prime Minister Golda Meir in her statement that there is no Palestinian people and by the claim by Minister of Defense Moshe Dayan that "Sharm el-Sheik without peace is preferable to peace without Sharm el-Sheik". Young Labor movement leaders who started their career in the IDF, like Yigal Alon and Moshe Dayan, began to compete with each other in providing support for the new settlement project in the areas conquered in 1967. Hankering after fertile new lands, the kibbutz movement settled in the Jordan valley and the Golan Heights. It took until 1973, with the *Yom Kippur* war, for the chickens to come home to roost: the Golda Meir government was dismissed at once and the Labor movement lost power in the 1977 elections.

One cannot overlook that the lack of vision was also the result of US policy and the unlimited international support which it granted to Israel both diplomatically and in increasing financial aid and arms as part of its Cold War strategy. But when the United States understood, as a result of the 1974 oil boycott, that it must exert pressure on Israel to reach a polit-ical settlement with Egypt and to retreat from Sinai, the Labor government led by Yitzhak Rabin was incapable of undertaking the task. Paradoxically, it was the "rightist" Prime Minister, Menahem Begin, elected in 1977, who accepted the demands of the US administration to compromise with Egyptian President Anwar Sadat and to retreat from Egyptian territory to the pre-1967 international border.

The ascent of the Begin government, and peace with Egypt following the Labor party's loss of public credibility, created a break between the terms "left" and "right" and between the political and economic content of these party blocs. By now, the basis for much of the *Likud*'s support was *Mizrahi* (Oriental or *Sephardi*) Jews, most of whom belonged to the lower classes, while the "left" voters came largely from the *Ashkenazi* (European) middle classes. On the political level, it was the Labor party which took the initiative after the 1967 war to start the drive for settle-ment in the occupied areas, which was to be intensified by the *Likud*. It was the "right" that after 1977 retreated from Sinai, signed a peace agreement with Egypt, and in the framework of these agreements recognized the "legitimate rights of the Palestinian people".

"Right" and "left" were transformed since 1977 into symbols of two hostile "cultural camps" with an ethnic class basis, and not of political camps with different views on political, social and economic issues. These groups did not mobilize supporters on the basis of their interests or views, but by appealing to the identity and the status symbols of their "cultural camp". These symbols also represented different attitudes to the Palestinian "other". The "leftist" discourse demanded control over the Palestinians on the basis of modern and rational reasons, i.e. security, while seemingly ready for compromise on democratic grounds, fearing what is paradoxically called "the demographic threat". As against this, the "right" was identified with the ethnic-Jewish orientation to a "greater Israel" and the unity of the Jewish people. However, as regards the Palestinians, the main difference between the two camps was largely rhetorical. In practice both blocs supported the continuation of the occupation and expanding the establishment of Jewish settlements on Palestinian land; both "blamed" Arafat and the PLO leadership for refusing to recognize Israel, thus justifying the continued Israeli rule over the West Bank and Gaza. The outstanding political expression of the broad common denominator between *Likud* and Labor was of course the national unity coalition governments in the period between 1984 and 1990. After 1967, the occupation of the West Bank and Gaza Strip became the most important guarantee for the maintenance of the "nation in conflict".

The crisis of "peace imagination"

The Oslo process and the changes of the 1990s

The popular Palestinian uprising which broke out at the end of 1987 marked a breaking point and put an end to that inertia which had characterized the Israeli occupation since 1967. What was called the first *Intifada* came as a surprise to the Israeli public. Many Israelis were shocked at the extent of force used in suppressing the Palestinians but the security discourse had up to then been fed by images of the danger to Israel of Palestinian resistance. The *Intifada* suddenly showed that those involved were men, women and children fighting for their basic human and political rights against an army of occupation. The self-image of the Israelis and of the security myth were badly damaged.

When the *Intifada* broke out, it to a large extent undid the Israeli belief that had granted the occupation its stability – namely, the unreserved legitimization granted by the majority of the Israeli public to the oppressive actions against the occupied Palestinian population. In the light of the challenge to this legitimacy, the military echelon came to the conclusion that the *Intifada* could not be suppressed by force and that a political solution was required. The clearest voice of the military logic demanding negotiations with the Palestinians was that of Defense Minister Yitzhak Rabin.

Rabin, who was strongly identified with the military establishment, became the leader of the opposition to the *Likud* government and finally led the Labor party to victory in 1992. Since leaving the "unity government" and going into opposition in 1990, the Labor party had been compelled to present an alternative to the rigid policies of Prime Minister Yitzhak Shamir. However, while undergoing a degree of internal democratization, it was still far from developing a completely new strategy for the State of Israel. Nevertheless it looked for a moment as if the Labor party was recovering and restoring that ability to lead which it had lost in 1977. Between 1992 and 1995 it appeared like a party redefining the goals of the state not only as regards the Palestinians and the peace option, but also as regards social and economic policies: this involved determining new priorities for investment in the infrastructure – education, transportation and developing the areas of Israel's remote under-privileged "periphery". Israel's economy was opened up for the first time to the world market with capital drawn in from abroad on a commercial basis and investors beginning to take an interest in Israel's economic potential in times of peace. Things seemed to be looking up.

However, in spite of the above it is important to note opposite tendencies which also existed during Rabin's term of office:

1 *The "imagined peace".* Even before the ink was dry on the signatures to the agreement between the PLO and Israel, a blind eye was being turned to the difficulties to be expected in the process. The leaders of the "left" and its principle spokespeople, having declared victory over the "right", now foresaw the Oslo process as "irreversible", and necessarily leading to the recognition of a Palestinian state. There was a tendency here to ignore both the need to dismantle the occupation apparatus, and the political struggle that was to be expected against the opponents of the process – particularly the extremist settlers and the religious camp. Underestimating this opposition was one of the main factors determining the failure of Oslo.

2 *The security discourse.* The process of dialogue with the Palestinians did not come about as the result of recognition of their individual and

collective rights, but from the practical recognition that Israel lacked the military and moral strength to defeat them. The discourse was and remains a security-oriented discourse of a "nation in conflict". When it was argued that at present "there is no military solution" to the conflict, the implication of this statement remained that if and when such a solution exists, it may be implemented.[9]

3 *Increasing settlement.* Far from being stopped, settlement in the occupied territories was actually intensified. The number of settlers in the West Bank and the Gaza Strip, without East Jerusalem, grew between 1993 and 2000 from 100,000 to 200,000 (in 2003 it had risen to 230,000). Increased settlement also necessitated growing military control over the Palestinians, and the construction of by-pass roads only for settlers, according to the Apartheid model, as well as the expropriation of more and more Palestinian land.

These trends contradicted the positive attitudes of the majority of the public who believed that the peace process was moving forward. Yitzhak Rabin held in his hands most of the power in designing the relations with the Palestinians and it was he himself who articulated the interests of the army and of the business community which supported the process. However, in his shadow the Labor party as such was virtually neutralized, as was its main political partner, *Meretz*. Neither was actively involved in shaping policy toward the Palestinians. Since the public already "imagined" the peace, the parties turned to what I have termed the "post-conflict agenda". This agenda related to questions of economic policy, social issues, religion–state and ethnic relations, and civil rights. Although most Israeli politics since 1993 dealt with these subjects, they were issues on which the "left" parties lacked a clear and crystallized stance. Thus it ensued that instead of the traditional "left–right" discourse, new identities, groups and organizations dealing primarily with the "new agenda" came to the fore. As for the "left" parties, they did not succeed in moving over from their old and traditional agenda of the "nation in conflict" to the new post-conflict agenda. This is the source of the central failure of the "left". In the spirit of the imagined peace, it helped in the de-politicization of relations with the Palestinians, neglecting what should have been top priority, namely dismantling the occupation apparatus. On the other hand, it was unable to formulate a new winning strategy and coalition of forces on post-conflict affairs. The neo-liberal economic positions of the "leftist" camp stood out particularly, with the promotion of the privatization process and the free market. This was combined with generating anti-Arab feelings, and a condescending attitude to everything Eastern (Orientalism) in which anti-*Mizrahi* sentiments were not lacking.

These policies truly catered to the interests and expressed the views of the secular *Ashkenazi* middle and upper class supporters of the "left" parties but prevented the reshaping of policies to meet changing circumstances. With the de-politicization of the peace process, these parties were dragged into a pursuit of the immediate needs of their constituency at the expense of tackling the grave difficulties involved in the peace process.

There was something ostrich-like in this policy of neglecting the controversial political situation. It reached its highest point with the assassination of Yitzhak Rabin and its aftermath. The concentration of power in his hands, as the symbol of Israel's security myth, along with the ineffective functioning of Labor and *Meretz* as leading political parties, facilitated the collapse of the "left" following the assassination. Though the immediate reaction of the public in the wake of the assassination was opposition to the extremist settlers, the leadership of the "left" failed to convey a correct political interpretation of the assassination and to draw the necessary conclusions. On the contrary, the dominant narrative adopted by the public opinion was that of the extreme right, which claimed that the murder was the result of "polarization" within the Jewish public. It was as if Rabin's verbal debates with the settlers had created the atmosphere which led to his being killed. The anti-democratic significance of the occupation, of military rule and of the settlements, was not discussed. The conclusion was that an effort must be made at reconciliation with the extremist religious settlers. Rather than politicizing the peace with the Palestinians, there was a reformulation on the "left" of the "nation in conflict", readapted to the imagined peace: now the common goal was securing "peace among the Jews".

Post-Rabin policies

The winning slogan of Bibi Netanyahu in the 1996 elections, "Bibi is good for the Jews" expressed the belief that following Rabin's assassination, peace among the Jews was what was needed. However, Bibi only succeeded in the polls preceding the elections through changing his attitude to the Oslo process, and committing himself to honor the agreements and talk to Arafat. Since most of the public has already "imagined" the peace and taken it for granted, the elections could not be won under the slogan of a "greater Israel". However, the imagined peace did not commit its supporters to any concrete action, such as stopping settlement, or ending the occupation. Netanyahu proved that he was not even committed to conduct negotiations with the Palestinians on the territorial issue because in the agreement, the extent of Israeli retreat from the occupied territories in stages was for Israel to decide.

The period of Netanyahu's government also witnessed an increasing lack of faith of Israelis in their political parties and the growth of "post conflict" approaches in old and new parties. Thus the *Shinui* party gained increasing credibility and rose from six mandates in 1999 to 15 in the 2003 elections. This was the expression of voters from the "left" who underwent the process mentioned above of de-politicization as a result of the imagined peace. As for the Labor party, it declined consistently following Rabin's murder: from 44 mandates in 1992, to 32 in 1996, 26 in 1999, and only 19 in 2003. From great hopes for a "leftist" renewal in 1992 there remained only a shadow. The Barak government constituted the last nail in the coffin of the "left". Having won a large majority in the direct elections for Prime Minister in 1999, within a year Barak lost all the credit he had won. The view commonly held that this was due to his own personal failure overlooks several basic facts which bear witness to the Labor party's state of collapse even at the time of Barak's election.

In the 1999 elections Labor and *Meretz* lost 20 mandates from the 56 they had won in 1992. In his new government Barak failed to build a coalition against the occupation and even included the National Religious Party, which represented the most extremist settlers. In his first year Barak did not hold negotiations with the Palestinians; during the intensive Camp David negotiations his Government coalition controlled only 32 mandates (Labor and the Center Party. *Meretz* had left the government – significantly not over the peace process, which it supported, but over its disagreement on post-conflict educational issues with the ultra-religious *Mizrachi* party, *Shas*). With the failure of the negotiations and the outbreak of the second *Intifada*, Barak lost the confidence both of the *Knesset* and of the public. After the Labor party's subsequent failure in the elections for Prime Minister in 2001, it joined a strongly rightist government under Sharon's leadership. This offered the clearest indication that it had no significant disagreement over continuing the increasing repression in the territories and nullifying the Oslo process. These factors prove not that the "left" disintegrated as a result of the Barak government, but the opposite: Barak's failure was the consequence of the prior process of the "left's" ideological disintegration and its inability to rethink the concept of the "nation in conflict". This erosion, as noted, had started with the murder of Rabin and Barak was incapable of stopping the rot.

Conclusion

Why, then, did the political camp called "left" disintegrate in the wake of the Oslo process and the assassination of Rabin? Following the Gulf War and after the US exerted pressure on Israel, the required conditions for a solution to the conflict and for Israel's abandoning its control over the Palestinians had been created. The *Likud* had neither interest in such a historical shift nor the ability to lead it. Thus the Labor party had a rare historical opportunity to restore its leading national role through bringing Israel back to its internationally recognized pre-1967 borders, and building a democratic state.

However, putting and end to the protracted conflict involved a major realignment which included evacuation of the settlements in the territories occupied in 1967, and freeing the Palestinian people from occupation. This demanded the deconstruction of the old "nation in conflict" and the construction of a new type of "Israeli-ism", no longer motivated by the reaction to an external enemy as the unifying element of the nation. This reconstruction would have to be capable of including different socio-cultural groups, conducting an internal dialogue within the coalition, and making decisions within agreed democratic forms.

The "left" failed this challenge completely. Rather than waging a struggle against the forces opposing Oslo, it gave into them. It failed to build a post-conflict coalition capable of legitimizing the ending of the occupation. The "left" parties also felt threatened by the demands of its own supporters for a post-conflict agenda. The Oslo period involved demands not only of the Palestinians, but also of the ultra-orthodox for more budgets; of the *Mizrahim* for land, housing and cultural autonomy; of newcomers from the former USSR for cultural recognition and the integration of non-Jewish immigrants; not to speak of the continued demand of Palestinian Israeli citizens for civic equality. All these were perceived as a threat to the homogeneous nation constructed under the rule of the veteran secular *Ashkenazi* elite.

This "nation in conflict" had been maintained by the Labor Zionist movement only with the help of an "external enemy". From the moment that Israel recognized the PLO and started to conduct negotiations with Arafat, the Israelis imagined that peace had been attained and began to involve themselves in post-conflict agendas. From that moment the "nation in conflict" concept, and the hegemonic position of the "leftist" *Ashkenazi* elite, were challenged. Against this challenge the parties of the "left" responded with arrogance and withdrawal. This reaction revealed the absence of a clear distinction between the social groups supporting the "left" (secular *Ashkenazi*) and the political parties (Labor and *Meretz*).

High-status groups believing in their cultural superiority tend to close their ranks and seek exclusivity in order to maintain their power. As against this, political parties must strive to expand their public support by building broad coalitions of varied interests and social groups. In this sense the "left" behaved not like parties but as direct representatives of the dominant secular *Ashkenazi* status groups. They felt themselves threatened by the many demands upon them with the rise of the post-conflict agenda and the decline of the "nation in conflict" concept as a response to the imagined peace.

Until the Camp David conference was convened there was no public debate of any of the relevant questions that were to be discussed there, not the question of dismantling the settlements, not Jerusalem, not refugees and not the Holy places.[10] Rather, the government coalition was deteriorating due to debates on post-conflict issues, which preoccupied Israeli public opinion too. The "left" parties never adequately tackled the major issues of ending the occupation and the political struggle against the extremist ideological settlers and their supporters.

This discrepancy between, on the one hand, the interests and views of their supporters on post-conflict issues, and on the other hand, promoting a real peace strategy, caused the "left" parties eventually to be abandoned by their own voters. Ever since the failure of Camp David, and particularly with the outbreak in 2000 of the second *Intifada*, the "leftist" status group was inclined to return to its pre-Oslo identity of a "nation in conflict". Some of them still voted for Barak in 2001 and for Labor and *Meretz* in 2003, but a large part of them went over to supporting Sharon's policy of violent confrontation and backed Labor's joining Sharon's national coalition after 2001. The concept of the "left" as supporting the ending of the occupation through peaceful negotiations with the Palestinian leadership was eradicated during Barak's period in office.

After the elections of 2003, Sharon established a secular *Ashkenazi* coalition without either the "leftist parties", the ultra-orthodox, the Arabs or the *Mizrahim*. Yet this was a better reflection of the renewed nationalist discourse of many members of the "leftist" cultural community than had been provided by the parties of the "left". Under Sharon, moreover, they felt more protected from the post-conflict demands of the marginalized groups. Since the 2003 elections the weakened "left" has remained in opposition, without a relevant strategy or coalition of forces and interests capable of providing an alternative to Sharon's militant nationalism. Such an alternative would demand a new agenda, incorporating reconciliation with Palestinian society, but also with various parts of Israeli society. This would include both *Mizrahim* and *Ashkenazim* and would be founded on redefining a common multi-cultural national identity, allowing the different groups who make up the society to live together without needing an "external enemy". The "left" has yet to start the job of rebuilding itself as an alternative to that very "nation in conflict" that they themselves had invented and institutionalized in the past, and which they never really abandoned. Only when this *radical* change takes place, be it by the existing parties or by new forces, will we be able to speak not of the "left" but of the left, without the quotes.

Notes

1 From hereon I will write "left" under quotes in order to emphasize my criticism of the concept.

2 For land displacement see Kimmerling, *Zionism and Territory* (Berkeley: California, 1983); for the Labor displacement see Shafir, *Land, Labor and the Origins of the Israeli–Palestinian Conflict* (New York: Cambridge University Press, 1989) and for the role of the military in building the "nation in conflict ('nation in arms' according to his terminology)" among the Zionist-Socialist youth, see Ben-Eliezer, *The Making of Israeli Militarism* (Bloomington: Indiana University Press, 1998).

3 For *Mapai* see Sternhell, *The Founding Myths of Israel: Nationalism, Socialism and the Making of the Jewish State* (Princeton: Princeton University Press, 1997); for the Marxist Zionist groups see E. Margalit, *Anatomy of the Left* (Tel Aviv: Peretz Publishers, 1976).

4 The *Histadrut*, established in 1920, was the roof organization that controlled all the economic activities and social services. *Mapai*, established in 1930, was the ruling party in the Histadrut and in the World Zionist Organization (since 1933) in coalition with other Zionist-Socialist parties.

5 Y. Shapiro, *The Formative Years of the Israeli Labor Party: The Organization of Power* (London: Sage Publications, 1976).

6 L. Grinberg, *The* Histadrut *above All* (Jerusalem: Nevo Publications, 1993).

7 Y. Ben Porat, *Arab Working Force in Israel* (Jerusalem: Falk Institution, 1966).

8 L. Grinberg, The Crisis of Statehood: "A Weak State and Strong Political Institutions," *Journal of Theoretical Politics* 5, 1993.

9 The main problem of the "military solution" is moral: Do the soldiers and the public opinion believe in the legitimacy of the use of violence? This question was raised in 1982, during the Lebanon War. This was interpreted as a political war, what Begin has called a "war of choice". For this reason in 1987 there was no legitimacy in the use of the military violence needed to repress the Intifada. Only when the old belief of a "war of no choice" was reconstructed, after the Camp David conference in July 2000, was the military able to mobilize the moral support of Jewish public opinion to repress the second Intifada with unrestrained amounts of violence.

10 This is the reason why, despite the fact that Barak offered in Camp David to annex 11 percent of the West Bank to Israel (80 percent of the settlers), the offer was called "the best offer Israel can make".

Jewish National Self-Determination at the Crossroads

9

HILLEL SCHENKER

Despite the breakdown in the peace process and the tragic escalation of mutual violence, surveys carried out by the Steinmetz Peace Center at Tel Aviv University, the Dachaf Institute and others indicate that a majority of the Israeli Jews continue to support a two-state solution based upon a withdrawal from virtually all of the West Bank and the Gaza Strip, including the return of most of the settlers to Israel proper. The core group supporting this approach does not consist of post-Zionists or non-Zionists, a miniscule part of the Israeli public, but rather of people who look at the Israeli–Palestinian conflict via the prism of the liberal-left Zionist narrative.

In presenting a concise presentation of that narrative, which should be understood by anyone interested in resolving the conflict, it is necessary to go back to the sources. No, not to some Biblical promise of a God-given right to land in the Middle East. The modern Jewish national movement was not based on the word of the Scriptures, or inspired by rabbinical pronouncements. It was a late nineteenth–early twentieth century secular movement for national self-determination, influenced by the wave of nationalist yearnings that swept Europe, a rebellion against the passive wait-for-the-eventual-coming-of-the-Messiah then espoused by the overwhelming majority of the Jewish religious establishment.

Not a land without a people

Why did the founders focus on that small patch of land in the heart of the Middle East by the Mediterranean Sea, that had been ruled by the Greeks,

Romans, Crusaders, Moslems, and at the time of the genesis of the movement, by the Ottoman Turks? Because that is where the Jewish nation coalesced about 4,000 years ago. That is where the Jews had enjoyed periods of independent national sovereignty, the land described in the historical record of the Jewish people known as the Five Books of Moses. It was from here that they had been exiled twice, most recently at the beginning of the first millennium; it was the place where small enclaves of Jews had always remained (the secluded Galilean town of Peki'in, and Shfaram near Mt. Carmel and the bay of Haifa); where many Jews had converted to Islam to survive; and where Jews began to return from the Diaspora in the fifteenth century to the four "Holy Cities" – Jerusalem, Safed, Tiberias and Hebron.

The founders of the modern Jewish national movement looked for a location that would be an antidote to Jewish vulnerability in Western, Central and Eastern Europe where the overwhelming majority of world Jewry resided. This powerlessness expressed itself in cyclical expulsions from most European countries, the Spanish Inquisition, deadly pogroms in Eastern Europe and modern anti-Semitism in enlightened Western Europe. The Nazi Holocaust was yet to come. It was natural that the Jewish people looked toward the land of the origins of its nationhood, the land of Canaan, Palestine, or *Eretz Yisrael* as they called it.

The problem, of course, was that, after the Jewish dispersion to the far corners of the globe, another ethnic community began to coalesce in the area, what we now know as the Palestinian nation. A distinct Palestinian nationhood only began to evolve in the 1920s in the wake of the conflict with modern Zionism and the evaporation of the "Southern Syria" concept, finally crystallizing with the collapse of Nasserite pan-Arabism. The historical fact is that Israel/Palestine was not "a land without a people for a people without a land", according to the phrase originally popularized by British Zionist writer Israel Zangwill.

While the founder of modern Zionism and of the Zionist Congress, assimilated liberal Viennese Jewish journalist Theodor Herzl, may have downplayed and virtually ignored the presence of the Arabs, others did not. His rival and the leading advocate of cultural Zionism, Ahad Ha'am (Asher Ginsberg), wrote about the presence of another people in the land. The young David Ben-Gurion, who became the political leader of Labor Zionism, entered into a series of dialogues with the local Arabs that he wrote about in *Encounters with Arab Leaders*, though Arabic was not among the many languages he learned. The ideologue of the Socialist-Zionists, the Russian Jew Ber Borochov, actually believed that Jewish and Arab workers would unite against the exploitative *effendi* bosses and that class solidarity would help to overcome cultural and ethnic differences.

Shattered illusions

Whatever they may have believed in Europe and other parts of the Jewish Diaspora, the moment the modern secular Zionists from the first and second *Aliya* (waves of immigration) arrived in the Middle East in the 1880s and early 1900s, it was clear that they encountered the presence of the local Arabs. How did they respond it? The first major artists of the Jewish *Yishuv* (pre-state community), Reuven Rubin, Nachum Gutman and Abel Pen, painted romantic images of the local Arabs as a role model to be admired. Rubin even painted some self-portraits in which he darkened his image to become more oriental. Many in the *Yishuv* also made an effort to learn spoken Arabic, and Middle Eastern themes entered into the popular and classical music written by Jewish composers. The *Sephardi* Jews in Jerusalem and other towns, who began to arrive after the expulsion of the Jews from Spain in 1492, already knew Arabic, as did the early arrivals from Yemen.

The Arab riots of 1929 and 1936 ended this idyllic image. Though the rebellions were aimed as much against the British Mandate as against the Jews, they shattered any illusions of a nonviolent reemergence of a Jewish national home. In response to this new understanding, the right-wing Revisionist Zionist leader Ze'ev Jabotinsky called for the establishment of an "iron wall", the cultivation of a military and societal power that could withstand any Arab resistance until the Arabs would resign themselves to the Jewish presence in Zion. But both before and after the establishment of the State of Israel, the Revisionists were in the minority, and in 1935 they even founded an alternative New Zionist Organization that had little political impact on the historical developments.

The mainstream Labor Zionist movement, which set the dominant tone on the ground and in the leadership of the *Yishuv*'s institutions, in cooperation with the liberal Zionists led by World Zionst Organization President Prof. Chaim Weizmann, advocated the establishment of an autonomous Jewish community in the land, the building of a viable economy and society with a defensive military capacity, spearheaded by the pre-state *Haganah* and *Palmach*. They established a network of kibbutzim (collective settlements), *moshavim* (small-holders cooperative agricultural communities), and a series of cooperative economic enterprises under the auspices of the *Histadrut* Labor Federation. Their slogan was "one more goat and one more dunam", i.e. the gradual development of an autonomous Jewish community. By the time the State of Israel was established in 1948, half of the economy was under one or another form of public control. In contemporary terms, the approach was very similar to Third Way social-democracy.

Bi-nationalism

There was a third response. The left-wing Socialist-Zionist *Hashomer Hatzair* and *Kibbutz Artzi* movements advocated the establishment of an autonomous Jewish community in cooperation with the local Arab population. When the fate of the British Mandate was on the line at the fledgling United Nations in 1946–7, they advocated the establishment of a bi-national Jewish-Arab state rather than partition. A noted critic of contemporary Israeli government policy, Prof. Noam Chomsky, subscribed to this view. Other advocates of bi-nationalism came from the small *Ichud* and *Brit Shalom* groups, led by Prof. Martin Buber ("I and Thou"); Dr. Judah Magnes (first president of the Hebrew University); Henrietta Szold (founder of the Hadassah Women's Zionist Organization), and others. In the book *Culture and Resistance*, Edward Sa'id quoted Magnes as having said, "Let's try to think in terms quite morally and profoundly about the Arabs. Let's think in terms of their presence, not their absence." Sa'id both admired and dismissed the Buber intellectual group, respecting the "individuals" but not the movement. The *Hashomer Hatzair* movement was the mainstay of the *Mapam* Socialist-Zionist party, the second largest party with 19 (out of 120) seats in the first *Knesset*, now part of *Meretz*.

World War II was obviously a turning point. While some Zionist right-wing elements (future prime minister Yitzhak Shamir and his dissident *Lehi* or Stern group) explored the possibility of cooperation with Italian fascists against the British, the mainstream liberal-left Zionists joined the Jewish Brigade to fight alongside the British army against the Nazis and to concurrently develop their own military skills for future battles to come. At the same time, the leader of the Palestinian community, Hadj Amin El-Husseini, made the unfortunate choice of siding with the Nazis against the British, according to the principle of "the enemy of my enemy are my friends".

Of course, the primary aspect of World War II that affected developments was the Holocaust, the murder of six million European Jews, one-third of the Jewish people. This clearly was the background for the support of the necessary two-thirds majority in the United Nations for the 1947 Partition Plan (UN Resolution 181). As we all know, the leadership of the Jewish *Yishuv* accepted it, while the Arab states rejected it. Since the Palestinians did not have a sovereign authority at the time, they weren't really in a position to accept or reject the plan. However the local Palestinian leadership and community actively opposed the establishment of a Jewish state in the area designated for the Jews. Today, in retrospect, a number of Palestinian leaders, among them Prof. Sari Nusseibeh and

Ziad Abu-Zayyad, have said that the Palestinian leadership should have accepted the partition plan, to guarantee the creation of an independent Palestinian state in part of Palestine. But at that moment in their national development, it was impossible.

In the early years of the State of Israel, the governments were dominated by the Labor Zionists (*Mapai*), led by the first Prime Minister David Ben-Gurion. The left-Zionist *Mapam* party was sometimes a partner and sometimes in opposition, while the liberal Zionists were always partners. The right-wing *Herut* party (forerunner of today's *Likud*), like the Communists, was blacklisted by Ben-Gurion as parties not to be accepted in principle to the government coalition.

During the first two decades of the state's existence there were no serious official attempts to resolve the Israeli–Arab conflict. The Palestine Liberation Organization (PLO) was only founded, under Egyptian auspices, in 1964; *Fatah* was founded by Yasser Arafat and his associates in Kuwait in 1959, and its first attempt at military action was carried out in 1964. It was only after the 1967 Arab débâcle that *Fatah* assumed control of the PLO in 1968, thus creating a serious independent Palestinian address. Some historians believe that in any case Ben-Gurion found the lack of a possibility for serious dialogue with Arabs and Palestinians to be convenient, as he wished to concentrate on strengthening the economic, social and military foundations of the new state.

New Outlook

In 1957, the liberal and left Zionists, together with a number of Israeli Arab citizens, came together to create an initiative whose goal was to establish "a medium for the clarification of problems concerning peace and cooperation among all the people of the Middle East." They established *New Outlook*, an English language monthly based in Tel Aviv, a magazine which also was to serve as a catalyst for initiatives toward dialogue and peace. This project brought together some of the major supporters of the liberal-left Zionist narrative. They were inspired by Martin Buber's theories of dialogue, and the editors met regularly with the elderly professor in his Jerusalem home.

Although originally an editorial collective, the driving force and founding editor was Simha Flapan, who had been a leader of *Mapam* and later wrote two seminal books on the conflict, *Zionism and the Palestinians* in 1979 and *The Birth of Israel: Myths and Realities* in 1987. Some consider him to have been one of the first "new historians". In addition to other leading *Mapam* members, the initiators included prominent liberals such as *Ha'aretz* daily publisher and editor Gershon Shocken (then an MK) and Minister Moshe Kol of the Independent Liberal party. Also involved were two Israeli Arab MKs for the *Mapam* party, Rustum Bastuni and Abdul Aziz Zu'bi, who after the '67 war observed that "my state is at war with my people." *New Outlook* received the financial backing and political support of the liberal Dr. Nahum Goldmann, Chaim Weizmann's successor as President of the World Zionist Organization, who wrote an article in the initial edition entitled "Hands proffered in friendship".

Ben-Gurion attacked the initiative from the *Knesset* podium, saying that it sowed illusions of possibilities for dialogue and peace that were unrealistic. It should be recalled that, during this period, whenever Israeli academics participated in international symposia, Arab intellectuals would move from their seats to ensure that they weren't sitting alongside the Israelis, out of fear of criticism they might receive back home.

Another skeptical response came from an Egyptian in Moscow. The occasion was the Soviet backed international youth festival. One of the Israeli delegates was Latif Dori, Flapan's young Iraqi-born assistant in *Mapam*'s Arab Affairs Department, and today a *Meretz* activist with widespread contacts among the Palestinians and Egyptians. Flapan suggested that he take 50 copies of the initial issue of *New Outlook*, which had just been published in July 1957, to distribute at the conference. When a young Egyptian received it, his response was: "This magazine is a fraud. It must be propaganda created by the Israeli foreign ministry to create an impression that Israel is really interested in peace. Look, it says volume 1, number 1. That's proof it's a fraud." Dori assured him that this was a genuine initiative, and took his address, promising to send further issues via third-party Europeans. They met again in 1977, when the Egyptian accompanied President Anwar El-Sadat on his historic visit to Jerusalem. This time the Egyptian said, "You were right. It was a genuine initiative, and we read it with great interest on a regular basis."

According to the liberal-left Zionist narrative, the 1967 Six Day War was a turning point. Until then, the Arab perception may have been that the State of Israel was a temporary phenomenon in the Middle East, something like the Crusader kingdom, doomed to disappear. The overwhelming victory in the war against the Egyptian, Jordanian and Syrian armies demonstrated, in the eyes of the Arabs, that Israel was a rooted phenomenon, with a strong economy, society and military capacity. That was the beginning of an Arab realization that it was necessary to come to terms with Israel's existence in the region. It was Dr. Meir Pa'il, former head of the IDF Officers Training College, a military historian and later an MK for the left-Zionist *Moked* and *Sheli* parties, who promoted the idea that "the occupied West Bank and Gaza Strip were negotiating cards for peace". Former Prime Minister Ben-Gurion agreed with him in his old age, saying that everything, except the Golan Heights and East Jerusalem, should be returned to the Arabs (he didn't say Palestinians) in exchange for peace.

The settlement issue

The liberal-left Zionists were divided in their attitude toward settlements in the post-1967 occupied territories. The mainstream Labor Zionists, who continued to dominate government policy until 1977, believed that most of the territories would eventually be returned in exchange for peace. They supported the establishment of a limited number of settlements, for security reasons (the Alon plan), under the assumption that they would be included within the permanent boundaries of the state under the rubric of "border rectifications". The left-Zionist *Mapam* party was opposed to the establishment of any settlements on the other side of the Green Line, i.e. the 1967 borders (with the exception of a kibbutz called Geshur which when settling in 1974 on the ridge of the Golan Heights, declared that "it would be disbanded if it became an obstacle to a peace agreement with Syria". Mesmerized by the "miraculous" victory in 1967, a small group of Labor Zionists, among them veteran *Kibbutz Hameuchad* movement ideologue Yitzhak Tabenkin and poet Natan Alterman, helped to establish the Movement for a Greater Israel , which won broad public support for the establishment of settlements in the newly "liberated" territories.

The religious *Gush Emunim* (Bloc of the Faithful) settlement movement was only founded in 1974, aiming through settlement to ward off any "territorial compromise" following the shock of the 1973 *Yom Kippur* War. Its seeds were sewn during the Passover holiday in 1968, when nationalist Rabbi Moshe Levinger rented a few rooms in the Park Hotel in Hebron "to celebrate Passover", a gathering that became the basis for the first Jewish settlement in Hebron.

In December 1975, there was a critical struggle over the attempt to establish an illegal settlement near the ancient West Bank town of Sebastia. Labor Prime Minister Yitzhak Rabin was opposed to the initiative, while his security adviser Ariel Sharon actively supported the *Gush Emunim* venture led by Rabbi Levinger. Foreign Minister Shimon Peres backed a compromise resolution of the crisis. The settlers were removed from the site, but eventually won the day when they established an alternative settlement nearby, Kedumim, which still stands.

Rabin never backed the settlement activity, even stating when he first entered politics in 1974 that he wouldn't mind "visiting Gush Etzion (a settlement bloc near Jerusalem) with a visa". In the early 1990s, during his second term in office, he entered into sharp confrontation with the settlers, calling them "propellers" who revolve around, signifying nothing. The settlers' anger at this criticism generated the atmosphere in right-wing circles that promoted and sanctioned the Prime Minister's demonization and later led to his assassination by the nationalistic religious student Yigal Amir.

When the right-wing *Likud* party, led by Prime Minister Menahem Begin, came to power for the first time in 1977, there were only about 7,000 settlers in the occupied territories. Begin declared that "we have the full right to settle in all parts of *Eretz Yisrael*". For the first time, unrestricted settlement activity had full government backing. Today, in 2003, there are about 230,000 settlers, and they constitute a serious obstacle to a peace agreement with the Palestinians. The overwhelming majority of the supporters of the liberal-left Zionist narrative believe that most or all of the settlements should be evacuated in exchange for peace.

An address for dialogue

The first authorized PLO encounters with Israelis after the 1967 watershed were carried out by PLO European representatives such as Sa'id Hammami (London) and Dr. Issam Sartawi (Paris) in the early 1970s. They began by meeting with members of the small and peripheral anti-Zionist *Matzpen* group, but these meetings had absolutely no impact on Israeli society. Arafat and his associates, Abu Ayyad, Abu Jihad, Khaled El-Hassan and Abu Mazen who supported these contacts, understood that they had to reach out to more mainstream Israeli elements. With the foundation of the Israeli Council for Israeli-Palestinian Peace in 1976, the Palestinians got an address for dialogue from the Zionist and non-Zionist (but not anti-Zionist) liberal-left.

Most of the leaders of the initiative were from the newly formed *Sheli* peace party, among them Arie (Lova) Eliav, former Director General of the Labor Party, retired generals Prof. Matti Peled and Dr. Meir Pail, non-Zionist Uri Avnery from the *Haolam Hazeh* magazine and party, Dr. Ya'acov Arnon, former Director General of the Finance Ministry and Yossi Amitai, a Middle East expert and a member of a *Hashomer Hatzair* kibbutz. They were backed by Flapan and most of the New Outlook group. Thus began a series of dialogues with Hammami and Sartawi, both of whom were later assassinated by PLO rejectionists, and with Chairman Arafat himself. Since Peled had served together with Yitzhak Rabin on the

IDF General Staff during the 1967 war, it was arranged that the Prime Minister would get direct reports immediately after the meetings.

In 1978, New Outlook initiated a two-day dialogue at the American Colony (the East Jerusalem hotel that had once been owned by the Husseini family and is now a center for foreign correspondents and diplomat meetings). This was eventually published under the title *When Enemies Dare to Talk* (Croom Helm, 1979). Again the Israeli participants were supporters of the liberal-left Zionist narrative: among them future *Meretz* leader MK Shulamit Aloni; MK Eliav; Amitai; Prof. Yehoshafat Harkabi, a retired general and former head of IDF Military Intelligence; Prof. Shimon Shamir, later Israeli ambassador both to Egypt and Jordan; journalists Amos Elon (*Ha'aretz)* and Hanna Zemer (*Davar*, the *Histadrut* and Labor Party affiliated daily); leading writers Amos Oz and A. B. Yehoshua (*Meretz* supporters today); Dr. Arnon and others. Among the Palestinian participants were Anwar Nussiebeh, former Jordanian Defense Minister and father of Dr. Sari Nussiebeh; Dr. Haydar Abdul Shafi from Gaza, later the Palestinian keynote speaker at the 1991 Madrid Conference; Bethlehem Mayor Elias Friej; Ibrahim Dakkak, head of the West Bank Engineering Union; Ziad Abu-Zayyad, *Al Fajr* journalist and later Minister of Jerusalem Affairs for the Palestinian Authority; Prof. Nafez Nazal and others. For many, on both sides, this was the first in-depth meeting with "the other".

In 1980, *Al-Fajr*, the East Jerusalem-based Palestinian daily that served as the organ for PLO views in the occupied territories, began publishing an English-language edition. In the first issue they published an editorial that concluded with an outstretched hand for dialogue with peace-loving Israelis. The editors of *New Outlook* responded to the challenge, and subsequent meetings eventually led to the 1989 *New Outlook–Al Fajr* "Road to Peace" conference at Columbia University in New York, cosponsored by American Friends of Peace Now and Edward Sa'id's American Council for Palestine Affairs. This was during the period when Israeli law forbade contacts with PLO representatives "except within academic circumstances".

Among the 25 Israeli participants were *Ratz* (Citizen's Rights) Party leader MK Shulamit Aloni and *Mapam* MK Yair Tzaban, both future ministers in Rabin's 1992 government; former MK and Peace Now spokesperson Dr. Mordechai Bar-On; kibbutz member and former Deputy Air Force Commander Dr. Giora Foreman; Prof. and future MK Naomi Hazan; writer Yoram Kaniuk; *New Outlook* editor and former Secretary of the *Kibbutz Artzi-Hashomer Hatzair* movement Chaim Shur; Dan Darin, a future Deputy Mayor of Tel Aviv; and the leaders of Peace Now.

The leaders of the Palestinian delegation were Dr. Nabil Sha'ath, now Palestinian Authority Minister of International Affairs; Dr. Afif Safiyeh, now PLO ambassador to Great Britain and the Vatican; Faisal Husseini; Edward Sa'id; *Al-Fajr* Editor Hanna Siniora; Ziad Abu-Zayyad; Prof. Hannan Ashrawi; Prof. Ibrahim Abu-Lughod; deposed Hebron Mayor Mustapha Natshe; Noga Tadross, assistant to Farouk Kadoumi, head of the PLO Foreign Affairs Department; and others. In the background was PLO UN Observer Dr. Nassar El-Kidwa (Arafat's nephew). The keynote Israeli speaker was Prof. Harkabi, while the keynote Palestinian speaker was Dr. Sha'ath. Dr. Sha'ath later said "it was this encounter with mainstream Israelis that convinced me that there was an Israeli partner for peace". He told this writer that this was the bottom line of his post-conference report to the PLO leadership-in-exile in Tunis.

When Yitzhak Rabin was elected Prime Minister in 1992, his government was composed almost entirely of ministers who supported the liberal-left Zionist narrative. It was during this period that members of future Labor Minister Dr. Yossi Beilin's group, Dr. Ron Pundak and Dr. Yair Hirschfeld, began the back-channel talks with Palestinians such as Hasan Asfur and Abu Ala (Ahmed Qureia) in Norway that eventually led to the Oslo Accords. The dialogue had moved from Peace Now and the slightly more radical *Meretz* and Peace Now to the mainstream centrist social-democratic Labor Party. The signing of the Declaration of Principles (DOP) signaled the mutual recognition of Israel, the product of the Jewish movement for national self-determination, and the PLO, the Palestinian national liberation organization.

This was the crossroad from which the peace option could emerge. Most supporters of the liberal-left Zionist narrative now believed that a peaceful two-state solution, a return to the principle of partition, was inevitable. This perception crashed with the failure of the Camp David talks in the summer of 2000 and the outbreak of the bloody second *Intifada*, which at the time of writing (December 2003) has cost over 800 Israeli and 2,000 Palestinian lives.

Barak: a generous offer?

At this point the supporters of the liberal-left Zionist narrative split over the reasons for the failure. Many accepted the explanation presented by Labor Prime Minister Ehud Barak, backed by American President Bill Clinton, that PLO leader Yasser Arafat, when the chips were down, had rejected the most generous Israeli offer possible that could have formed the basis for an end to the conflict. They were also traumatized by the outbreak of the second *Intifada*, and particularly by the horrible wave of inhuman suicide bombers that struck at the civilian population throughout the country. Others, a minority, believe that Barak's offer was not as generous as the PR spin portrayed it and that it was understandable that the Palestinians could not accept it.

I believe that all three parties share blame for the failure. The Israeli position could have been more forthcoming, along the lines of the positions presented at the follow-up Taba talks in January 2001, when it was too late. The Americans could have been more affective mediators (President Carter in 1978 was a better mediator than Clinton in 2000) and should have insisted that the talks continue. The Palestinians should have responded more positively to Israel's authentic offer, even if flawed. Arafat should have understood that for a short time there existed a historic window of opportunity for the establishment of a viable Palestinian state alongside the State of Israel. The Palestinian leader's failure to understand this and act upon it ensured Ariel Sharon's election in February of 2002. It could have been foreseen that President George W. Bush would not turn out to be an effective mediator. The best evaluation of the failure was provided by Robert Malley and Hussein Aha in their article "Camp David: The Tragedy of Errors" (*The New York Review of Books*, August 9, 2001).

While the right-wing Netanyahu (1996–9) and Sharon (2001–the present) government had no intention of continuing the Oslo process toward a viable two-state solution, the Rabin, Peres and Barak governments share responsibility for not ending the settlement process. This inability to change the settlement policy suggested to many Palestinians, incorrectly in my view, that the Labor-*Meretz* governments were insincere about their intention to end the conflict. In particular, Rabin missed an opportunity following right-wing extremist Baruch Goldstein's 1994 massacre of thirty Palestinians in the Tomb of the Patriarchs, to remove the Jewish settlement from the heart of Hebron, when he could have easily received the support of the majority of the Jewish Israelis for such a move. Rabin and Barak's exaggerated reliance on military measures as a counterpoint to terrorism, rather than seeking a fundamental resolution of the conflict, didn't help either. On the other hand, Arafat's unwillingness, or inability, to end the suicide bombings against civilians in Jerusalem, Haifa and Tel Aviv, appeared to send a message that Palestinians simply don't want to accept an Israeli presence in the region.

A two-state solution

So where do we stand today? A wave of pessimism has swept over many supporters of the liberal-left Zionist narrative, as effectively articulated in the article by Labor MK Avraham Burg, "The End of Zionism?" published as chapter 5 in this book. Burg, once a member of Peace Now, was injured when a hand grenade was thrown by a right-wing Israeli at a rally in 1983 against the Lebanon war. He served as Chairman of the most important international Zionist body, the Jewish Agency, and then as Speaker of the *Knesset*. Burg has written that the demographic aspect of the conflict is crucial since between the Jordan and the Mediterranean there is no longer a clear Jewish majority, and the only way to maintain a Jewish and democratic state is to remove all the settlements in the West Bank and Gaza and draw an internationally recognized border between the Jewish national home and the Palestinian national home, namely the two-state solution.

Today there are potentially four ways of resolving the demographic dilemma: (1) To repartition the land between the Jordan river and the Mediterranean sea; (2) To return to the bi-national idea; (3) To annex the West Bank and Gaza without providing democratic rights to the Palestinians; and (4) To expel the Palestinians from the area. No significant Israeli factor is considering the last option.

As for the bi-national idea – a few Israeli Zionist and post-Zionist intellectuals have raised it, either as an ideal, or as a default option (Dr. Meron Benvenisti), because the two societies are so intertwined as a result of the settlement policy that it is too late to repartition the land. But both Israelis and Palestinians are too mutually scarred and traumatized by the escalating cycle of violence to seriously opt for a bi-national solution at this stage. In addition, the overwhelming majority within both societies clearly prefers a national state. We live in a period of nationalism. The European Union to the contrary, Yugoslavia has split into five going on to six separate national entities, Czechoslovakia has become the Czech Republic and Slovakia, and the Soviet Union has become . . . etc. So why should Israel and Palestine be any different? Maybe in the future, two separate Israeli and Palestinian states will evolve into a federation or confederation. But not now. From the purely Israeli point of view, restoring the country's declining economic growth depends primarily on a viable and peaceful two-state political solution.

The latest attempt to formulate a just, political non-violent resolution of the conflict is the Geneva Accords, published in November 2003. Once again, following the path charted by the earlier practitioners of Israeli–Palestinian dialogue, it was initiated on the Israeli side by supporters of the liberal-left Zionist narrative. The innovative Yossi Beilin (who left the Labor party and is today a member of *Meretz*) was joined in the final stages of the process by MK Burg; former general and Labor Party leader MK Amram Mitzna; *Meretz* MK Chaim Oron; writer Amos Oz and others. Worked out with former Palestinian minister Yasser Abed Rabo and young Fatah leaders supported by Marwan Barghouti (currently in an Israeli prison), the detailed understanding provides a model for a future political agreement based upon a two-state solution along the lines of the 1967 borders. It would include mutual territorial exchanges enabling 75 percent of the settlers close to the Green line to remain within the State of Israel, in exchange for resettlement of refugees in potentially fertile border land to be ceded by Israel. The preamble states that, "This agreement expresses the recognition of the Jewish people's right to a state and the recognition of the right of the Palestinian nation to a state, without damaging the right to equality of the citizens of both sides." This formulation is a fulfillment of the dreams of the founders of liberal-left Zionism.

It also hints at one of the dilemmas that will still remain after the realization of a two-state solution. After the establishment of a Palestinian state in the West Bank, Gaza and East Jerusalem, there will still remain a sizable minority of over one million Palestinian Israeli citizens within the State of Israel, nearly 20 percent of the population. The formula that is evolving in liberal circles is that Israel will be "a Jewish state and the state of all its citizens", ensuring that Israel will remain both a Jewish and a democratic state which guarantees its predominantly Jewish identity, and equal rights for the minority group.

As one of the young Palestinian participants in the final negotiations on the Geneva Accords told author Amos Oz, "Perhaps we can now see on the horizon the end of the hundred year war between Jews and Palestinians. But now begins a bitter struggle between those within both nations who support compromise and peace and a fanatical coalition of Israeli and Palestinian extremists". Because of the current level of mistrust between Israelis and Palestinians, it is assumed that no solution will be possible without significant international mediation and support, whether via the Road Map advocated by the American, Russian, European, UN Quartet, or any other international mechanism.

The alternative is a continuation of the current violent stalemate, which will eat away at the economic and social fabric of both Israeli and Palestinian societies. If we continue the Biblical eye for an eye, or sometimes two eyes for an eye, we may eventually reach the Samson option, in which the whole Israeli–Palestinian Middle Eastern house would collapse.

10

Left Out – the Ecological Paradox of the Israeli Left

ALON TAL

From the emergence of David Ben-Gurion as the key power broker within the pre-state Zionist movement in the 1930s until the election of Menahem Begin and the *Likud* party in 1977, leftist or Labor Zionism dominated the Israeli political system. It was also during this period that environmental degradation in Israel reached hazardous levels. By the mid-1970s, air pollution in Israel's cities exceeded international standards and Israel's own newly promulgated air-quality criteria. With a few exceptions like the Jordan River tributaries, all the country's streams and rivers were contaminated by sewage. Tar on the Mediterranean beaches was an unbearable annoyance that reflected a very sick Mediterranean sea. Drinking water was chronically unhealthy, especially among Israel's Palestinian Arab citizens, and dysentery a common malady. Noise, litter and other nuisances are an inseparable part of the contemporary Israeli experience.

There was a connection between these two phenomena – Labor rule and ecological neglect. The same political ideology that fueled the estab-lishment of Israel and its remarkably successful initial development paid little attention to the attendant environmental devastation. Leftist Zionist politicians in the early days of the state were more aware of the environ-mental conditions than is commonly perceived. Simcha Blass was Israel's leading figure in water management during the 1950s. His autobiography explains that decision makers were cognizant of the salinization of the coastal aquifer from over-pumping. They simply perceived it as an unfor-tunate exigency required for creating a prosperous agrarian economy and gainful employment for the hundreds of thousands of immigrants pouring into the country. Minutes from early *Knesset* debates show a host of politicians bemoaning the sullying of their Promised Land.

Yigal Alon, the deputy Prime Minister from the Labor Party, reported to Israel's *Knesset* in a special 1973 session, that: "in the past decade chemical production increased 160 percent and production of detergents 100 percent. Israel showed the third highest use of coal and fuel per head in the world. During this decade, agricultural land use increased only 5 percent but the use of nitrate fertilizers 40 percent. Energy consumption is increasing 10–12 percent a year. If we add the fact that Israel already uses more than 90 percent of the water sources at its disposal, that special meteorological conditions will not allow good dispersal of pollutants in the atmosphere, that there is a trend toward large concentrations of residents in the coastal region and a rising standard of living – then we can see the severity of the environmental problems which are likely to arise in Israel if proper measures are not taken".

A feeble record

Most of these hazards have only grown worse. A government study released in 2003 estimates that 1400 Israelis die prematurely each year from air pollution exposures. Israel's two main aquifers are more polluted than ever. With the growing population came urban sprawl, staggering loss of open spaces and the disappearance of entire landscapes like the Sharon region. Biodiversity preservation, perhaps the most impressive achievement of Israel's first fifty years, is alarmingly in decline.

There are a few encouraging trends that deserve mention. Thirty years ago, Lake Kinneret (the Sea of Galilee) was on the verge of eutrophication, once the Huleh wetlands had been drained and could not provide a natural "sink" to filter out nutrients. It suffered from sewage discharges, runoff from dairies and massive loadings that reached the shore. Due to painstaking watershed management, the lake water quality has taken a turn for the better. Also, with international agreements protecting the Mediterranean, the tar concentrations on the beaches have also dropped. These items are proof that Israel's environmental history need not have been so negative.

One can make historical excuses for the ecologically obtuse Zionist leaders, who saw themselves as "Socialists" and oversaw the country for the first half of Israel's history. Yet one would have imagined that the Labor movement, and political parties which regarded themselves as belonging to the left, would have integrated the ecological impulse into their ideological commitments. Failing this, it can be reasonably argued that the left must bear responsibility for Israel's most acute environmental problems. Politicians on the left with green susceptibilities often find themselves at odds with the prevailing views in their parties. Leftist party platforms in Israel typically espouse an ambitious ecological manifesto but the gap between promise and performance is conspicuous, in spite of the desire to imitate trendy progressive political slogans from around the world. Why has the Israeli left's environmental record been so feeble? How could it attempt to redefine itself in ecological affairs?

Seeking nature

The great irony about Labor Zionism's position on the environment is that it could have been different. Unlike many leftist political movements around the world, Zionist Socialism in the early part of the twentieth century harbored strong convictions about stewardship and intimacy with the land. This was a political movement that was informed as much by Tolstoy as it was by Marx. After two thousand years of Exile, it thought that a new Jewish state ruled by workers in the homeland had not only to create a harmonious egalitarian society, but equally, it had to facilitate reconciliation between the Jewish people and its land.

The most prominent advocate in this realm was the philosopher/farmer Aharon David Gordon. Far from being a politician, Gordon was a retired Russian estate manager, who moved to Palestine in 1904 at the age of forty-seven. His choice of *Aliya* was a conscious rejection of urban, Diaspora life and values, and in particular the traditional Jewish alienation from the soil. Because of his sincerity, seniority and indifference to politics, Gordon enjoyed a particularly revered status among the labor-oriented Jewish immigrants of his day, who later were to lead to the establishment of the State of Israel.

In Gordon's view, unlike the Jewish migration to America that was primarily motivated by materialism or economic advantage, a Jewish renaissance in Israel should constitute a true revolution that embraced a fuller, more meaningful life. Part of the equation was "the religion of labor", spiritual edification through manual work on the land. The parallel impulse was unmistakably environmental and today would be categorized as "deep ecology".

Gordon wrote in *The Human and Nature* that "it is clear that man-as-man always needs to be among nature. For nature is for a man who truly feels and knows, what water is for a fish. It is not just something to look at, for man's very soul is in need of it . . . Moreover, the more man develops and the more his internal emotions and awareness become deeper and broader, and his knowledge becomes richer, so is he in greater need of direct attachment to nature."

This "green" philosophical perspective was bolstered by a rich liturgy of poems and songs. and perpetuated through an educational curriculum that targeted children from preschool and made nature studies into the most prestigious classes. As such, this pro-environmental proclivity was quickly integrated into leftist Zionist ideology of the time, at least at the level of official dogma. Some fifty years later, even Prime Minister Ben-Gurion, often considered the quintessential advocate of aggressive economic development, would deliver an impassioned speech in Israel's *Knesset* on nature and its preservation, extolling "the unencumbered connection between the natural landscape of this land and its history".

And yet, as he and his associates saw it, creating an economic infrastructure that could accommodate the hundreds of thousands of immigrants and fielding a military force capable of withstanding growing Arab hostility, must have complete priority. The ruralist idealization of farming would survive on the left on paper, while the commitment to preservation and environmental health would be put aside. This undoubtedly had much to do with the huge leverage that kibbutzim and the agricultural sector wielded in Israel's political arena at the time.

Ultimately, little of the Gordonian secular redemption package found an expression in Israeli public policy. In 1953 it was Labor politicians like Pinhas Lavon who rejected the pleas of zoologists and ecologists against draining the Huleh swamp. The Israeli left lost sight of the natural harmony that was a critical component of its original agrarian ideology. In the end, the drainage project, designed to create more farmland, turned out to be an ecological disaster, and recently a reflooding initiative began.

As time went on, in the "real world" rough and tumble of security, jobs, housing, planning commissions, industrial policies and water management, the old romantic environmental notions sounded nostalgic but impractical among most Labor politicians. An example was Prime Minister Golda Meir's dismissive rejection in the early 1970s of *Likud* Knesset Member Yosef Tamir's personal plea to create an environmental agency. Indeed, Yigal Alon, a kibbutz member and one of the "greener" Labor leaders, had to sneak a proposal to create such an agency through the Israeli cabinet when Meir was abroad meeting President Richard Nixon.

There were certainly those in the leftist camp who retained a fierce commitment to the natural world and to an environmentally friendly Jewish state. The Society for the Protection of Nature in Israel quickly became the largest organization of its kind in Israel during the 1950s through the initiative and political patronage of kibbutz members and

Mapai politicians. For its first thirty years, its organization and constitution reflected kibbutz culture, preferring to be managed by a "secretary" than a "director".

The Society relied heavily on Labor politicians who were sympathetic to their message for funding and for political patronage. Thus, novelist (and *Mapai Knesset* Member) S. Yizhar was instrumental in shepherding the Society's vision of a Nature Reserve Authority through the parliament in the early 1960s. He did so against the odds, defying party bosses, like the director-general of the Prime Minister's Office, Teddy Kollek, who took a less environmental stance.

It is also important to note that even the advocates of nature held a somewhat narrow view of environmental interests. The mounting pollution problem of Israel's cities was definitely not on their agendas. Rather, it would be rightist and centrist politicians, such as Shimon Kanovich, Yosef Tamir or Yedidyah Be'eri who made somewhat quixotic efforts to address these dynamics. Thus, it was *Likud* politician Ronni Milo who championed the establishment of a Ministry of the Environment and initially held the Cabinet post. The relatively high exposures to environmental hazards suffered by Israel's Arab citizens were on the agenda neither of left nor of right.

It should not be inferred from this cursory review that the left has been less sensitive to environmental problems than Israel's right-wing parties. The truth is that neither embraced these issues in a serious, systematic way. The emergence of environmentalism was more linked to the personal and even heroic inclinations of individuals then to the political or ideological habitat in which they dwelled. In any case, by the time Israel became an independent state, little was left of the early Labor-romantic vision of harmony between Jews and their land Today, it is hard to find even remnants of the original Gordonian impulse among leftist politicians and parties.

The left and the environment

In considering Israel's recent political divisions it is important to dispel the misconceptions harbored outside, and to a lesser extent inside, of Israel that perceives the environment as an issue primarily of concern to the left. The traditional Democratic/Republican dichotomy in the US regarding many environmental issues perpetuates such perceptions. Regardless of international trends, there is little empirical evidence to support such a perception in Israel.

To be sure, Hebrew University political scientist Avner de-Shalit conducted a survey in the 1990s among workers at the Society for Protection of Nature in Israel in which he discovered a disproportionately large number of workers who identified politically with the *Meretz* party, the most leftist of Israel's Zionist parties. Moreover, in several consecutive elections, the *Meretz* platform was justifiably singled out as being the most ardently pro-environmental. De-Shalit concluded that in practice *Meretz* functioned as Israel's "de facto" green party.

But in the decade that has meanwhile elapsed, reality has not supported an equating of the "left" with environmental interests in Israel. Israel's Labor Party cannot honestly claim any particularly redeeming environmental inclinations. When the Ministry of Environment was first established, the battle for clean air policy pitted pro-environmental right-wing *Likud* politicians Milo and Justice Minister Dan Meridor, against Labor's Treasury and Energy Ministers Shimon Peres and Moshe Shahal, who opposed emission standards. The only occasion on which a Labor politician, Daliah Itsik, served as Minister of Environment in 1999, she sniveled to the press that Prime Minister Barak was punishing her with an insulting appointment. Her performance in the job was not much more enthusiastic and she hastened to take the post of Minister of Industry and Commerce at the first opportunity. Labor Prime Ministers continued their party's tradition of railroading through every available development project (except railroads), regardless of the ecological ramifications.

Meretz may have a more legitimate basis for boasting an environmental record. Yossi Sarid, the long-time chairman of the party is still considered to have been Israel's most conscientious Minister of Environment for the three years of impressive service that that he gave between 1993 and 1996. While at the helm he was a charismatic advocate for open space and tougher pollution enforcement policies in the Cabinet, increased the ministry's budget three-fold, expanding its authority and fashioning guidelines for the future. Yet, despite his pledges to the contrary, the moment that an opportunity to fill a more "prestigious" ministerial portfolio (Minister of Education) presented itself, Sarid, too, abandoned his post. At the same time, the *Meretz* party and its representatives frequently failed to internalize the ecological commitments reflected in its own platform.

For example, when Professor Amnon Rubenstein, a senior *Meretz* leader, served as chairman of the *Knesset*'s Constitution Committee, he backed the private company that had won the contract to pave the trans-Israel highway. Despite an extensive attack on the highway on ecological grounds in the *Meretz* platform, and a firm party commitment to stop it at all costs, Rubenstein essentially saved the project, whose economic feasibility had become dubious. Similarly there is the critical issue of open space preservation, where Meretz's platform is extremely vociferous in favor of conservation policies. However, the disproportionately large kibbutz lobby within the party made *Meretz* at best, a non-player in the currently raging societal debate over the legitimacy of re-zoning agricultural lands for commercial purposes. Yet this is probably the most important public debate of its kind ever held in Israel.

The Communist-led non-Zionist *Hadash* party has shown a general tendency to side with environmental interests. But based on its legislative initiatives and campaigns, the environment has never been a party priority. As Arab constituents dominate its electoral support and the current *Knesset* faction includes no Jews at all, its agenda is generally focused on issues of discrimination and occupation rather than environmental justice.

Indeed, in several instances it has been right-wing, or capitalist, parties that have taken the lead in championing Israel's environmental causes. Extreme "hawk" and *Likud* member, Uzi Landau, emerged as the leading campaigner for coastal preservation. He also opposed the trans-Israel highway. It was the free-market *Shinui* party Chairman, Yosef Lapid, who penned the only piece of innovative Israeli environmental legislation of the past ten years, a bill that created a Commissioner for Future Generations to review all proposed legislation and government positions from the perspective of inter-generational equity. Indeed, the same *Shinui* party was the only one that requested the Ministry of Environment portfolio in coalitional negotiations – something *Meretz* chose not to do two years earlier.

While individual politicians, such as *Meretz* MK Mossi Raz, emerged for a brief period as the darling of Israel's environmental movement, often they were a lone voice within their party (Raz was not elected to the 15th *Knesset* in 2003). When awards were given out by environmentalists for parliamentary performance that year, right-wing politicians such as Michael Nudelman (*Yisrael Beitenu*) or the *Likud*'s Nehama Ronen outnumbered the champions of the environment from the left. Indeed in the contrasting "dirty dozen" list, where environmental groups named vilified anti-environmental politicians, the Labor Party was prominent.

The inability of Green parties in Israel to capture the hearts (and ballots) of the public in general elections suggests that the Israeli public does not place its environmental problems near the top of its national agenda. In two electoral attempts, the Green party has made a weak showing, hardly mustering more than 15,000 votes. This was only a fraction of the "Green Leaf" pro-cannabis party's support and was not nearly enough to cross the threshold into parliamentary representation. Nonetheless, at a local level there have been some surprising success stories. For instance, Haifa architect Shmuel Gilbert's "Our Haifa-the Greens" list did well enough in the 1998 elections to make him head of the opposition. Gilbert joined forces with independent Yonah Yahav (formerly Labor) in 2003 to win control of the city council, affording him the position of deputy to Mayor Yahav, and head of the powerful planning and building commission. But, here again, the Greens' partner in the elections was not *Meretz* or a leftist oriented party but the free-market *Shinui* party. This suggests that political affiliation is a poor predictor of a politician's environmental orientation. Personal upbringing, and socialization, rather than party platform or tradition seem to be the dominant factor in shaping the environmental commitment of Israeli politicians.

The irrelevance of political ideology in environmental affairs is considered by many Israeli Green activists to be a blessing. If environmentalism were the sole domain of the leftist political spectrum, they say, surely it would be to the country's ecological detriment, especially during the present period when the left's geo-political positions are so unpopular among the Israeli public. Yet the Israeli left has a responsibility to take the environment seriously. Certainly, political expediency justifies it. The success of Green factions in local elections indicates that there will come a day when the Israeli public, like that of many European countries, rewards political parties with a real commitment to the environment. Any new perspective of social justice that the Israeli left will promote must include environmental objectives.

Toward a new vision of justice and the environment

It is time for the Israeli left to rediscover some of its early ecological zeal. Part of this vision involves the recognition that a Jewish state must maintain a nurturing and protective relationship with the land. This means that a healthy society is not only measured in narrow terms of economic prosperity or egalitarian distribution of resources and opportunity, important as they are. It is time to adopt an applied definition of "sustainability" that has become such a central precept of the world's present environmental jargon. In practice it means that several subtle and not-so-subtle shifts in conventional values and policies among leftist and Labor parties in Israel are overdue. Here are a few of the necessary items for such an agenda:

Rethinking ruralism

The citizens in the state of Israel live predominantly in cities and towns.

This phenomenon will continue to grow more pronounced. It dictates that open spaces are more important than ever for the mental and spiritual well-being of the nation. As agriculture becomes less relevant economically, its significance grows as a landscape resource for internal and external tourism, and as an inspirational connection to a more agrarian heritage, for both Jews and Arabs. It is also a critical hedge against sprawl and other encroachments on habitat.

Agricultural living should retain a special place in the leftist identity, but needs to evolve to meet a new economic and ecological reality. In a planet where there are chronic calorie shortages, food production remains among the most honorable of professionals. Israel should subsidize an agriculture that is less reliant on chemical pesticides and Thai laborers, and that is irrigated almost exclusively with tertiary-treated effluents. It is important that the left, with its rich history of agricultural involvement, join forces with Israel's growing Green community to save open spaces through the preservation of a gentler agricultural sector. In this spirit, speculation and lucrative compensation for re-zoning agricultural lands should be rejected for what they are: greed and exploitation of historical status to the detriment of the quality of life of present and future generations.

Rethinking immigration

The initial commitment to Jewish immigration was common to all the Zionist political factions. This position was an expression of basic tribal solidarity. Israeli leaders, especially after the Holocaust, had lived in the Diaspora and understood the threat of anti-Semitism. Immigration to Israel offered an immediate solution. Later, the impulse was driven by demographic concerns and an unabashed desire for security. David Ben-Gurion was always forthright in his belief that Israel didn't have enough Jewish soldiers.

Such logic no longer holds today. Not many Jewish communities are threatened by anti-Semitism, and the Israeli army has sufficient troops. A far more serious threat to Jewish well-being is ecological. There is not a single category in Israel's present environmental crisis that cannot be linked to the astonishing increase in population of one million newcomers per decade. In a word, if Israel does not curb its demographic growth rate immediately, even the most conscientious environmental policy will fall short, and the country's environmental indicators will continue to reflect the massive exceeding of the land's carrying capacity.

There are three engines that drive population increase:

- high Arab birth-rates,
- high Orthodox Jewish birth-rate, and
- immigration.

The left cannot begin to address the first two phenomena without a real commitment to reforming the third. While according to the Law of Return any Jewish immigrant to the country will be welcome, financial incentives are no longer justifiable. Neither should Zionist emissaries be sent to the four corners of the earth to recruit potential Israelis. The insurgence of non-Jewish immigrants from the former Soviet Union during the past decade is certain to appear disingenuous to Arab citizens, and there should be stricter immigration criteria. In short, the Ingathering of the Exiles should no longer be an item on the agenda – and must be replaced by serious efforts to achieve zero population growth. The question of the size of families is a sensitive issue to be sure, but all who are serious about creating a minimal quality of life for the whole population in the future will have to take the stand that large families are environmentally irresponsible.

Rethinking cooperation with Israeli Arabs and Palestinians

The continuous drop in Arab Israeli support for leftist parties, and their preference for national Arab parties, reflects a failure which must be faced squarely. To regain Arab Israeli involvement and confidence, promises are no longer enough, for too many have been made and broken. Real contributions to the quality of life for Arab citizens must be assured on the ground. The gap between Israeli Arab and Jewish environmental exposures, and the glaring discrimination in access to key resources, is well documented. It is time that the left made environmental justice, founded on Jewish–Arab equality, a central part of its agenda, and this not only in word but above all in deed. This constitutes a concrete expression of the traditional Biblical commitment to respect the disenfranchised minority in Israeli society. The environment is also one of the areas where coexistence activities are not perceived primarily as symbolic, but have tangible benefits for Arabs and Jews.

While he was Minister of Environment, *Meretz* leader Yossi Sarid internalized this approach and implemented a program of affirmative action, establishing a disproportionately large number of environmental protection units among Arab municipalities. Yet inadequate funding has continuously undermined these units and many have closed. The complete absence of any protest by the political parties left the sincerity of Sarid's achievement in question. Environmental justice is a prolonged process and its results are not seen overnight. This shows that on such issues, the left need more ideological stamina.

As a viable Palestinian state eventually takes hold, the environment offers enormous potential for reestablishing the trust that has been the ultimate victim of the past three years of violence. It is no coincidence that from the outset of the present peace process, the environment was considered to be among the most promising confidence-building measures. Whether in power or not, the left should bring its many environmental experts to the negotiating table with their Palestinian colleagues, and only limitations of space prevent us from entering in detail into the agenda of such discussions. While politicians quibble over borders, an ongoing dialogue should deal with promoting common sewage effluent and car exhaust standards, shared strategies for pesticide-use reduction, or biodiversity preservation plans. These and other ecological issues may ripen to become the true fruits of peace: mutual benefits in quality of life that come from a common recognition that this good land of Israel/Palestine has to support two nations and can only do so sustainably if they marshal all their resources to that end, together.

Rethinking definitions of justice

Socialistic political ideologies were born out of a sense of outrage that free market and Fascist governance were inherently unjust. A leftist political platform can only survive in the age of globalization if it evolves to embrace a richer and more universal meaning of equity. Internationally, the environmental consequences of free trade have galvanized and unified the left. In Israel, this has remained a non-issue.

Before deciding how to serve society, it would well to consider whom it includes. For starters, the response in Israel must include and integrate the natural world. Israel is home to 2600 plant species (130 endemic to Israel) and 700 vertebrates. But after four decades, this stability is being challenged. The left should insist that the interests of the natural world be considered, especially in a period when the country continues to make dramatic and often irreversible development decisions.

The community of concern needs to be even broader. Just because the *Knesset* created a framework for considering the interests of future generations, this does not mean that all political parties are actually doing so. The left's vision of justice must contain a strong inter-generational element. This tiny Land of Israel is all that our generation, or any generation of Israelis, will ever have in which to find spiritual inspiration and make peace with other creatures of the planet. When speaking of "a better life", following decades of development and economic rewards for almost all sectors of Israeli society, it is time to bring this ethos of progress to non-economic spheres. We must now foster an enduring harmony with our natural resources and physical environment. Even if romantic Socialistic founders of Israel belong to the past, looking forward, we must insist that future generations are left a land that continues to hold the same beauty and holiness that once inspired the Biblical prophets.

References

Alon, Yigal 1973: "International Environment Day", *Biosphera* 73 (7), 1973.
Avineri, Shlomo 1991: *The Making of Modern Zionism, the Intellectual Origins of the Jewish State*. New York: Basic Books.
Blass, Simcha 1973: *Water in Strife and Action*. Givataim: Masada.
De-Shalit, Avner 1995: From the Political to the Objective: the Dialectics of Zionism and the Environment. *Environmental Politics* 4, 1995.
—— 1994: Where Environmentalists Hide? In Robin Twite and Robin Menczel (eds.) *Our Shared Environment*. Jerusalem: IPCRI, 1994.
Divrei HaKnesset (Israel's Parliamentary Minutes) 1993: Speech by David Ben-Gurion.
Don-Yehiya, Eliezer and Liegman, Charles 1983: *Civil Religion in Israel*. Berkeley: University of California Press.
Garfinkle, Adam 1997: *Politics and Society in Modern Israel, Myths and Realities*. Armonk, New York: M.E. Sharp.
Gordon, Aharon David 1951: *The Human and Nature*. Jerusalem: The Zionist Library.
Herzberg, Arthur 1966: *The Zionist Idea*. New York: Harper and Row.
Schwartz, Eylon 1999: Changing Paradigms in Israeli Environmental Education. http://www.heschelcenter.org/paradigms_eng.html.
Tal, Alon 2002: *Pollution in a Promised Land, an Environmental History of Israel*. Berkeley: University of California Press.

11

The Left Needs
Two Banners

VICTOR CYGIELMAN

Who is left? Take for example an Israeli who demands social justice and defends the rights of the exploited and underprivileged in Israeli society yet ignores the suffering of the Palestinians under Israeli occupation, or the discrimination against Palestinian Israelis: can he or she be considered part of the left? Or conversely, take for example those who demand an end to the occupation and back the right of the Palestinian people to establish an independent state alongside Israel, yet ignore the glaring socio-economic gap in Israeli society and current efforts to destroy the trade unions: can they be considered part of the left? In both cases, the answer is a resounding "No".

The fact that these two seemingly separate categories are so totally intertwined is a basic component of Israel's complex political and socio-economic reality. This linkage explains and reflects the distinctive challenges confronting the left in Israel. It is a left that over the years has increasingly been losing electoral support and in the last two elections took an unprecedented beating from Ariel Sharon's *Likud* party. How did this happen?

A discredited ideology

There are three main factors which can help us to explain the dwindling influence of the left and of leftish ideologies. The first factor was the dismantling in 1991 of the Soviet Union and the collapse of the "Socialist" regimes of other Communist-led European countries. These regimes, which were political and economic disasters, naturally discredited Socialist ideology and Socialist parties everywhere. Communists had argued for years that the lack of political freedom in these countries was offset by the economic progress and the higher living standards. In the end they, too, had to agree that this "Socialist" economic model was also a lie. No social and economic betterment can be achieved and maintained under a one party rule where free trade unions are suppressed.

In the wake of what was called "the collapse of Communism", preaching the superiority of capitalist state structures became the name of the game. These structures were indeed characterized by their democratic institutions but also by a society in which dog eats dog and maximum profit is the supreme value and norm. In this discourse, the prevalent model is, of course, what is called "the American way of life".

The security syndrome

The second factor is Israel's security situation. Its battle for survival in 1948/49, and the successive wars with its Arab neighbors, created and shaped a mentality in which Israel's security is the paramount concern, overshadowing all other considerations, be they political, social, or economic.

This became particularly valid since the war in June 1967. The military confrontation and Israel's victory brought about the occupation of vast tracts of Palestinian land. The legacy it left in the form of the occupation has been maintained up to our days: 36 years of arbitrary rule over a captive population numbering close to 3.5 million men, women and children and actively resisting its subjugation. Palestinian terror against Israeli civilians strengthened this "security syndrome" while the overall struggle for social justice continued to deteriorate in Israeli society.

Israel's founding fathers strove to build a socialist-oriented welfare state functioning in a capitalist society, based on a mixture of private and public enterprises. A visitor once asked David Ben-Gurion, Israel's first prime minister and a dominant figure in its early years, why Israel should be viewed if not as a fully, then at least as a partly socialist country. B-G would point to the *Histadrut,* the powerful labor and trade union movement that also encompassed a host of communal and cooperative enterprises: these included the agricultural settlements (kibbutz and moshav); industrial and transport cooperatives (e.g. bus and trucking companies) and a huge construction enterprise like *Solel Boneh* ("paving and constructing"). All these played a major role in the economy before and after independence.

However, though the kibbutzim functioned internally as fully socialist societies, the factories they owned were run on a strictly capitalistic basis. The workers employed by the kibbutz in these factories tended to come from what were called "development towns", mainly populated by Jews who had immigrated from the Arab countries. There was a built-in contradiction here since the employer and the worker had different interests, occasionally even resulting in a strike by the workers against their kibbutz bosses. One result was that the *Mizrahi* worker was alienated from the ruling "leftist" parties, which workers perceived both as exploiters and as hypocrites. The *Mizrahim* preferred the rightist *Likud party* with its appealing populist, demagogic and nationalistic slogans.

The growth of the *Likud*, and its electoral victories over the Labor movement since 1977, were accompanied not only by the decline of the kibbutz movement, but also by overall socio-economic policies veering more and more toward "Thatcherism": under successive Likud governments, these policies which since the 1970s saw the dissolution of the *Histadrut*'s powerful industrial empire and increasing privatization, in recent years resulted in the dwindling of the welfare state and the steady erosion of its achievements.

As in the United States, it is the economically weaker social strata who bear the brunt of Netanyahu's economic "reforms". No wonder that in Israel's Americanized society, the gap between the 10 percent with the highest income and the 10 percent with the lowest, is continuously growing. Moreover, in the wake of the *Intifada* and the continuing armed Israeli–Palestinian conflict, Israel is suffering from a serious economic crisis: foreign capital has fled, investments for initiating new economic projects have reached an all-time low, and the level of unemployment has attained new heights.

An enduring curse?

The third factor relates to the peace camp itself. In Israel, the peace movement is dominated by middle- and upper-class *Ashkenazi* intelligentsia, who generally vote Labor or Meretz. On the other hand the bulk of the *Mizrahi* population supports the Likud and other nationalist parties, where religion nourishes chauvinist feelings and vice versa. In this paradox, the rich vote left and the poor vote right, the latter against their own interests in view of Netanyahu's socio-economic policies. The question is – is this an unavoidable feature, a sort of enduring curse, on the Israeli political scene?

As the song puts it, "it ain't necessarily so". But certain conditions must be met, and the first is that there is no hope for building an effective center-left coalition without detaching a significant part of the *Mizrahi* vote from the nationalist-religious parties.

Though there is no prospect for serious economic recovery as long as the armed Israeli–Palestinian conflict continues, one cannot expect Israeli workers to put aside their struggle for social justice until peace is won. Unless the leftish leaders of the peace camp simultaneously raise two banners – the banner of peace and the banner of social justice – they will be unable to win over part of the *Mizrahi* electorate so as to obtain a majority in elections.

Another condition is that the Israeli peace camp itself must cease to be a monopoly of the established *Ashkenazi* part of the population. Surely the time has come for the peace movement in Israel to recognize the importance in all peace activity and forums of a *Mizrahi* presence, of *Mizrahi* intellectuals and activists, Needless to say, these must not be "token *Mizrahim*" but authentic representatives of the Mizrahi public.

Until these two conditions are fulfilled, the left will be doomed to remain in its minority status as well-meaning but impotent seekers of peace, cut off from the real demands and aspirations of most of the Israeli people.

Views from the Left

The Roots of Israel's Economic Crisis

TAMAR GOZANSKY

The June 1967 war, which brought about the Israeli occupation of the Palestinian territories, accelerated the militarization of the Israeli economy and society. At the beginning of the twenty-first century this is an economy also increasingly influenced by its unprecedented concentration of finance capital. This has resulted in unemployment and economic hardship for entire sectors of Jews and Arabs in the population. Yet despite the heavy cost of the continuing rule over the Palestinian territories conquered in 1967, the West Bank including East Jerusalem, and the Gaza Strip, the Israeli establishment has been prepared to pay the price rather than accept the establishment of a viable Palestinian state alongside Israel.

The feeling of euphoria that followed the 1967 war and the increase in business opportunities resulting from the occupation created a sense of economic prosperity in the country. This followed a period of harsh recession. Israeli military control of the territories was now exploited for the expansion of the domestic market by Israeli companies (consumption items, investment, financial services, insurance, etc.) by an additional 2.5 million consumers, and for the employment and exploitation of tens, and later hundreds, of thousands of Palestinian workers earning less and receiving fewer social benefits than Israeli workers.[1]

When they are permitted to work in Israel, Palestinian workers are employed mainly in two sectors: construction and agriculture. Half of the workers in these two sectors are non-Israelis, either Palestinians or migrant workers. According to the statistics of the *Histadrut* Labor Federation (2003), in 2001 the average wage for an Israeli construction worker was NIS 6,423, as opposed to NIS 4,412 for a migrant worker and NIS 2,302 for a Palestinian worker from the occupied territories.

Expropriation, settlement, military economy

The continuation of the Israeli–Palestinian conflict created a population of modern colonists who live in the Israeli settlements in the territories occupied since 1967. As in other colonial situations, these settlers form a socio-political lobby with right-wing annexationist parties pushing for the continuation of the occupation (what the settlers call "defending our homes"). According to data of the Central Bureau of Statistics for the second half of the year 2003 (which do not include the Jews living in Jewish neighborhoods in greater Jerusalem formerly Palestinian-owned and annexed to Israel in 1967), some 230,000 settlers were living in 143 settlements in the West Bank and Gaza Strip.

The first settlements were established in the occupied territories in 1968, shortly after the end of the war, with government approval (in advance or retroactively) and financing, under close military security, and on expropriated Palestinian lands. The government fully subsidized the physical infrastructure, family housing, construction and public services, which are known to be more modern and extensive than those inside Israel, and which employ some 40 percent of the settler workforce. Security also constitutes a profitable economic branch.[2]

The occupation accelerated Israel's transformation into a "war society" where top priority was given to the army, the military budget, army service, and the development of military industries. But as the burden of military expenditures grew, and as social polarization increased in Israeli society, it lost its old self-confidence and was overtaken by a sense of siege and fear. The Israeli government exploited these feelings of anxiety in order to continue the occupation, financing it at the expense of civil investments and welfare state benefits of the Israeli population.

It is important to note that while they received large tax breaks, at no stage did the large corporations in Israel make do with the handsome profits they garnered from the occupation. As early as the 1970s they increased their efforts to achieve speculative financial profits, for example in the period 1972–82 by manipulating bank shares, whose huge profits were tax-exempt. At the same time local and foreign financial companies were lobbying for the privatization, which was soon to be implemented, of Israel's government-owned and publicly-owned companies and services.

Israel's transition to a stagflation economy, which also took place in the 1970s, together with the socio-political earthquake cause by the *Yom Kippur* war of October 1973 led to a change of government. In the 1977 general elections the Labor Party was defeated and the *Likud* Party headed by Menahem Begin came to power for the first time. This change in political leadership, which has lasted, except for short periods, up to now, continued on a three-track policy: maintaining the occupation, assuring the profits of the large companies, and eroding the welfare state.

After 1977, the *Likud* government gave a new impetus to the settlements, ruling in 1979 that it was possible to unilaterally declare land in the territories as "state land" (with no need for any "security" argument) and to build settlements on it. At the same time, in the framework of its neo-liberal economic policies, at the end of 1979 the government allowed Israelis to purchase land privately in the territories. Less than three years later, in April 1982, the establishment of privately initiated settlements in the occupied territories was permitted. (For the record, Ariel Sharon was defense minister at that time.)

Economic crisis

The first Palestinian *Intifada*, which erupted at the end of 1987, increased the cost of Israel's military control of the territories and decreased the corporate profits guaranteed by this control. Because of the *Intifada*, work permits for Palestinians were cancelled in the early 1990s and the government decided to allow Israeli employers to replace their Palestinian workers with migrant laborers. Without work in Israel, the incomes of Palestinian families in the occupied territories decreased by at least 50 percent. As a result of the destruction of their economy, Palestinians purchased much less from Israeli companies, but even today they remain dependent on Israeli products and thus continue to be part of the "expanded Israeli market".

The long-lasting economic crisis, which had begun in Israel in 1996, intensified and deepened on an unprecedented scale following the renewal of Israeli military actions in the occupied territories, which continued on and off throughout the second half of the 1990s. The situation deteriorated following Ariel Sharon's provocative visit in September 2000 to the area of the historic mosques in Jerusalem and the repression by force of Palestinian protests, leading to the outbreak of the second *Intifada*.

During the course of the conflict since the end of the year 2000 an ongoing closure has been imposed on Palestinian cities and villages, internal economic life was strangled and the Palestinian economy collapsed. Few Palestinian workers have been permitted to work in Israel and unemployment among Palestinians now exceeds 50 percent of the workforce (in Gaza – 65 percent); and the majority of Palestinian families live on less than $1 a day per person.

As for the Israeli economy, the war situation has caused a rapid rise in military expenditures in the state budget, which has grown to about 10 percent of the gross domestic product (GDP). The continuing occupation, and the perpetuation of the war, have engendered a vicious cycle of killings and suicide bombings, undermining the sense of security in Israel. The effect on the Israeli economy is significant: a serious crisis in the construction industry, with a wave of dismissals of building workers; and a two-thirds decrease in the number of tourists visiting Israel in 2002, as against 1999, putting tens of thousands employed in the tourist trade out of work. The accumulated damage to the business sector (in annual terms) from October 2000 to June 2002 was 12.5 percent.[3] Also, the flow of Israeli capital abroad has increased, as have foreign financial investments earning quick profits from the high Israeli interest rate (in mid-2003 the basic interest rate in Israel was eight times higher than that in the US).

The war also led to a one percent decrease in Israel's GDP in each of the years 2001 and 2002. On a per capita basis, the picture is even worse: the per capita GDP went down from $18,000 in 2000 to $14,000 in 2002.[4] If at the end of the 1990s Israel's GDP put it in the third decile of countries worldwide, even ahead of some of the developed European countries, by 2002 Israel had regressed to the fifth decile, alongside undeveloped Third World countries.[5] The increase in military expenditures and the long-term political decision to give preference to maintaining the occupied territories and settlements intensified Israel's socio-economic crisis.

A "new Middle East"?

These problems led various Israeli governments to seek ways to create a situation whereby the occupation would continue, but within the framework of Palestinian self-rule as in the 1993 Oslo accords, signed by a Labor government. The 1994 Paris Agreement, the economic annex of the Oslo Accords, intentionally left all the Palestinian territories in the condition of an economic appendix to Israel. The Oslo Accords were intended to create more favorable conditions for business and investments by Israeli companies both in the territories and in Arab countries, a "New Middle East" in the words of Shimon Peres.[6] This was cut short by the assassination of Prime Minister Rabin in 1995 and the return of the *Likud* (headed by Netanyahu) to power in the 1996 elections.

In 2002 the American government initiated the Road Map plan. From the point of view of the Israeli government, the implementation of the Road Map is supposed to enable the continuation of the Israeli occupation in at least half of the West Bank and leave most of the settlers in their homes. A sort of Palestinian state (a "temporary state") will be established in only half of the West Bank and the Gaza Strip, but this state will continue to be dependent on Israel in every way. Israel's large investment in the "separation fence", or wall is intended to unilaterally determine the border between Israel and Palestine and to ensure the inclusion of most of the settlements inside Israeli territory.

Parallel to and in close connection with the militarization of the economy and society, the great complex of monopolies and cartels, mergers and takeovers, which began to dominate the world economy in the 1980s and '90s, also took root in Israel. It reached a high point during the Sharon governments (of 2001 and 2003), with Benyamin Netanyahu as Finance minister.

State capitalism

The economic regime in Israel from the establishment of the state in 1948 until the June 1967 war had been characterized by the expansion of the local capital market; capital import on a large scale; the addition of large numbers of Jewish immigrants as workers and consumers; and the expropriation of most of the lands owned by Palestinian Arab citizens.

The expansion policy of the Israeli capitalist economy depended largely on intensive governmental intervention in the areas of investment, the import of capital, urban and rural development but also on building social services (the most important of which was the establishment of the National Insurance Institute in 1954). In the face of the relative weakness of the Israeli bourgeoisie in the 1950s and '60s, the government took upon itself the task of subsidizing new factories and developing those that had been established during the British Mandate, such as the Electric Corporation and the oil refineries. The governments headed by *Mapai* (which in the course of the years changed its name to the Labor Alignment, and later to the Labor Party) combined incentives to private capital with direct government investments in infrastructure, including the construction of apartments for sale and rent.[7]

Israeli governments worked in close cooperation with the three major banks at that time: Bank Leumi (established in 1920 by the Zionist movement), the Discount Bank (established in 1935 as a private bank by the Recanati family), and Bank Hapoalim (established in 1921 by the *Histadrut* General Labor Federation according to an agreement with the

Zionist Organization). In addition to the veteran investment companies (PEC, Palestine Economic Corporation, and AMPAL, American-Palestine Trading Corporation), collaboration between American entrepreneurs and the banks, and generous government incentives, led to the establishment in the 1960s of four investment companies which quickly became the dominant forces in the Israeli economy: Rassco, the Israel Investors Company, the Clal Company and the Israel Company.

In Israel's era of state capitalism, the governmental sector had played a major role in the economy. In 1967 the number of government companies (including subsidiaries) reached some 250, and the government's percentage of their capital amounted to 55 percent. During these years the economic institutions under the supervision of the "Workers' Company" of the *Histadrut* also played a dominant role. In 1965, some 24 percent of all wage workers in Israel were employed by companies and cooperatives connected to the *Histadrut*.[8] But contrary to what the heads of *Mapai* tried to claim then, the public economy, based on its two principal components – the government and the *Histadrut* – was never a socialist economy, but rather an economy based on state capitalism, which fulfilled the expectations of the big banks and the private investment companies. Moreover, as the years passed the corporations succeeded in crushing the public sector, first and foremost the *Histadrut* sector, taking control of its companies and factories. Corporate capital replaced public capital.

From the 1970s privatization was rampant. During these years the Israeli economy went from the model of expansionist capitalist economy to the economic model based on stagflation. This transition was accompanied by a government policy that turned its back on active involvement in economic development and adopted a different goal, in the course of time developing a no-growth economy, in which inflation existed together with unemployment.[9]

That same *Likud* government that initiated "liberalization" in the area of Jewish acquisition of land in the occupied territories, also initiated "liberalization" in the area of foreign currency. In October 1977, the *Likud* government officially announced the removal of supervision over foreign currency and an exchange rate regulated according to economic developments; cancellation of the purchase tax while raising the VAT from 8 percent to 12 percent; cancellation of most subsidies for basic food products and a rise in the prices of electricity, water, and public transportation. These measures, together with inflating the rates of the bank shares, led to hyper-inflation that reached 400 percent in 1984.[10]

Privatization and concentration of capital

In the 1980s, after the speculative stock-exchange bubble burst (the bank shares crisis erupted in 1983 and forced the government to "nationalize" four big banks) the large corporations increasingly pressured the government to make structural changes in its policy, preferring tax breaks for the private sector profit over budgets for the welfare state. In 2003, as opposed to 1986, the rate of corporate tax had decreased from 61 percent to 36 percent and employers' payments to national insurance had fallen from 15 percent to 4 percent of their workers' wages.

At the same time, the *Likud* (and Labor) governments accelerated the privatization of the government companies in various branches – chemicals, gas, construction, communications and aviation, as well as the banks that had been "nationalized". The *Histadrut* "Workers Company", which included the large industrial concern *Koor*, the investment company *AMPAL*, and *Bank Hapo'alim,* was dismantled and privatized in the 1990s. From the 1990s onward there were waves of takeovers, with large companies acquiring each other, and of merger agreements, resulting in groups representing foreign capital strengthening their control over the Israeli economy.

These processes created an unprecedented concentration of capital in Israel. A survey conducted by the Tel Aviv Stock Exchange revealed that six families controlled 40 percent of the value of the shares traded on the stock exchange: the Recanati family (Discount Bank, IDB); the Ofer brothers (*Mizrahi* Bank, shipbuilding); the Bronfman and Culver families (*Koor*, aviation, Tadiran); the Arison family (*Bank Hapoalim, Koor, Solel Boneh*); and Dankner investments (*Bank Hapoalim* and *Koor*).[11] These six families control 12 of the 17 economic conglomerates in Israel, and their total sales amount to 10 percent of Israel's annual GDP. As a result of their dominant status, the capital groups of these families made some 90 percent of the net profit of these 17 economic conglomerates.[12] This centralization is of especially great significance in the area of the commercial media, particularly newspapers, the commercial television channels and cable television. The control of this economic branch is in the hands of the banks (*Hapoalim* and Discount), the families who own the daily newspapers (Moses, Fishman, Nimrodi), and foreign companies. This control enables them to concentrate far-reaching political power in their hands.[13]

This explains why foreign corporations and entrepreneurs today own 50 percent of the 20 largest companies in Israel that trade on the stock exchange, including banks, and companies involved in high-tech, chemicals and drugs, insurance and investment. Israeli governments, which should according to their Zionist ideology create and maintain an independent national state, have given up the goal of achieving political and economic independence. Israel is becoming increasingly integrated into the American military strategy and into the global expansion of multinational companies based in the US. The refusal of the American government, which grants more aid per head to Israel than to any other country, to allow Israeli military industries to compete with those in America – and Israel's obligation to purchase the maximum amount of military equipment in the US – led to a crisis in Israel's military–industrial complex. What Israel calls its "integration into international financial markets" comes at a high price, expressed in billions of dollars of annual interest payments.

Poverty and unemployment

The ever deepening structural crisis of the economy has been accompanied by the institutionalization of unemployment (more than 10 percent of the workforce), and unprecedented gaps in income levels, hitting the poorer sections of the population in general, including women, old people, children, large families, one-parent families, the disabled, etc. Among the victims was the Arab sector, which has always suffered as a national minority from grave economic discrimination (double the unemployment rate of the Jewish sector).

Following the policies of the IMF and the World Bank, Israeli governments too blamed the economic crisis and the government's growing budget deficit on social welfare expenditures, the size of the public sector, and the "unreadiness to work" of the unemployed. The government cut health and education budgets and withdrew from the area of public housing (except for the settlements). Contrary to government propaganda about the oversized public sector, public expenditure in Israel, relative to production, is slightly higher than in Europe not because of social spending, but because of military spending. Without the exceptionally high military expenditures public spending in Israel is similar to the norm in Europe.[14]

According to recent National Insurance Institute (NII) statistics, the number of families living in poverty on the basis of their incomes (before welfare payments and direct taxes) is 32 percent of all families in Israel and 36 percent of the children in Israel. After the welfare payments and direct taxes, 18 percent of the families and 25 percent of the children live under the poverty line. Contrary to the public stereotype, poverty is not necessarily linked to the unemployment of the head of the family. The statistics demonstrate that more than half of those found beneath the poverty line (52 percent) live in families where there is a wage earner. The proportion of those living in families with a wage earner, among all those living below the poverty line, grew from 33 percent in 1990 to 45.2 percent in 2000. At the same time the rate of those living in poverty among all the wage-earning families grew from 14 percent in 1990 to 22 percent in 1998. In other words, the wage erosion caused by the rapid polarization in incomes, and the growth of employment by manpower companies, push tens of thousands of wage-earning families under the poverty line. At the same time unemployment in the first half of 2003 went up to 285,000, or 10.8 percent of the workforce.

The "Plan for the Recovery of the Israeli Economy" submitted by Finance Minister Benyamin Netanyahu to the *Knesset* in April 2003 was an expression of these policies; it is unprecedented even in international terms. For example, according to the NII, the old-age pension for a single individual will drop from 16 percent of the average wage in 2001 to 11 percent of the average wage in 2020. The cut in child allowances, cumulative from January 2001 till the end of 2006, will take away 17 percent of the allowance of a family with one or two children, 38 percent of the allowance of a family with three children, and 73 percent of the allowance of a family with 7–8 children. As a result of this policy, the rate of children in Israel living under the poverty line will grow from one-third to one-half; among Arab children the rate will grow from one out of two children to two out of three children.

The neo-liberal policies encourage the employment of workers via manpower companies and contractors, employment by personal contracts rather than collective agreements, and the employment of migrant laborers. According to *Histadrut* estimates, 10 percent of salaried workers in Israel, some 180,000 men and women, are employed at the minimum wage by manpower companies. They are denied the rights attained by the workers in this sector won over the years by the trade union movement. Sixteen percent of all workers employed in the public sector are employed via manpower companies, and this figure rises to 33 percent for government workers.[15]

To this sector of workers without rights must be added the migrant laborers. Like the Palestinian workers, most receive less than the minimum wage, without benefits like overtime pay and annual vacations. In mid-2003 it was estimated that some 300,000 migrant laborers (with and without legal work permits) are employed in Israel, and they constitute some 16 percent of all wage earners. Thus, these two groups of exploited workers – manpower company employees and migrant laborers – already make up about a quarter of the workers in Israel, and in economic branches such as agriculture, construction, nursing, and security they account for more than half.

The processes referred to above, along with the privatization of the huge *Histadrut* health fund (in 1995), reduced the number of labor union members in Israel to one-third of all wage earners. Since most wage earners in Israel are employed in workplaces that are not organized, the main labor struggles and strikes take place in the public sector (government ministries and public companies like the Electric Corporation, local authorities, universities, etc.). The government, in a Thatcherist spirit, is acting to further limit the freedom of workers to organize and strike by means of legislation.

The price is double

The neo-liberal policy dictated by the American government, the IMF and the World Bank was officially adopted at the end of the 1970s, and since then has been continued by all Israeli governments (*Likud* and Labor). It has been the workers and the poorer sectors of the population who have had to pay both the cost of the economic policy and the cost of continuing occupation and wars. Under these conditions, it is objectively impossible to separate the struggle for a just and stable peace based on the establishment of an independent Palestinian state alongside Israel on the June 4, 1967 borders, from the struggle against rightist economic policies and for the protection of social services, full employment, equality and social justice.

One of the difficult problems of the Israeli left is that, in practice, these two crucial struggles are usually conducted separately. In most cases, those who demand the dismantlement of the settlements and the withdrawal of the Israeli army from all the Palestinian territories, do not at the same time demand the dismantlement of the oligarchic and centralized rule of capital in Israel – and the other way around. The *Histadrut* and the trade unions, which oppose government economic policy, do not take a stand against the occupation and its heavy socio-economic cost; while the peace movement, which for years has struggled against the occupation and its crimes, does not mobilize for the social struggle.

The ethno-centric character of Israeli democracy, the institutionalized anti-Arab discrimination in all areas (budgets, housing, the establishment of new towns, education, infrastructure) and the systematic overall discrimination against Arab citizens who constitute 20 percent of Israel's population – all these factors place obstacles in the way of building a joint

Jewish–Arab struggle. Yet this is crucial for the success of any political and social campaign.

In theoretical terms, the Israeli left has to cope both with the nationalist, racist and social demagogy of the right, which preaches a "Greater Israel", and with the tradition of what the Labor party called "constructive socialism" which preaches the upbuilding of the country by the labor movement in cooperation with capital.

Obstacles facing the Israeli left

At the outset of the twenty-first century, the ongoing occupation and the government's economic policies have, both together and separately, reached a dead end. According to the public opinion polls most Israelis support a withdrawal from the territories and oppose the government's economic plan. It would thus appear that conditions are ripe for conducting a popular struggle for peace and social justice. However, in the socio-political reality of Israel today, opposition to the occupation and to the ever-widening social gaps has still to overcome the obstacles presented by nationalistic reactions to events and the exploitation of Israel's security problems. The hysteria of the "struggle against terrorism" fanned by the Bush administration rides the same wave that holds aloft the *Likud* government and the Israeli right-wing. With the aid of generals, academics, the mass media, economic "experts" and political commentators, the government is still able to successfully persuade most of the public that there is no "partner for peace", that "the struggle against terror" has priority and that this demands "economic sacrifice".

One of the most serious problems on the way to presenting an alternative social policy is the opportunistic position of the *Histadrut* leadership, which lacks any vision of fundamental social change. The majority of this leadership supports the privatization of government companies and social services, goes along with the growing phenomenon of manpower companies, ignores the distress of migrant and Palestinian workers, and accepts the government's claim that workers must also contribute to reducing the budget deficit via wage cuts.

The political parties in Israel (except, in this writer's opinion, for the Israeli Communist Party and *Hadash*) in the main support neo-liberal policies. They are far removed from any kind of critical thinking *vis-à-vis* capitalism as a socio-economic system, and most reject even the moderate Social-Democratic version of this criticism. As a result, even those parties in opposition to the right-wing government and the settlers do not offer a comprehensive principled alternative to the government's neo-liberal conceptions. Under these conditions what is required is a campaign which combines the political and social struggles, and which integrates the efforts of peace, social, and environmental organizations, youth and women's movements, Jews and Arabs, under a common umbrella. This broad coalition must present the fundamental alternative: a democratic society aspiring to equality and social justice and living in peaceful co-existence with its neighbors.

Notes

1 Ze'ev Schiff and Ehud Ya'ari, *Intifada* (Jerusalem and Tel Aviv: Schoken Press, 1990).
2 Shulamit Carmi and Henry Rosenfeld, "The Political Economy of the Militarist Nationalism in Israel", in *Israeli Society: a Critical Look* (Tel Aviv: Brarot Press, 1993.)
3 Zvi Sussman, "Government Policy in an Economy in Crisis: War, the High-Tech Crisis and World Recession" in *The Allocation of Resources to Social Services, 2002* (Jerusalem: Center for the Study of Social Policy in Israel, 2002).
4 Bank of Israel, *The Economy and Economic Policy, 2002.*
5 Ya'akov Lifshitz, "Economy during a Low-Grade War: a Reevaluation of the Dilemma 'Guns or Butter'", in Ibid.
6 Efraim Davidi, "Globalization and Economy in the Middle East – a Peace of Markets or a Peace of Flags?", *Palestine–Israel Journal* 7 1, 2 (2000).
7 Tamar Gozansky, *Economic Independence – How?* (Tel Aviv: Iyun Press, 1968); Shlomo Frankel and Shimshon Bichle, *The Nobility, Israel's Financial Elite* (Tel Aviv: Kadim Press, 1984).
8 *The Histadrut, the Workers' Economy 1960–1965* (Tel Aviv: The Institute for Economic and Social Research, 1967).
9 Esther Alexander, *The Power of Equality in the Economy – the Israeli Economy in the 1980s, the True Picture* (Tel Aviv: HaKibbutz Hameuchad Press, 1990).
10 Ya'akov Reuveni, "The Political Economy of the Likud 1977–1984: a Diagnostical Examination", *Economic Quarterly* 126, October 1985.
11 Shimshon Bichler and Yehonatan Nitzan, *From War Profits to Peace Dividends* (Jerusalem: Carmel Press, 2001).
12 Dun and Bradstreet, *Dun's 100 Israel's Largest Enterprises, 2002.*
13 Ari Shavit, "The Citizens Moses and Fishman", *Ha'aretz,* February 18, 2002.
14 Arnon Gafny and Zvi Sussman, "The Democracy of Welfare – for Increased Social Involvement by the Government in the Market Economy Regime", in *The Allocation of Resources.*
15 *Histadrut* Industrial Democracy and Manpower Companies Section, *Manpower Companies, the Present Situation,* May, 2003.

13 The Dilemmas of Israeli Education

SHULAMIT ALONI

When the State of Israel was established in 1948, the largest party in the Jewish population was *Mapai*, by definition a Socialist-Zionist party, now called the Labor party (at the time, the term Social Democratic was not yet popular). To the left was *Mapam*, a Zionist party with a Soviet orientation. Still further left was the Jewish-Arab Communist Party that, although not Zionist, still supported the concept of the partition of the country into Jewish and Arab states. The conservative General Zionist party was located in the center, and there was also a small classical capitalist "Independent Liberal Party".

On the right was the *Herut* (Freedom) party established by members of the militant underground *Irgun* movement that supported a Greater Israel on both banks of the Jordan River and opposed the partition of the country.

The pre-state "Revisionist" Zionists, later to become *Herut*, took on many rudiments of Italian fascism in their early days: extreme nationalism, the unity of the nation, discipline, sacrifice, and the primacy of the state over the rights of the worker or the individual.

The religious sector

Alongside these parties were, and still are, the religious Zionist parties, which originally had general and workers' wings, the latter establishing their own communal and cooperative agricultural settlements, like *Mapai* and *Mapam*. All the religious Zionist parties joined in 1956 to form the

National Religious Party (NRP or *Mafdal* in Hebrew). This party underwent a process of transformation in both the political and the religious spheres, moving from moderation to extreme, militant, right-wing and even racist views, presenting the Jews as the "Chosen People" with divine rights over the entire country. On the other hand, all rights, individual or collective, were denied for the Palestinian population of the land. Since the 1980s, the NRP has located itself to the right of the *Likud* (formed from *Herut* and the General Zionists in 1973).

It is important to note that, to this day, there also exists an anti-Zionist or non-Zionist ultra-orthodox religious stream with its own system of education. On the eve of the establishment of the State of Israel it ensured the status of its "independent" education within the framework of what is known today as the religious *status quo*, defined in a letter from the Jewish Agency to the ultra-orthodox *Agudat Yisrael* dated 1947. Over the years, this ultra-orthodox Judaism has invested great efforts in maintaining and expanding its educational networks.

Labor "from dawn to dusk"

At the time of the establishment of the state there were three educational streams, general, workers' and religious. The workers' educational movement, with a wide network of institutions owned by the labor movement, was educating to the values of labor, agriculture, and the establishment of a just, exemplary socialist society. Moreover, this was undoubtedly a Zionist-nationalist education. Although inherently secular, it was imbued with love for the homeland and for the sources and historical narratives of the people of Israel, the Hebrew language and Hebrew literature and culture. Characteristic of those times, the educational institutions of the workers' movement had an anthem that began with the words: "We are all workers, we labor the whole day through, we work with our hands from dawn to dusk, by the sweat of our brows we will eat our bread . . . in song and joy."

With the establishment of the state, Ben-Gurion determined that the government must emphasize the primacy of the state over all the pre-state voluntary organizations – hence the establishment of the Israel Defense Forces and the abolition of "political" armies from Mandate days like the kibbutz-oriented *Palmach*, and the *Irgun*. The same principle applied to education, all of which came under the auspices of the state. It was easy enough to dismantle the workers' stream because Ben-Gurion's party controlled it. However, with the abolition of separate streams in 1953, religious education, which was also incorporated into the national educational framework, had its own demands. It was granted an independent unit of its own with its curriculum stressing religion, similar to but not identical with the general curriculum. In these schools, to this day only Rabbis and religious teachers are employed as teachers.

Educational goals

In 1949, a law was passed making free education compulsory for children between the ages of five to 14, a year of nursery school and eight years in primary school. The goals of national education, as they were defined in 1953, reflected the spirit of the times as well as the needs of the religious community. The definition in the second paragraph of the law states "The purpose of national education is to found primary education in the State on values of Israeli culture and scientific achievements; on love of the homeland and loyalty to the State and the Israeli people; on a belief in agricultural work, labor and pioneering; and on striving for a society built on freedom, equality, tolerance, mutual aid and love of the human race."

The following points are worthy of attention:

1   There is no mention of the minorities living in Israel or their heritage and needs.
2   Scientific achievements are lauded but not the foundations of science, and therefore there is no education in research (in order to appease the religious community for whom much research was tantamount to heresy).
3   There was an emphasis on agriculture and labor and not on industry and commerce because the latter are "bourgeois" and Diaspora-oriented, and not socialist.
4   There is no mention of human rights, human autonomy, gender equality or relations with other nations of the world. Neither is there any mention of freedom of conscience or religious freedom.

These goals were considered valid until the middle of the 1990s when, after protracted efforts, they were changed. In the new era, the national and religious–traditional emphasis remained. However, it is no coincidence that there is still no mention of individual rights, the rights of the "other", research, development, creativity, and intellectual curiosity.

What of the institutions of ultra-orthodox education, both of *Agudat Yisrael* and the bigger *Sephardi* Shas movement? Up to the time of writing, there has been no outside control over the content of their curriculum. The 1947 *status quo* agreement promised a degree of educational autonomy, and a commitment not to harm religious consciousness. However, the state would obviously determine a minimum of compulsory subjects such as Hebrew language, history, science, etc. This clause in the agreement was not implemented in the ultra-orthodox schools. Deliberately or not, the emphasis on "Torah education" at the expense of general subjects has perpetuated backwardness in their communities.

On the national level, after 1977, an extra year of compulsory free education was added – the ninth grade – and nursery school began at the age of four, but this was not free, even in areas of weaker populations. There was compulsory, free nursery school only from the age of five. Over the years there has been a growth of various types of "complementary education" in order to augment and enrich what is learned in the educational system. This is of course only available to those parents with the means to pay for it. It therefore discriminates at all age levels against pupils from poor homes. Yet it is they who may be most in need of help in their studies because they come from backgrounds where their parents cannot always help them. On the other hand, some success was recorded in attempts to introduce integration in order to mix pupils from weaker and stronger background for the benefit of new immigrants and the weaker pupil. Important educational work was carried out by the Zionist youth movements, representing the whole spectrum of political views, left and right, religious and secular. Today, when ideologies play a lesser role than before, the influence of these movements has declined.

A political "revolution"

Significant changes in the content of national education began with the 1977 upheaval, when *Mapai* lost the elections to the nationalist *Likud* party led by former *Irgun* underground leader Menahem Begin. He and his party, which were associated with the concept of "Greater Israel", came to power after the occupation of the West Bank and the Gaza Strip during the Six Day War in 1967. The *Likud* was joined by the National Religious Party, one of whose younger leaders Zevulun Hammer, became Minister of Education in the new right-wing settler-oriented government.

The minister introduced intensive religious education into state schools, as was considered appropriate for the Chosen people in the Promised Land. Fully paid Rabbis were placed in national schools (at the expense of geography and science teachers) and untrained women teachers doing their national service taught in the lower classes, introduced obligatory religious rituals. This was the beginning of a period of religious missionary-ism in state schools. In the religious state schools Messianic indoctrination was bolstered, stressing exclusive Jewish rights to the whole land. The minister organized a "scientific" conference in Jerusalem in order to prove that evolution and Darwinism are inherently foolish and that we should return to the biblical story of the Creation in Genesis. There was even an attempt to change nursery school songs. In a *Hannukah* song, the words "miracles and wonders wrought by the *Maccabees*" were replaced by "miracles and wonders *wrought by the Lord* for the Maccabees".

During the years Zevulun Hammer served as Minister of Education, followed by Yitzhak Levy (also from the NRP), plans for putting into practice study programs for science, civics and humanist Judaism were abandoned. Outstanding professors who had prepared these courses were fired or forced to resign. The Reform and Conservative Movements in Judaism were of course ignored. In place of the secular humanist direction fundamental to the educational philosophy of the early days of the state came a nationalistic orthodox religious approach.

The impact of occupation

Clearly, what happened in the field of education did not occur in a vacuum. Special schools for Jews and Arabs oriented toward a humanistic education reach only a small minority of the population and received little government support. New policies were adopted expressing the rejection of the old political–educational values. These changes reflected the dominant developments in Israeli society as a whole. The occupation of 1967, the shock of the *Yom Kippur* War in 1973 and the *Likud* victory in the 1977 elections, all brought about a complete change in the relative strength of right and left. The declining Labor Party, though active in the Socialist International, was moving toward support for market capitalism, privatization and globalization. The focal point on Israel's political landscape was the occupation, the settlements and the immorality of Israel's policy toward the Palestinian people. On these issues Labor reacted too late if at all. Similarly during the 1982 Lebanon war the Labor Party voted to support the government and, therefore, the annexation of the Golan Heights. Only after the failure in Lebanon became apparent in public opinion did Labor come around to opposing the war and demand that the IDF retreat.

As for Labor's opponents, the rightist camp became more nationalistic in its foreign policy and is becoming more Thatcherist in its economic policy. Although many voters from the poorer sections of the population supported the *Likud*, that party was increasingly hostile to the welfare state or to addressing the glaring socio-economic gap. Under the *Likud*, an unbridled capitalism is flourishing, the rich are becoming richer and the poor poorer. Migrant laborers, numbering some 300,000, who suffer from cruel exploitation, are building the country. Civil rights and equal rights for women are low on the agenda. In a racist spirit, the *Likud*'s coalition partners from the NRP and the settler movement are becoming more ethnocentric, denying the rights of the Palestinian people, taking over from their rightful owners every possible unit of land in the territories, destroying Arab property, uprooting ancient olive trees and systematically expanding illegal Jewish settlement.

It is not surprising that the unbridled resistance to the Oslo Accords originated among these same rightist-religious politicians and particularly the settlers. Neither is it unexpected that they were the source of the demonstrations against Rabin, of hatred, incitement and, finally, political murder in order to stop the peace process.

The period of the Oslo Accords and the short-lived Rabin government (1992–5) saw both political and economic progress. Peace seemed to be drawing nearer and there was a new confidence at home and abroad in the economy. There also took place something akin to an "educational revolution". Education became a top priority, with its budget almost equaling that for security. The curriculum was reformed to include subjects like civics, human rights, the different streams in Judaism. and other subjects formerly shunned. Teacher training was advanced. A long school day was introduced, starting in weaker population areas, for the benefit of children and working mothers. Colleges were opened all over the country, broadening the number of young people able to receive higher education. A start was made to tackle the backward state of education in the Arab sector, which required a special effort in view of the discrimination which it had suffered for so many years.

"Left" and "right"

Israeli society is split over political, social, religious and ethnic issues but it would appear that in the Jewish state the usual division of the population into right and left on a class basis is no longer appropriate. The differences are, for example, more in approaches to the Palestinian people and the occupation, marking the dividing line between "hawks" and "doves". Today, now that the right has been in power for most of the period since 1977, the Palestinians have no state of their own and are more humiliated and economically depressed than ever. There are, as we have seen, basic differences in the image of Israeli society, on subjects like democracy; civil rights; discrimination according to race, religion or gender; religious pluralism; concern for minorities; the role of the army and the dangers of militarism.

These are among the dilemmas which are also expressed in education. They revolve not only around the low level of knowledge in by Israel international standards. There is also the choice between an education which is increasingly religious and nationalistic and one which is pluralistic and democratic. The latter is unlikely to flourish in an atmosphere of paranoia, where generals and ex-generals constantly warn the public, and little children are taught in school that the Jewish people is on the verge of destruction. An alternative educational philosophy would be founded on a strong, confident but peace-loving society which is aware that the threat to drive us into the sea derives primarily from propaganda by militarist political circles.

Needed – a constitution

We are now in a situation in which the mainstream left constitutes a weak and vacillating opposition, lacking leadership and presenting no viable alternative policies. The Labor party is paralyzed and its strength is decreasing from election to election. The urge for power constantly draws it into coalitions with the right, though this is against its political interests, leaving wide sections of the public apathetic to its fate.

Ours is not a "normal" society which evolved over centuries. We are a country without recognized borders and without a constitution. Many of the new immigrants who came from Eastern Europe and the Mediterranean countries lacked experience of democracy, as people who lived as a minority in their countries and fought to survive. Uniting a people coming home from the ends of the earth demands and still necessitates a constitution so as to define and teach the rights and obligations of citizenship in a new sovereign state. We lack a sense of security in spite of our strong armed forces as we witness nauseating and inexcusable acts by terrorist suicide bombers in our buses and cafes, inevitably increasing hatred of "the other". Our children are taught that our army is "the most ethical in the world" yet they watch our soldiers using Palestinians as "human shields" despite this being illegal as well as immoral.

The society developing here in Israel is very far from the "exemplary society" envisaged by the fathers of Zionism, which was to provide the guidelines for our educational project. The shadow of the protracted occupation touches the lives of all Israelis and follows us everywhere. The arrogance of power latent in the occupation seems unlimited when 18-

year old boys are sent to destroy buildings or drag people from their beds in the middle of the night, all in the sacred but manipulated name of "security".

Therefore, in a society which has lost its way in the search for truth and honesty, it is hard to distinguish along normal political lines between "right" and "left". Lacking an accepted code of ethics, it is not easy to undertake a consistent and truthful teaching of values. All our educational endeavor depends upon our ability, which has been eroded over the years, to honor both our own human rights and the rights of others. Such an education cannot abide manifestations like occupation or religious coercion: it must be founded on the principles of democracy and freedom of speech, conscience and choice, as promised in Israel's 1948 Declaration of Independence on "freedom, just and peace, as envisaged by the prophets of Israel".

The Israeli Woman and the Feminist Commitment

14

ERELLA SHADMI

Why is it that in the Hebrew language the words for man (*gever*) and for heroism (*g'vurah*) come from the same root? It is because of the traditionally inferior position of the woman in Israel society, so largely dominated by militarism, nationalism and religious fundamentalism. Within this scale of values the woman cannot expect equality and many would primarily restrict her role to motherhood and family. This is a "private" sphere but in it, every newborn Jewish baby may be seen as a statistic in the "demographic race" against the Palestinians, and as a "future soldier". The goal of Israeli feminism is to transform society so the existing gender relations will be eliminated.

Israel's economic policies dictate that women's salaries, working conditions, promotion rights and retirement conditions are inferior to those of men. The options for decent employment and higher education for poor *Mizrahi*, Russian[1] and Palestinian-Israeli[2] women, are minimal. The public sector, the largest employer of women, has been the main victim since the mid-1980s of budget cuts, privatization and exploitation by manpower companies. Women are also the main sufferers from the most recent cutbacks in the social services – health, welfare, children's and old-age allowances.

Gender is thus deeply rooted in the structure of Israeli society, along with other patterns of discrimination, both national, racial and ethnic. All these forms of oppression crisscross and construct a patriarchal and racially structured capitalist regime. Yet both before and after feminism evolved in Israeli politics, gender was never a central issue in the politics of the "left", posing the question whether these politics have really been "left" at all. Left politics in the sense of aiming to uproot all forms of oppression and discrimination had to wait for feminism to become really left. In an attempt to enquire whether Israeli feminism has lived up to this expectation, this article will take a critical look at three landmarks in the history of Israeli feminism: the feminist outcry of the early 1970s, Women in Black (1988), and the single-mother protest led by Vicki Knafo in 2003.

Feminism in the 1970s and beyond

The new feminist activism of the 1970s was focused on issues like equal pay for equal work, the right to abortion, day-care centers and male violence. Feminists also organized study and consciousness-raising groups and the first national femininist conferences. They established the first women's centers Kol Ha'isha and Tsena u'rinah;[3] a feminist publishing house, "The Second Sex"; Alef, the first lesbian feminist organization; and "No to violence against women". New feminist literature and journals appeared. Toward the end of the first decade of feminism, the first center for battered women and sexual assualt victims had been opened. All this attracted media attention, often hostile.

The feminist upsurge was encouraged not only by a more pluralistic atmosphere and the increasing awareness of discrimination against women in Israel, but also by growing feminist aspirations in the West, imported by newcomers. These new, mainly radical initiatives were far from the centers of power, unaffiliated with any political party and often from leftish male politics. (The Likud first won power from Labor in 1977.) They were not associated with older traditional women's organizations. Since they saw the liberation of women as part of the transformation of society, they were among the first to challenge what they saw as the omnipotence of the state in Israel. They also set out to shake the Zionist myth that Israel had achieved gender equality. Many of them did not completely cut themselves off from the mainstream and maintained pro-Zionist positions, but all were radical and critical of Israeli society.

Thirty years on, one can see that public awareness to discrimination and to many other women's issues has increased. In areas like male violence against women and equal opportunity in employment, more legislation has been introduced. There are more women writers and artists, more academic research and publications. An impressive network of feminist organizations – radical, political, governmental and non-governmental – is now active. While some provide legal counseling or deal with legislation and protection, education and health, others represent specific constituencies such as *Mizrahi*, religious or lesbian women, or Palestinian women.

Feminist ideas are now more visible in the grass-roots politics of peace, social justice and environmental organizations, and in political parties. Most government departments today have offices for women's issues. Most universities and colleges offer feminist studies. In short, the feminist seed seems to have been implanted throughout Israeli society. Nevertheless, there remain the issues first of whether and how this implantation basically changed the position of Israeli women, and second – whether it has been "left". The answers are interrelated.

Non-radical feminism

All in all, the condition of the Israeli woman has hardly changed for the better. Gender and other forms of discrimination against women, be they founded on racial, ethnic or class issues, have scarcely been touched. Male violence against women and inequality in the labor market are still prevelant. I would suggest that the limitations of left feminist politics are to be found in their elitism, their middle-class *Ashkenazi* composition and agenda, and their distance from *Mizrahi*, working-class, and poor women. All these factors blind them to the racial character of women's oppression and cast doubt on the effectiveness and "leftism" of Israeli feminism.

However, this is not all. As privatization expands, the Israeli welfare state unburdens itself of many functions (like education, housing and health) onto women's organizations. These consequently become increasingly service-oriented, complementing the state rather than challenging it. The leftist political orientation remains only in relatively few radical feminist organizations.

The problem has been exacerbated since the *Al-Aqsa Intifada* of September 2000 by the growing anti-liberal neo-Zionist trend in an Israeli society whose capitalist regime has long been accepted by all the political parties. This trend comes at the expense of tolerance and multiculturalism and endorses masculinity and traditional femininity. It is also characterized by an alliance between the nationalistic–religious rightist circles and secularists with liberal outlooks, both mainly *Ashkenazi* and middle class. Again, the main victims are women, especially from the *Mizrahi* and Palestinian populations.

In these circumstances, radical feminists are marginalized and efforts are made to co-opt them into accepting "feminism from above" as promoted by the establishment, rather than as part of a wider social transformation. This sort of non-radical feminism sponsors middle-class women's interests, such as sexual equality in the work place and representation in politics. The demands of radical and *Mizrahi* feminists to uproot gender and race oppression and to transform social institutions are met with silence or with apprehension. Even many radical feminist groups fail to face up fully to issues of race and class. As for most of the women's organizations, they conform with the mainstream approach and accept the non-political rules of the game. Such a situation poses the question whether any women's "left" politics is left in Israel The only exception may be found in *Mizrahi* feminism and among a few radical feminists, but they tend to be marginalized within the general feminist movement.

Women and peace activism

The 1980s saw an unprecedented upsurge in women's peace activism. First, women constituted the majority of the peace camp in Israel. Second, women-only peace groups began to appear after the Lebanon war (1982) and even more so in the period of the first *Intifada* (1987–93). Among these were Women against Silence, *Reshet*; the Women's Network for Peace; *Shani*, Women for Peace; Bat Shalom in Jerusalem; and Women in Black. Later came Four Mothers, protesting against the Israeli occupation in Lebanon; New Profile, working against the militarization of Israeli society; *Machsom* Watch overseeing checkpoints in the occupied territories; and the Women's Coalition for a Just Peace, a coalition of ten womens' peace movements, including most of the above.

How can this wide involvement of women in the struggle for peace be explained? Some associate it with the supposedly mothering, peace-loving nature of women. Others stress socio-political phenomena like protest against the low participation of women in conventional political life and the struggle against ultra-nationalism, militarization and religious fundamentalism in Israeli society. Also, it must not be forgotten that this was a time when in its very essence, the *Intifada*, with its overriding violence and brutality, had a particularly strong impact on women. All these factors can explain the urge by women to broaden their activism in the peace movements: theirs was a protest against the dangers they saw for themselves and for their children from an increasingly security-dominated and male-dominated Israeli society.

Though in many respects Women in Black of the first *Intifada* and the Women's Coalition for a Just Peace (CWJP) of the *Al-Aqsa Intifada* are similar to other peace movements, their leading roles, their world reputation, their radicalism and innovative methods of work make them worthy of a closer look in order to better understand leftist women's activism.

The work of Women in Black, a network of silent weekly vigils standing once a week in central locations all over the country since January 1988, has been characterized by three novel forms. First, using their own bodies in a vigil questioned the traditional role ascribed to women and their bodies as a patriarchal function. It also establishes the connection between the Israeli occupation of foreign land and male occupation of women's body. Second, using of the color black to express sorrow over the occupation, echoing female mourning practices in the Middle East. Third, winning a high public profile through a regular and consistent schedule of protests in every corner of the country, exposing large numbers of people from different walks of life to the message of the Women in Black.

In spite of the insults and violent sexist comments hurled at them, in their new and original strategy the Women in Black went beyond political parties, interest groups and elections. They neither accumulated power nor socialized with politicians or media personalities. Yet their combination of womanhood and ever-present protest probably drove home the injustice of the occupation to a hitherto unknown extent. Like it or not, the public was forced to take notice of the Women in Black and they were to become an inseparable part of the whole Israeli landscape.

New voice, old problems

In November 2000, twelve years after Women in Black was established and five weeks after the outbreak of the *Al-Aqsa Intifada*, a few members of Women in Black founded the Coalition of Women for a Just Peace (CWJP). This was during a period of change in public opinion in general and in the peace movement in particular. There was growing disbelief among Israelis in Palestinian support for peace and in Arafat's honesty in conducting peace negotiations. Militaristic and nationalistic sentiments were spreading, no meaningful political opposition was apparent and neither, for the most part, was the voice of the peace camp heard. Though facing indifference, mockery and even violence, the Coalition spoke up courageously for peace at home and won the attention of women around the world, who established their own vigils in support of the Coalition.

Women in Black and the Coalition for a Just Peace share the problem of a membership largely composed of well educated and relatively privileged *Ashkenazi* women. This enables them to work courageously against powerful political streams with which they are familiar because of their background; on the other hand, it strengthens the tendency for them to develop into conformist movements, blind to society's racialized power structure.

Their ethnic and class composition makes non-*Ashkenazi* women feel uncomfortable in their ranks. Working-class and *Mizrahi* women can only be alienated by women who assume that everyone must be familiar with the highbrow language, terminology and texts whose use is taken for granted, not to speak of shared memories of youth movements and middle-class life style.

Neither do Ashkenazi middle-class feminists acknowledge the connection between peace, ethnicity and class. When Arab culture is downplayed, a *Mizrahi* who also defines herself as an Arab Jewess in a state fighting the Arab world, experiences a schism rather than a sense of solidarity. The primarily middle-class *Ashkenazi* composition of many feminist groups expresses the class and ethnic hegemony in Israeli society as a whole and is not unique to the two movements discussed here. It is shared by most of the peace camp and feminists movement. Among the outstanding exceptions were the Black Panthers of the 1970s, and the present *Mizrahi* Democratic Rainbow and *Achoti* (My sister).

Can the "*Ashkenazi* elitism", be overcome? The Coalition, at any rate, has taken the first steps toward taking up issues of social justice and ecology as well as peace. One indication of this is the Coalition's support for the single mothers' protest. I attribute this change in women's politics to their understanding that remaining silent at a time when the social gaps in Israeli society are growing so ominously, may isolate them and threaten their positon.

This feeling of isolation of what was once a leading feminist group (a feeling experienced by other left and peace groups in Israel) is also a result of the emergence during the 1990s of several identity-specific women's frameworks – ultra-orthodox, national religious, Palestinian Arab, lesbian and *Mizrahi*. They are critical of the old feminist leadership, pressing them to combine the struggles for peace and social justice.[4]

In doing so, they would strengthen their contact with a growing number of long-standing grass-root organizations and movements be they mainstream like WIZO or *Na'amat* or more radical like *Isha Leisha* and *Kol Haisha*, mixed groups like *Yadid* and Community Advocacy, and the *Mizrahi* feminist organization, *Achoti*. Apart from the services they have rendered to women all over the country, including the generally neglected periphery areas, such groups have contributed to raising political and social as well as feminist consciousness.

What the analysis presented here suggests is that *Ashkenazi* women react to the threat to their privileged positioning in two contradictory ways: on the one hand, by seeking power through allying themselves with

Ashkenazi hegemony and Western feminists like themselves; on the other hand, by slowly begining to alter both those racist attitudes. and the practices which accompany them in the work. The latter is, as we shall show, the only option for new women's left politics.

Single mothers: a new feminist protest

On July 1, 2003 harsh government measures taken as part of the new economic plan went into effect at the expense of the poor, the homeless, and the unemployed. Among those most drastically hit were 150,000 single mothers. One of them, Vicki Knafo, a part-time working mother of *Mizrahi* origin from Mitzpeh Ramon, a poor southern development town, suddenly moved from anonymity to the national headlines when she decided on a week-long protest march to Jerusalem. Hundreds of single mothers and their supporters hit the roads in solidarity with her, ending up encamped outside government offices in Jerusalem. Public attention was recently aroused by the protests of the physically disabled and the homeless, but the single mothers are more than another interest group because their protest is, perhaps unconsciously, feminist.

What the single mothers ask, as both Yali Hahsash[5] and Smadar Lavie[6] argue, is simply to have the option of a decent life and to be a mother without a male provider or a profession. What stands in their way is a state that fails to provide work, education and vocational training, creating an economic structure in which women, especially single mothers from backward areas like Knafo, cannot provide for their livelihood. The reality in which they live is merciless: little opportunity to find work; manpower companies offering temporary work with low pay and no social security; corporations that move to Jordan or the Far East in a search for cheaper labor; and hundreds of thousands of migrant laborers. Knafo and the single mothers call for a state that does not force them into a traditional heterosexual family, blocking their range of free choice.

The Israeli govermental policy of "radical capitalism" means an endless expansion of what is expected from mothers. It privatizes the education system and creates the conditions under which only women with either the money and skills, or a male provider, can survive. Other mothers, often poor *Mizrahi* women, face the risk, either that the parents will be blamed for the failure of their children, of that their children will be taken away by the authorities. Thus, the struggle is not only on the right to have a family without a male provider; it is also on the social construction of motherhood. Knafo and the single mothers are engaged in left politics at its best.

The singular and courageous move of the single mothers stimulated a wider resistance movement that is also feminist in its ways of organizing and coalition-building, including kibbutzim, the labor movement, the Reform movement and community centers, as well as feminist and women's organizations. They provided the camp dwellers with food, sanitation facilities, summer camps for the children, legal counseling and even entertainment. Apart from *Shatil*, an organization offering counseling to social change groups, there was no coordination of these efforts and no political manipulation was involved.

They were feminist in spirit – no hierarchy, decisions made collectively, each person giving as much as she or he could. The activity was non-partisan yet political, empowering to many women. It refused to be appropriated by political forces. As for the latter point, this lack of structure was indeed to take its toll. Yet on the whole, this undubtedly was feminist polititics in action. Whether bypassing the political structure was wise is debatable. But the protest was feminist in another crucial aspect: it gave hint of a new alliance which has the potential to effect real change in Israeli society, as advocated by radical and *Mizrahi* feminists. It draws the contour lines of the new left in the era of late capitalism and globalization: It would bring together people from poor development towns and cities, kibbutzim and workers from urban neighborhoods, *Ashkenazi* radicals and underprivileged *Mizrahi* women, religious and secular, old-timers and new immigrants from Russia and Ethiopia along with Palestinian Arabs.

This sort of alliance would not be associated with traditional left organizations but would be held together by a belief in social justice and social responsibility. It is a left that is consciously feminist and antiracist; embracing all the relevant groups involved, and aware of the role of religion in global politics. This new left is not communist or socialist-oriented as much as it is anti-domination. Moreover, it supplements the important but insufficient work of human and civil-rights and peace groups, which have not paid adequate attention to the material conditions and rights of the disenfranchised.

The new alliance stands in sharp contrast to the constituency of the current government, whose policies give priority to settlers in the occupied territories. The settlers in the West Bank and Gaza Strip are well aware that the new alliance lays bare how high is the economic price of this policy, and who pays it. They know that the price is said to be paid by "all Israelis" in the name of "national unity" but that the main burden for sustaining the ongoing military operations of the IDF and the interests of the settlers is actually borne by the poor and the undeprivileged. The supporters of the government constituency include neo-conservatives and neo-liberals, who share the economic doctrine of "small government". This category embraces, among others, many *Ashkenazi* middle class former peace supporters. Ironically, one can also find here feminists afraid to lose the gains they had made through feminism. And, finally, there are some *Mizrahi* people who feel alienated from a movement thus expressing a protest by *Mizrahim* and by the poor.

From the point of view of an establishment not lacking racist and sexist tendencies, the single mothers posed a threat to the existing order which had to be silenced. After an initially enthusiastic welcome, the single mothers found themselve encountering reproach, hostility and defamation. Only time will tell how effective the single mothers protest was and will be. However, its scope and the influence upon it of feminist ideas show to what extent, in spite of all the problems, these ideas have penetrated Israeli society. In the last decade, too, the *Mizrahi* critique has become more prominent and its mouthpiece, *Achoti* (My sister) worked in Mitzpeh Ramon, helping local women fired from their work in an attempt to set up an autonomous cooperative. Its work no doubt made a crucial impact on women like Vicky Knafo.

The feminist "threat"

In explaining the different stages in feminist history from the 1970s and 1980s to 2004, I have tried to show how the movement moved from a marginalized position into playing an important role in leftist Israeli politics. I have also shown that women's left politics recorded a number of achievements: in building a network of services for women, and in its meaningful contribution to gender discourse, to women's political consciousness, and to left politics.

The feminist movement strove with increasing success to link the struggles for gender and ethnic justice. Nevertheless, feminist politics faced three particular problems: First in its becoming a network of service organizations rather than a radical movement; second, in attempts from within and without the women's movement to de-radicalize and de-politicize it; third, in the reluctance on the part of too many feminists and non-feminists to recognize racism as a feminist issue These three problems constrain the struggle to transform society and women's position within it. They also repress the "leftism" of women's politics.

The contribution of the contemporary feminist movement to the single mothers' protest shows that it has achieved a degree of viability and stability. Yet it cannot rest upon its laurels for there are those who will do all in their power to co-opt it, seeing in this sort of feminism a major threat to society as it exists and functions today. The ability of feminism to counter all attempts to depoliticize it will enable it to make its own specific radical contribute to the left. This in turn will determine what role it can play in the aspirations of the leftist camp to transform not only the women's lot within society, but society itself.

Notes

1 The issue of women from the former Soviet Union has not been addressed here.
2 This chapter deals only with Jewish women. The position of the Arab woman in Israel is mentioned elsewhere in this book but it needs and deserves a full and in-depth treatment which space restrictions prevent me from presenting in this chapter.
3 This socio-economic analysis is based particularly on the following writers: Yif'at Hill, "From Work to Hell", paper delivered at the *Achoti* Conference, Jaffa, Community Center, June 19, 2003; Barbara Swirsky, "Israeli Women on the Production Line", in Annette Poentas and Barbara Erenriech, *Women on the Global Production Line* (Tel Aviv: *Breirot*, 1986 [Hebrew]); Barbara Swirski, *A Year of Economic Harms to Women* (Tel Aviv: *Adva*, 2003); Shlomo Swirski and Eti Konors-Atias, *The 2002 Social Situation* (Tel Aviv: Adva); Orly Benjamin, "Violating Women's Citizenship: Pink Collar Temporary Workers in the Israeli Public Sector", paper presented at the Gender, Work and Organization Conference, June 25–27, 2003, Keele University, United Kingdom.
4 For a fuller analysis of the ideas presented in this section, see Erella Shadmi, "Between Resistance and Compliance Feminism and Nationalism: Women in Black in Israel" in *Women's Studies International Forum* 23/1 (2000): 23–34, and Erella Shadmi, "The Paradoxes of Whiteness: The Contemporary Women's Peace Movement in Israel", paper presented at the international conference of the International Sociological Association, Brisbane, Australia, July 7–14, 2002.
5 Yali Hahshash, "Reproduction Policy in Israel: Motherhood, Capitalism and Racism" (working title), unpublished MA thesis, Jewish History Department, Haifa University, Israel.
6 Smadar Lavie, Vicki Knafo and the Law of Arrangements, e-mail sent to *Achoti* mail group, July 9, 2003.

15

The *Mizrahim*: Challenging the Ethos of the Melting Pot

HENRIETTA DAHAN-KALEV

Though the subject is often misrepresented and distorted, what is sometimes called Israel's "*Mizrahi* problem" is not the specific problem of those Jews who came to Israel from the Arab and Islamic countries. The ethnic split or divide within the country's Jewish population was and is the problem of the State of Israel and of Israeli society as a whole. Its roots go back about a century ago to the ideological Zionist convictions of Israel's largely *Ashkenazi* founding fathers.[1] My approach is founded on the premise that the establishment of the original institutions, both pre-state and post-state, of Zionism and of Israel, carried the seed of discrimination and suppression of the *Mizrahim*, and not only of the *Mizrahim*.[2]

In this respect, the Jews who came from Arab and Islamic countries were far from being alone. In the State of Israel, others who were seen and defined by the Jewish authorities as "minorities" were also to suffer, particularly the Arabs who stayed in the state after its establishment in 1948. From its early days, when Theodor Herzl (1860–1904) convened the first Zionist Congress in Basle, Switzerland in 1897, Zionism was a Euro-centered movement, with all the accompanying implications. It thus involves a superior and arrogant attitude to "the Orient".[3] Consequently, Israel was and remains a Euro-centered state, with deeply rooted discrimination in its institutions, in its norms, and in its political life.

Apart from the *Mizrahim* there are, therefore, numerous additional dimensions to this discrimination. It stands out most prominently today in Israel's attitude to the Palestinians in the occupied territories on the one hand, and to Palestinian Israeli citizens on the other. It is also expressed in other ways: in the attitude to migrant foreign laborers, to non-Jewish immigrants from the former USSR, and to all those who because of the color of their skin (Ethiopian immigrants), their religion or their nationality, are unable or do not want to be assimilated into the existing Israeli society and its norms.

"We don't want Israelis to become Arabs"

In the process of absorbing newcomers from the Diaspora in the early years of statehood, two major waves of mass immigration arrived: 335,000 survivors of the European Holocaust and 373,000 Jews from North Africa and Asia, who became known as *Mizrahim*. Israel's Jewish population in 1948 numbered 650,000, mainly *Ashkenazim*. There were major differences between the *Ashkenazim* and the non-European Jews. Most of the *Mizrahim* were religiously observant and followed their own traditional Jewish patterns of behavior. In Israel, however, these "Orientals" were confronted by the demand to discard what they were and transform themselves into "new Jews" in the framework of what Zionists called "merging the Exiles" (the so-called "melting pot" concept). They were "absorbed" by, and dependent on, officials who were largely *Ashkenazi* and understood neither their way of life, their family structure, nor their religious-oriented culture. The founding fathers and mothers, in determining the place and role of the immigrants according to their own criteria, failed to ask the newcomers for their opinion on their "new" identity.

The *Mizrahim*, then, were to a large extent clay in the hands of others, especially the ruling *Mapai* (Labor) party. They also provided cheap labor. In the Zionist settlement process they naturally received the less valuable lands in the periphery, where many under-privileged members of their new generations still live. The patterns of oppression and exclusion, both cultural and political, were drawn in accordance with the condescending and paternalistic approach of the "absorbers". (Among the occupational stereotypes in common usage were sayings like "My Yemenite cleans the floor well" or "My Moroccan does all the cooking".) The efficiency of the manipulations to which the *Mizrahim* were subjected, and their weakness as objects, rendered official discrimination superfluous, as opposed to the case of Palestinians, homosexuals and women, against whom discrimination was founded in the legal system.

In their values, history, traditions and language, the *Mizrahim* were therefore considered in the country's formative days to be alien from the "new Israel", even though by 1967 they constituted a majority of the Jewish population. Jewish Agency leader and future prime minister Levi Eshkol (of *Mapai*) called these newcomers "damaged human material", and future minister Moshe Kol (an "Independent Liberal") warned that "we may sink into a sea of Levantism".[4] Golda Meir asked publicly, "Shall we be able to elevate these immigrants to a suitable level of civilization?" In Howard M. Sachar's authoritative *A History of Israel*[5] where the above quotes are found, he states that "the idea of 'reforming the primitives', of transforming them along the European model, had been the dominant trend of Israel's acculturation effort from the onset of the post-state immigration . . . Until the mid-1960s the shopworn technique of 'merging the communities' (was) a euphemism for the assimilation of the Oriental Jews to the Europeans". One should not be surprised, then, to hear Ben-Gurion himself speaking of "human dust" and declaring that "we don't want Israelis to become Arabs".[6]

Ben-Gurion and his colleagues followed the Zionist imperative to open the gates of immigration to all Diaspora Jews, but aspired at the same time to construct a modern non-Diasporic society. There was a tendency to see the *Mizrahim* who came among the million and a half immigrants in Israel's first two decades as an object to be crushed and shaped, and not as a subject with a history and a will of its own. Considered alien and "other", they were even seen as liable to endanger the classical values of the society.

"Ashkenization"

In these circumstances the *Mizrahim* faced two alternatives. One was to cut themselves off, unwillingly, from their origins and shake off what was called "their traditional Diaspora ways". This demanded abandoning traditions which for hundreds of years had answered the needs of their individual and group existence, so as to assimilate into "Israeliness", which was in itself only in its infancy. The other alternative was to remain committed to their traditional position as Arab Jews. It was within this framework of a Euro-centered society in which Arabism was seen as a hostile and threatening culture that the multi-dimensional alienation and identity crisis of the *Mizrahim* developed.

One result was inevitably what is called in everyday language the "Ashkenization" process, characterized on the one hand by accommodation and adaptation while on the other hand, the particularist part of the identity becomes increasingly invisible. In this process, which generated much internal tension among Arab Jews, denial and suppression of former identities (Moroccan, Yemenite, Iraqi, etc.) was widespread among members of the second generation in Israel.

Yet the dominant trends in Israeli literature addressing "collective identity" hardly dealt with this crisis of identity experienced by masses of immigrants from Arab and Muslim countries. Inadequate attention has been devoted in academia to questions of alienation and cultural discrimination, or to the ramifications of the deconstruction and reconstruction of the *Mizrahi* identity. Perhaps more serious than other factors was the fact that the *Mizrahi* narrative itself was delegitimized, and this regardless of the extent to which people "assimilated", tried to conceal their color or their accent, or to jettison their traditions. Not only were they denied expression, for example, in those school textbooks which they themselves studied, but in the life of the state as a whole the *Mizrahim* were exposed to the inadequacy of their own identity as compared to other groups, be it the fighters in the 1948 War of Independence or the Holocaust survivors.

Tensions and tokenism

The *Mizrahim* were rarely interested in organizing on an ethnic basis against the state or against Israeli society. They aspired first and foremost to recognition as equal citizens for what they are, and not on condition that they change. In effect, to the extent that the *Mizrahim* were co-opted into the ruling establishment, this was carried out within a tokenist context. When they successfully penetrated into the government, they did so in one of the two ways possible in places where prejudice prevails. On the one hand, as we have noted, it was at the cost of Ashkenization,[7] involving Europeanization and a renouncing of their own historical and biographical narrative; on the other hand, it came through forcing themselves as tokens into the notch allocated to "professional Mizrahim" in political groupings trying to present a pluralistic image to the public. In our day there has indeed been a massive penetration of *Mizrahim* into the top echelons of the system, including the government and the army; however, as a rule such leaders were only able to make the grade if they were "Ashkenized" to some degree or another.

The economic, educational and cultural status of the *Mizrahim*[8] their politics, their own opinions and the opinions in the surrounding society about them – all were dictated and fashioned by others. They were promised that if they would only adapt, then a happy, homogenous, egalitarian and humanistic society awaited them. Though in the course of time they made progress in various spheres, there emerged a second generation with an identity of dependence, characterized by scattered and random patches of *Mizrahi* culture and folklore. The essence of this identity was a longing for resemblance, for being "similar to", for winning equality and self-definition "like everyone else".

Missed opportunities

Under government coalitions controlled until 1977 by the *Mapai* (Labor) party, whose political style has been compared to that of the Bolsheviks, the State of Israel missed two opportunities to open itself up to processes of pluralism. Whenever the *Mizrahim* took steps to organize protests, the Israeli establishment cruelly suppressed such efforts. This happened in 1959 in the riots in Wadi Salib, a dilapidated and overcrowded slum in the formerly Arab section of Haifa, where, in a violent mass protest, a couple of hundred demonstrators from the 15,000 under-privileged *Mizrahi* population caused extensive damage to property and in the end were forcibly dispersed by the police, and their leader jailed.

The second and better known opportunity came with the Black Panther demonstrations of 1971 against ethnic and economic discrimination. The movement originated in the impoverished Musrara quarter of Jerusalem where young *Mizrahim* initiated large-scale protest meetings and resorted to non-violent activities (like taking milk from well-established areas to be distributed in poor districts). While the Panthers succeeded in alerting public opinion to their cause, this led only to the establishment by the Ministry of Education of a Department for *Mizrahi* Jewish Heritage, or the opening of folklore exhibitions in the Israel Museum, the shrine of canonic Israeli cultural assets. However, a Black Panther list in the *Knesset* elections came to nothing, and the increasingly disunited movement, part of which was successfully co-opted by Israel's ruling circles, eventually disintegrated.

The oppressive structures which characterized the treatment of "the *Mizrahi* problem" in Israel's pre-state and post-state political life continue to operate in other sectors, including Arabs, Russian and Ethiopian immigrants and migrant laborers. The result is that in contemporary Israeli society, those who cannot be assimilated will have to put up with an appropriately low status, economic as well as political. The same means used in early periods to weaken the *Mizrahim* and push them into the periphery are still practiced *vis-à-vis* other groups.

Narrative and dialogue

The importance of assuring a full and legitimate presentation of the *Mizrahi* narrative cannot be underestimated. What will this do to children who will learn, alongside stories of the struggle for independence and on the Holocaust, the story of their own past, with the annals of all ethnic groups presented in equal dimensions, and without attempts at denial, by teachers and educators, *Mizrahim* and *Askenazim* alike? What will it do to young teachers who will have to give lessons to pupils from mixed *Ashkenazi–Mizrahi* families on how the *Ashkenazi* side of their family carried out discriminatory policies against the *Mizrahi* side? Providing equal rights for the *Mizrahi* narrative demands political courage and a readiness to encourage, rather than stifle, the dialogue which will surely emerge from presenting the past as it really was.

Today it is too late for the *Mizrahim* to respond to their situation through resuscitation, possibly nostalgic, of their Arab past. What is needed is not to negate the emptiness of modernity. *Mizrahim* who decided on a critical stance *vis-à-vis* their place in Israeli society may well have discovered that their position was intrinsically tied to a critique of modernity and the West. However, failure to give credit to and legitimize modernity does not involve a desire to return to pre-modernity. We are dealing with a process that is simply irreversible and the struggle of the *Mizrahim* is to develop and express post-modern cultural and political viewpoints.

This also behoves delving deeply into the highly complex tensions in which these cultures are immersed. From dealing with the confrontation between the Arab-Muslim and the Western-Christian civilizations one can derive an understanding of the confrontation between the Judeo-Christian-European and the Jewish–Arab-Moslem culture. In the tension between the European-Western and the Arab-Muslim civilizations, the "*Mizrahi* problem" can be viewed as one of its local, though of course special, expressions. Thus in this sense it is a particular case of the phenomenon of Orientalism, just as Zionism is a particular case of the phenomenon called Euro-centralism.

The struggle for legitimacy and equality

The *Mizrahim* are caught between the *Ashkenazim* from the point of view of their Jewishness, and the Arabs because this Jewishness is immersed in an Arab civilization. Yet they are punished and enfeebled by both groups. The legitimacy of the *Mizrahim* in Israel, or its denial, was dictated by the

Ashkenazi powers-that-be. Yet when all is said and done, what is called the "*Mizrahim* problem" actually represents the failure of the melting pot and a challenge to the ethos of "national unity". What remains of the classical concept of Israeliness, which was to be imposed on the *Mizrahim*, is a collection of ethnic rifts and socio-economic fragmentations, in which authentic identity is not preserved – neither for the *Sabra* (Israel-born), nor for the *Ashkenazi*, nor for the *Mizrahi*.

Whenever in the past the *Mizrahim* demanded to be recognized as equals, and organized to achieve their goal, they faced an uncompromising political response by the Ashkenazi "establishment" in defense of its traditional interests. Though future anticipated political struggles will be conducted in the framework of the appropriate ground rules and the rule of law, there is no reason to expect that they will be easy or tranquil. The struggle over categories like identity, memory and historical narratives molds not only social and cultural conditions in Israel's political discourse: it also touches upon the whole gamut of power relations in the state and society.

Notes

1 This is a concept which I hold both because I see myself as what I call an Arab Jew, and from many years of comprehensive research on the subject.

2 *Mizrahim*: Eastern, Oriental or *Sephardi* (literally Spanish). The European Jews were called *Ashkenazim*, the word meaning German but denoting all Jews from Central and Eastern Europe, and American Jews.

3 As analyzed by Edward Sa'id in his book *Orientalism* (Routledge and Kegan Paul, 1978).

4 See Haim Malca, *Yedioth Ahronoth*, September 4, 1998.

5 Howard M. Sachar, *A History of Israel* (Alfred A. Knopf, 1996).

6 See *Israel, Pluralism and the Conflict* by Sammy Smooha (University of California Press, 1998).

7 See F. Fanon's *Black Skin, White Mask*, 1967 New York. Grove Press.

8 For example, in the year 2001 the average income of native born *Ashkenazi* urban employees was over a third higher than that of *Mizrahim*; and there were twice as many *Ashkenazim* as *Mizrahim* studying at university. These figures concerning the younger generation in the two communities were published by the Adva Center. According to research conducted by the Van Leer Institute, *mizrahi* pupils have 43 percent less prospects of getting the *Bagrut* (matriculation) certificate than *Ashkenazi* pupils, and in the second generation, the gap is not decreasing (*Yedioth Ahronot*, February 2, 2004).

16 Jerusalem: Constructive Division or Spartaheid?

MENAHEM KLEIN

Jerusalem is a divided city. Only on the rarest of occasions will a person from East Jerusalem (*al-Quds*) and another from Western Jerusalem say "we" referring to the same city and its residents as if they were a collective. In the reality of the city as it is lived and perceived by Jerusalemites since the Israeli victory of 1967, Jerusalem is a divided and not a multi-cultural city. In a multi-cultured city, the orientation of the different groups points to the creation of a collective "we". On the other hand, in today's Jerusalem, which is more polarized than ever before, the orientation points to partition.

Polarization in Jerusalem is deeper than in Belfast. The bitterest confrontations in Belfast were conducted between people who spoke the same language, looked the same, shared similar eating and drinking habits, and even conducted mixed marriages between the two rival groups. All these characteristics, common to Catholics and Protestants in Belfast, are on the contrary, reasons for the very polarization to which we are referring in the case of Jerusalem.

An overall disparity

Though there has up to now been no physical wall dividing the city, the partition is nevertheless very real. We are speaking of two collective groups different in their nationality, in their history and mentality, in their religion, in their ethnic belonging, in their culture, in their language, in their political affinities, and in their representation in elected government institutions. They live in different residential areas and their hinterlands, both social and geographical, are different: so are their transportation and communication arrangements, their urban centers, their industrial zones, their educational systems from kindergarten to university, their community institutions, their health systems, and the authorities in their social life.

It is fairly obvious that there would thus be a disparity in their income, in their occupational "ladder" and in their participation in the labor market. The same also naturally applies in economic deprivation at all levels, in the infrastructure, in the provision of benefits by the state and the municipality and in the accessibility to investments. In all these areas one finds structural preference for the dominating Jewish party and discrimination against the dominated Arab-Palestinian party.

The interaction between the cities in Jerusalem is complex and dynamic. It operates mainly in defined geographical areas or in certain functional areas of meeting and contact, for example the labor market and tourist sites. These areas diminished since the start of the *al-Aqsa Intifada* in September 2000. This was not only because of the recession and the unemployment in the two economies and the disappearance of the tourists from Jerusalem. It was also caused by acts of terror and by the militarization of everyday life in Jerusalem, by mutual suspicion and by the preference of each population to seclude itself in its own area.

The urban, the religious and the political cities

The differences between the two ethnic communities have transformed Jerusalem into two cities, Western and Eastern, within which each one is composed of a complex of three cities: the urban city, the political city and the religious city. Each of these cities has its own institutions, center and periphery. One can identify various borderlines separating the two complexes, the Eastern and the Western. The borders are as follows:

1 *The demographic border*, namely the living and subsistence space of each one of the two groups. This is a dynamic line changing since 1967 in accordance with the construction and population of residential neighborhoods. In Jerusalem there is an almost total isolation in living and subsistence between Jews and Arabs. Only about one percent of the total residents of the Palestinian neighborhoods is Israeli-Jewish. This minority of Jewish settlers lives in an atmosphere of hostility toward the Palestinian majority, in fenced off and guarded localities within the Palestinian neighborhoods.

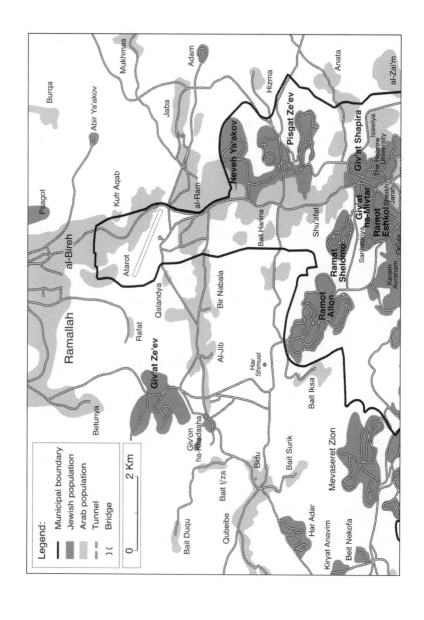

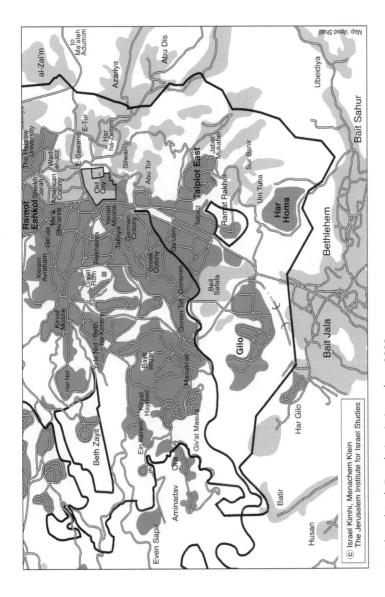

Jewish and Arab Population in Jerusalem, 2000.
Courtesy of The Jerusalem Institute for Israel Studies, Jerusalem.

2 The *border of Israel's effective rule*. This border crosses the demographic border, but for the most part not into the Arab territorial and functional depth. Thus, for example, the Shuafat (Shu'fat) refugee camp was never effectively under Israeli rule. Since the start of the *al-Aqsa Intifada*, Israeli rule has been less effective than at any time in the past. Israeli institutions that worked or provided services in East Jerusalem have retreated from there. This includes the construction by the Municipality of classrooms, or building by Israeli companies.

3 *The line of symbolic rule*. In those East Jerusalem zones where effective Israeli rule is limited, it exercises only a restricted symbolic rule. This can be seen in street signs or in law enforcement agencies. In this area, too, there has been corrosion since the *al-Aqsa Intifada*. This stands out particularly on the Temple Mount/*Haram al-Sharif* ("the Noble Sanctuary") where since 1967 Israeli rule has only been symbolic: it has in effect been administered by the Islamic *Waqf* which operated until 1994 under the auspices of Jordan, and since then under the auspices of the Palestinian Authority. From the start of the *al-Aqsa Intifada* till mid-2003, the *Waqf* (the Muslim religious endowment) unilaterally closed the Mount. A quiet agreement between the Waqf and the Israeli police brought about the reopening of the Mount to Israelis and Jews, but with certain limitations. The visitors are subject to supervision by the police and the *Waqf*, and people with an orthodox Jewish appearance are often not allowed to enter the site. Their entry is also restricted to days when there is no religious-national tension between Israelis and Palestinians, and when a quiet and unofficial agreement can be effective.

4 *The international border determined between Israel and Jordan in 1949*, which was breached by Israel when it conquered the Jordanian area in 1967. Israel's activities in Jerusalem transformed this border line into a mere legacy of history and of international law.

5 *Israel's annexation border* as determined by Israel at the end of June 1967, following its victory in the Six Day War. This is also the Jerusalem municipal border and it is much larger than the combination of the Israeli city and the former Jordanian city. The "united Jerusalem", which Israel created unilaterally, includes areas which were part of the West Bank under Jordanian rule. This line is not recognized by the international community. The urban growth of East Jerusalem and its spreading out toward the North, the East and the South also made this annexation border into a "virtual line". In certain places it even crosses through streets, houses, and apartments!

6 *The metropolitan border*. This is defined in terms of the day-to-day functioning and influence which the metropolitan focus exerts on the periphery, whose employment and services are provided by this focus.

Eastern and Western Jerusalem are two metropolitan foci, serving their separate hinterlands. In the East, the metropolitan border crosses the annexation line. East Jerusalem became a metropolis unintentionally. The large Israeli investment in building Jewish neighborhoods in the former Jordanian area was to lead to half the Jewish population of Jerusalem living there. This created a focus of employment and services for the Palestinians and made East Jerusalem into a metropolis.

Two processes limited the metropolitan influence of East Jerusalem. The first was the setting up by the Israeli authorities since the Gulf War of 1991 of roadblocks, and the imposition of closure and encirclement at different levels. The connections between the metropolitan focus and the periphery became more difficult than in the past, damaging both. Second, the Oslo Accords created a new political border in Jerusalem and its vicinity. Important cities neighboring Jerusalem, such as Ramallah and Bethlehem, which came to be totally controlled by the Palestinian Authority, were cut off, with the exception of the religious sphere, from the metropolitan focus of East Jerusalem. Though physical accessibility to Jerusalem is more difficult than in former times, it retains its place as a religious and symbolic center.

7 *The political border.* Until the Oslo Accords, from the Israeli point of view the political border was identical with the municipal border while from the Palestinian point of view, the political border ran along the lines of June 4, 1967. The Oslo Accords and the elections to the Palestinian Authority (PA) in January 1996 created a new line. In these accords, the Palestinian Authority was forbidden to work in East Jerusalem but this was permitted to the PLO. The PA was denied physical presence or administrative functions. This strengthened the collective Palestinian identity in Jerusalem and institutionalized the activities of political bodies on the PLO's behalf, and particularly Orient House. The Oslo Accords also determined that the residents of East Jerusalem in the area where Israeli law applies would be able to vote for, and be elected to, the institutions of the Palestinian Authority, though with different election arrangements.

The political border was founded not so much on the juridical status of East Jerusalem as an occupied area but rather on the fact that only 2–4 percent of the residents of East Jerusalem sought to be citizens of the State of Israel. A citizen has political rights on a national level, rights which are not enjoyed by a permanent resident. The right of a Palestinian in East Jerusalem to belong on the political level was recognized by Israel in the Oslo accords. To the political reality created by the Oslo Accords one must add what one might call a "change in consciousness" that took place in the wake of the discussions at Camp David 2000 on the permanent status in Jerusalem. These deliberations did not end with an agreement but they

broke the former Israeli taboo on the redrawing of the Jerusalem boundaries and on transferring Arab neighborhoods to Palestinian sovereignty.

The process of shaping the political border was blocked, and the
tendency perhaps even retreated, following the untimely death of Faisel
el-Husseini, the senior political personality in East Jerusalem, who was
the moving spirit behind a number of Palestinian institutions and mechanisms. His death in June 2001 created a vacuum both from a leadership
and from a moral point of view. This increased when in August 2001 the
government of Israel closed these institutions, of which Orient House was
the most prominent, and forced them to leave East Jerusalem for its
suburbs, from where they try to continue their work in the city.

8 *The line created by the complex of walls with which Israel has been
unilaterally enveloping East Jerusalem and its metropole since 2002.* On
the ground, up to now only part of the line has been built, but the government decided on its planned course in July 2003, and expropriation orders
for the land have already been issued. If and when the plan will be implemented, it will constitute the most dramatic change effected by Israel in
East Jerusalem since it was conquered and annexed in 1967.

From the geographical point of view this *de facto* complex of walls
changes the border of annexation. In many places the new line extends
into the West Bank beyond the 1967 annexation, but without officially
annexing the area. Israel is working to include Rachel's Tomb and and
the settlement Har Giloh in southern Jerusalem in the area of Israel, at the
expense of areas belonging to Bethlehem and Beith Jallah. Over and above
extending the area annexed, Israel wants to destroy Arab metropolitan
Jerusalem and control it without annexing it. It aspires to achieve this
through a wall enveloping all the following suburbs of East Jerusalem:
Anata, Hizma, Al Za'im, Al Ram, and Dahiat Al Barid, leaving them only
a narrow link with the Palestinian hinterland in the form of a cramped
road or tunnel under Israeli control. Only in a limited number of places
did Israel agree to relinquish suburbs which it included in "united
Jerusalem" in 1967: Kafr Aqab in the north and parts of Arab el-Sawahra
in the East.

Israel's proposed wall is intended to create Palestinian enclaves
surrounded by Israel in Sheih Sa'ad, Azariya and Abu-Dis. In densely
populated areas where there is no possibility of erecting a broad complex
of walls and obstacles, the concrete wall that Israel intends to build will
rise to a height of eight meters. In the center of Abu-Dis, Israel has already
built a concrete wall about two meters high on the 1967 annexation line,
dividing in two the neighborhood's main road. This wall divides the
section officially annexed to Israel from the section which in the near
future will be cut off from the West Bank and from Israel alike. The lower

wall is being replaced by one of eight meters, similar to what Israel is
building near Beith Hanina and Neveh Ya'akov in the north, and near
Rachel's Tomb in the south.

Assuring control

The plan called in Israel "enveloping Jerusalem" does not provide Israel
with effective control in the areas outside East Jerusalem, where about
130,000 Palestinian Arabs live. Neither does it increase Israel's symbolic
control over them. However, its planners want to contain every single one
of the Arab suburbs, cutting them off both from each other and from the
urban center of East Jerusalem. On the neighborhood level there will be
Palestinian automony for each separate neighborhood or suburb. Contact
with the central Palestinian government will be carried out through the
local Palestinian residents coming to the central Palestinian governmental
meeting point, and not through agents of the Palestinian central government coming to the neighborhood. Israeli supervision will be carried out
through its control over the road which is the main artery of the beseiged
suburb.

From the demographic point of view, Israel can claim that it is not
speaking of annexing some 130,000 residents into Israeli Jerusalem.
Demonsrating generosity and honoring international law, Israel seemingly permits the Arabs to maintain their connection with the Palestinian
hinterland. In effect, however, it is Israel which will control them, through
containing them for what are called security reasons.

Apart from the neighborhood level, a major change can be expected in
the metropolitan area. There will be a wall between each of the neighborhoods and the heart of East Jerusalem. If the Israeli plan will be
completed, about a quarter of a million Palestinian Arab residents of East
Jerusalem will be cut off from their social, political, economic, cultural
and language hinterland. This is about 10 percent of the total Palestinian
population in the West bank. As noted, the metropolitan connections of
East Jerusalem had been hard hit by Israeli measures since the early 1990s.
Now it can be expected that they will be destroyed. On the other hand,
nowadays the accessibility to West Jerusalem of those Palestinians who
are today permanent residents in Israel is not easy. Israel erected concrete
and earth barriers at the entrance to East Jerusalem neighborhoods
looking west, in order to restrict traffic to the few exit roads which Israel
can supervise. From time to time checkpoints are placed on these roads.
A mobile and rapidly changing line of checkpoints and inspection points
is also occasionally set up close either to the old international border or

to the "demographic border". These measures, imposed by Israeli soldiers and police on the Palestinians in East Jerusalem, emphasize the basic difference in their status as "others". Moreover, this is proof that steps like these are taken not only against the residents of the West Bank but also against East Jerusalem Palestinians, even if for the time being these measures are less harsh and systematic.

Israel declares that its intentions are exclusively for security purposes, but under this pretext the rightist Israeli government sets out to determine two political facts: first, to change that reality on the ground fashioned in Jerusalem by the Oslo Accords; and second, to do away as far as possible with the "change in consciousness" created in the year 2000 by the negotiations over permanent status in Jerusalem. The government is attempting to control the Arab metropolitan area of Jerusalem through weakening it, cutting it off from its natural hinterland in the West Bank, and dissecting it into small slices. The government's hope is that the condtions of life in these besieged areas will be so hard that most of the residents will prefer to leave. Moreover such policies will lead to a deterioration in the situation of Arab East Jerusalem which was annexed in 1967, and which has been discriminated against ever since. In such policies the Sharon government is also marking the borders of the authority of that sort of Palestinian state to which it can agree. The authority of the Palestinian state will be weak in metropolitan Jerusalem and non-existent in East Jerusalem.

In other words, Israel is trying to contain both the territory and the population and to develop levers of control over them, instead of sharing rule with the Palestrinians. What the Barak government proposed with the start of negotiations on permanent status for the urban and historical heart of East Jerusalem, the Sharon government proposes to the Palestinians only in distant suburbs scraped off the body of Jerusalem.

Israel is now attempting to achieve by means of destructive walls which will envelop the Palestinian neighborhoods what it was unable to achieve since 1967 through a belt of new construction with the building of new Jewish neighborhoods around the East Jerusalem Palestinian neighborhoods. In this way Israel "forced" Jewish-Arab demographic equality in the area annexed in 1967. In the talks in 2000 on permanent settlement, discussions took place on models of dividing both territory and control between Israel and the planned Palestinian state. Not satisfied with this, the Israeli government aspires to achieve exclusive Israeli control over all the area annexed in 1967. This demands the destruction of the demographic, urban and metropolitan reality which developed since 1967 in Arab Jerusalem. The East Jerusalem metropole must be destroyed first by damaging its periphery, second by weakening of the center itself, and third by cutting it off from its natural hinterland. All these measures are intended to perpetuate the control and the superiority of Jewish over Arab Jerusalem. The most appropiate name for this policy is "Spartaheid": Apartheid through the arguments and means employed by Greek Sparta.

Enveloping Jerusalem is an attractive line for Israel since it is built on the Zionist ethos of "taking our fate into our own hands", undertaking unilateral action and creating facts on the ground in accordance with exclusive Israeli interests. This ethos has an enormous attraction in Israel and it has only been strengthened by the assumption, a wrong one in my view, that "there is no partner for a peace arrangement" – or simply that "there is nobody to talk to". This has been the prevalent assumption since the summer of 2000: there is a great temptation to use unilateral action as an instrument that will be decisive in determining the wishes and deeds of the other party.

The *Intifada*, the swelling unemployment, the militarization of life in the city, the lack of a centralized and institutionalized authority which can impose the law in most areas of East Jerusalem – all had grave consequences. Places like el-Tur, Silwan, and Ras al-Amud found themselves on the way to becoming slums. The faster this process proceeds, the greater is the Israeli interest to constrict the Palestinian "other" with increasing severity so as to cut down to the minimum the damage it can do to the dominant majority.

Proposals doomed to failure

To sum up, the process of developing the borders in Jerusalem is characterized first and foremost by Israeli dominance. From the beginning Israel saw the Palestinians in Jerusalem as a threat in view of what is termed the "demographic problem". Israel's failure to restrict the number of the Palestinians in the city broke the taboo over dividing sovereignty in Jerusalem but also increased Israeli fears of the threat from the "other". Even without the penetration of the *Intifada* to West Jerusalem, Israel neither desired to propose, nor was capable of proposing, to East Jerusalem as a collective entity what was required: the sort of "positive discrimination" which could create full equality under Israeli sovereignty.

Neither could the Israelis agree to the transformation of Jerusalem into an open, equal and bi-national city which does not belong exclusively to either side. As they saw it, this would run counter not only to Israeli policy since 1948 but also to the self-determination of the State of Israel and the Zionist movement as Jewish entities. Moreover, Israel could not consent to the creation of a city which would be neutral, civic, nationally "blind", and would have an orientation toward providing the needs of the residents. After so many years of Israeli dominance, it would also be difficult to expect from the Israeli authorities to relate to the Palestinians as equals, be it on the municipal or the national level.

Therefore, the arrangements for partition between Israel and Palestine based on broad cooperation between equals and joint administration were doomed to failure. First, over and above the low institutional standards of the Palestinians, the Israeli consciousness of their own superiority had crystallized since 1967. Within it, an internal contradiction was revealed. The failure to deal with the "demographic threat" caused existential anxiety and a sense of challenge to the independent Jewish-Israeli identity. A feeling of Jewish-Israeli superiority was heightened by military power, by technological superiority and by possessing and maintaining the necessary tools for the retention of control. Equality in Jerusalem is prevented by a combination on the one hand of these feelings of superiority, and on the other hand of fear of the threat represented by "the other". Institutions like a roof municipality or common administration of the metropolitan space in the two parts of the city or in the old city, are not practical at least for the foreseeable future, attractive as they may be theoretically. The way to a settlement is through eliminating the alleged threat by means of partition. Second, the development of the borders to which we have referred is characterized by an increasing level of politicization. Far from moving further from Jerusalem, as the political process advances politics become more strongly riveted into the life of the city. There is little reason to assume that political set-ups in Israel and the Palestinian Authority will retreat from their deep direct involvement in Jerusalem since from their point of view, each one of them is speaking of their own capital city. Third, the process is characterized by its intractability. Border lines which in the past were for the most part flexible and passable are increasingly rigid as the result of the *Intifada* and the discussions on a permanent settlement.

Options for a divided city

The question is not whether Jerusalem will be divided but how it will be divided. Once the options of a bi-national city, a shared city and an equal city have been removed from the agenda, there remain only the following options.

First, *unilateral partition*, in which the Palestinian side would be even further weakened, split up into a number of fragmented geographical enclaves or neighborhoods, and lacking any form of political and community integration. It is hard to concur with the assumption that in the long run Israel can achieve its goal in this way. Apart from Jerusalem's centrality in Islam and in Palestinian nationalism, in the area where Israel wants to impose its rule about 10 percent of the overall population of the West bank is living. The Palestinians, the Arabs and the Muslims will not permit Israel to proceed with this option and at a certain stage they will assist the residents of East Jerusalem to become an active force rather than passive subjects.

A rigid partition imposed through an impenetrable wall as in Berlin until 1991, in Jerusalem from 1949 to 1967 or in Nicosia since 1974, would make the two parts of Jerusalem into borderline cities and bring about the deterioration of both of them. Physical partition, which creates not only a border but a multifaceted border regime facilitating frequent but controlled border crossing, would therefore be to the benefit of both parties.

The intention is not for two cities completely open to each other since this would mean placing the control points of the international border around and not between them. This would create a certain disconnection between the interior of the county and its capital. Were we not speaking of a capital city perhaps such a thing would be practical. Up to now, however, there has been no evidence that the ruling Israeli and Palestinian authorities are ready for this sort of arrangement, joining East and West Jerusalem at the expense of the links of each one with the hinterland in its own country. Moreover, as we have noted, this linkup would be forced rather than natural. The "faces" of West and East Jerusalem are not oriented to each other but to their ethnic hinterland. Consequently the reality demands drawing a clear border between West and East Jerusalem, according to the principle laid down by President Clinton: what is Arab is Palestinian, what is Jewish is Israeli. The delineation of the border will create a situation in which on both side the demographical reality will correspond with each party's authority, both effective and symbolical.

The border will be recognized both internationally and politically. The metropolis of East Jerusalem will be wholly open to its own natural hinterland. Roads will link the Arab neighborhoods to each other just as other roads will join the Jewish neighborhoods. All the citizens of Israel or Palestine will move freely within their own sovereign state. In those places where the two parties make use of the same road like the French Hill junction or Road No. 1, engineering solutions will be found.

Border crossings of different sorts will be built. Heavy traffic and busses will bring people and goods to terminals built at the entrances to the city near the bypass roads. As for private traffic, light vehicles and pedestrians, they will be able to cross at a series of border crossings, where a quick track will be built for Jerusalemites, enabling a quick and easy crossing for workers and business people. The border crossing will be along the seam line between Jerusalem and *al-Quds* but on main roads rather than on narrow ones. A dynamic will be created between the two cities while at the same time neither the sovereignty of each party nor their ability in certain cases to close the crossing, will be impaired. As to how people will cross over, an international unit will supervise implementation by the two sides. In the event of any controversy between them, a mechanism to resolve differences will be established. A border guard will be established by agreement, under international supervision. Its purpose would be to prevent any neglect of the border area, or its use in a manner harmful to the other party through construction, pollution etc. The physical separation and border obstacles in areas reflecting the religious-historical "bowl" of Jerusalem would be built with transparent material. The design and planning of the border will be opened by both parties to an international competition among architects and town planners.

While a roof municipality will not be established, there will be cooperation and coordination between the two municipalities. No settlers will remain living in Palestinian neighborhoods and special arrangements will be made for Holy Places of one party which will be under the sovereignty of another. These will assure freedom of worship and freedom of access to believers and visitors, as well as the maintenance of the sites. The Jewish side will enjoy freedom of access to the Jewish cemetery on the Mount of Olives with security being upheld by Jewish police.

There is a possibility of maintaining the Old City as an open city without rigid fences separating the Jewish Quarter, which will be under Jewish sovereignty, from the rest of the Quarters, which will be under Palestinian sovereignty. Entrance to the Old City will be free, with control operating only in exiting from there. A special fast lane for Israelis will ensure them a quick exit. Palestinians and tourists who did not enter from Israeli territory will have to show a visa.

The Temple Mount, as it is known to the Jews, or *al-Haram al-Sharif* as it is known in Islam, and what the Jews call the Western Wall – constitute one unit in Judaism and in Islam. The controversy over sovereignty must take this into account. There are, therefore, ony two possibilities. The first is to grant no political sovereignty over the Holy site. There would be no Palestinian sovereignty over the Temple Mount and Israel would withdraw its sovereignty over the Western Wall. In this case, the administration, but not the sovereignty, would be in the hands of the two parties. Alternatively, the sovereignty would be divided in such a way that the Temple Mount would be under Arab sovereignty and the prayer area of the Western Wall would be under Israeli sovereignty. Under both alternatives, the maintenance of Jewish interests on the Temple Mount would be secured through a representative international presence. The first option is more difficult to implement because it takes away from Israel something that absolutely belongs to it, and prevents the Palestinians from getting something that was not theirs. As for the second option, it denies Israel of only symbolic sovereignty, while meeting Jewish-Israeli interests.

Three stages

No arrangement can be made without it being preceded by an interim period. This can be broken down into three stages in accordance with the Road Map proposed in 2003 by the Quartet.

In the first stage there would be a freezing of the building of Israeli settlements within Palestinian neighborhoods in Jerusalem. The entry of settlers into the residential areas which they had acquired in the private market would be forbidden. House demolition by Israel in East Jerusalem would be halted. Also, there would be a building freeze in those sections relating to East Jerusalem in the master plan which Israel is preparing. Israel would cease the unilateral construction of the fence and the wall. The struggle against terror would be conducted through cooperation with the Palestinian security forces, following the return of the representatives of these forces to function in Jerusalem. This would be carried out in the framework of the same unofficial arrangements which pertained in Jerusalem until summer 2000. The two parties would be assisted by a special international force which would operate in the Jewish-Arab seam area alongside the two security forces.

Personal and public security would be restored to East Jerusalem through community involvement. Thus the boycott of identity cards for East Jerusalemites which Israel has imposed since 1996 would end and the identity cards would be returned to their owners. All the unilateral archeological excavations in particularly sensitive areas like the Temple Mount *al-Haram al-Sharif* and its environs would be halted immediately. Concerning services like the issue of passports and other documents by the Ministry of the Interior and the National Insurance Institute which the Israeli authorities provide to Palestinians in East Jerusalem, these procedures would be completely overhauled and vastly improved. The Palestinian institutions which Israel closed would be reopened and their proper and uninterrupted functioning assured. The two parties would encourage the development of the private sector and of civic Palestinian institutions. The aim would be to transfer authority, including the relevant budgetary allocations, from the Jerusalem municipality to the Palestine collective's administrative and representative institutions. This could be operated either on a neighborhood or on a functional basis.

Freedom of political organization and activity would be assured in East Jerusalem. Insofar as national elections would be held in the Palestinian territories, they would also be held in East Jerusalem in the same framework as those held in 1996. The two parties would declare their intention to reach a two-state solution in Mandatory Palestine, with their capitals in Jerusalem. Freedom of access to the whole Temple Mount *al-Haram al-Sharif* area would be assured as it was on the eve of the *Intifada* in the year 2000.

In the second stage, the processes of strengthening the Palestinian party and developing its overall potential, which would have started in the first stage, would be intensified. Comprehensive authority in urban affairs, including planning and construction, would be transferred to the Palestinian factors, and so would additional budgets. The Palestinian public and urban administration would be extended. Special efforts would be invested in the encouragement of investors and donors from abroad so as to improve the infrastructure and develop projects in East Jerusalem. Elected representatives of the Palestinian Parliament would be permitted to function in East Jerusalem.

In the third stage, the juridical–political framework for the permanent settlement in Jerusalem would be fashioned. This stage would see the termination of all the mutual demands of the parties. The authorities of the Palestinian State would officially replace the Israeli authorities in the eastern part of the city. The Palestinian Municipal Authority would commence to function officially and with full authority, and elections to its institutions would be held. A body coordinating between the two municipalities would be established in order to prevent one party damaging the interests of another. This body would also promote subjects of importance to both, including for example subjects like preservation and rehabilitation, highrise building and quality of the environment. Cooperation between the two police forces and the security services of the parties would be strengthened in order to solve local problems, including those likely to arise on special occasions, like mass pilgrimages to the Holy Places.

The left and Jerusalem

The Israeli left is afraid of Jerusalem. Jerusalem as the Holy City and the center of orthodox Jewish religion has always deterred the Zionist and the Israeli left. The mutual hostility between Jewish Orthodoxy and the left has accompanied the Zionist project from its beginnings. Jerusalem may have been the Holy City but it was never the focus of Zionist efforts and the left, rather than being attracted to it, the left was intimidated by it. This relationship continued after the establishment of the State of Israel. Divided between Israel and Jordan in the years 1949–67, Jerusalem was a provincial orthodox Jewish city compared to the city of Tel Aviv or the kibbutz movement, to which the Israeli left was attracted.

The Israeli victory in the 1967 war and the establishment of greater metropolitan Jerusalem under the leadership of Teddy Kollek changed the situation. Jerusalem was transformed from a provincial city into a mythological metropolis. However, the fear of the Holy City remained in the left. Instead of recoiling from Jerusalem's provincialism there came the fear of shattering the myth of a united Jerusalem. Only a small part of the Israeli left claimed that the subject was occupation and annexation, and not unity, and that in Jerusalem, too, Israel should return to the 1967 borders. However, within that left, there were few who could bolster this moral and political claim with adequate understanding of the facts – facts about the character of the Israeli control mechanism in East Jerusalem or the gap created under Israeli rule between Palestinian East Jerusalem and Jewish West Jerusalem.

Most of the Israeli left internalized the myth of a united Jerusalem and was afraid to touch it. Nowadays the leaders of the Zionist left should be ready to admit that in the year 2000 Ehud Barak outflanked them with the proposals he made on Jerusalem at Camp David. These proposals did indeed include preserving a sort of sovereignty over the Temple Mount *al-Haram al-Sharif* and changing the existing *status quo* there to Israel's benefit; also, Barak's proposals rejected the principle of an Israeli return to the 1967 borders and of imposing full Palestinian sovereignty on all the Palestinian neighborhoods in Jerusalem. Nevertheless, the proposals went beyond those which most of the leaders and activists of the left were ready on their part to adopt. If this was the case as regards the Israeli proposals at Camp David, how much more did it apply to proposals in the negotiations held at Taba in January 2001 on President Clinton's parameters.

Public support in Israel for Barak's "dovish" positions came not because of the backing they received from most of the leaders of the left, but because of the actual reality in Jerusalem. There is a great distance between the real Jerusalem and the mythical Jerusalem. The mythical Jerusalem is a "united Jerusalem" frozen in time since 1967. The real Jerusalem is a divided city lacking any *status quo*, where the Israeli–Palestinian cleavage grows increasingly deeper. Thirty-six years of Israeli rule in East Jerusalem has proved that the reality of the city can impose itself on anyone who attempts to deny it. It was not the leaders of the left who brought home this reality to the public consciousness. Ratherm it was the central stream in Israeli politics which did so when it made its negotiating proposals.

Any relevant stance on Jerusalem must be founded both on recognizing the dynamic reality in Jerusalem and responding to it accordingly. If in this spirit it wishes to be relevant, the left must overcome its fear of mystical Jerusalem and go beyond the concepts of the central stream. The left must state clearly that the borderlines determined by Israel at the end of June 1967 are not realistic, and are contrary to the Zionist interest. The radical left must admit that it is impossible in Jerusalem to return to the reality which pertained in the city on June 4, 1967, while the Palestinians can only be compensated territorially for the whole area on which Jewish neighborhoods were built in East Jerusalem. As for the mainstream left, it must admit that the *Intifada* deepened the division of the city and made the implementation of the Utopia of an open and egalitarian city impossible for an unknown length of time. These are the parameters for the sort of contemporary positions of the left which, while founded on understanding the reality on the ground, strive to put into motion the changes necessary for the benefit of both the Palestinian and the Israeli cities.

References

al-Jubeh, N. 2003: "The Social Development of Jerusalem: a City in Transition". In *Divided Cities in Transition*, Abraham Friedman and Rami Nasrallah (eds.), Jerusalem: The Jerusalem Institute for Israel Studies and the International Peace and Cooperation Center.

Eldar, A. 2003: "Carving up Jerusalem, for Security of Course". *Ha'aretz*, August 10, 2003.

—— 2003: "First They Take Over Someone's Land and Then They Sell it Cheap". *Ha'aretz*, January 15, 2003.

—— 2003: "Like Slums that Were Brought Together". *Ha'aretz*, December 30, 2002.

—— 2003: "They are Allowed to Sell Drugs, but Not to Fight Drugs on Behalf of The Palestinian Authority". *Ha'aretz*, February 4, 2003.

—— 2003: "Whoever Wasn't Fired because of the Cuts Was Fired Because of the Security Situation". *Ha'aretz*, January 1, 2001.

Hepburn, C. H. 1994: "Long Division and Ethnic Conflict: the Experience of Belfast". In Dunn Seamus (ed.), *Managing Divided Cities*, Keele: Keele University Press.

Klein, M. 2001: *Jerusalem, the Contested City*. C. Hurst and New York University Press.

—— 2003: *The Jerusalem Problem: the Struggle for Permanent Status*. Gainesville: The University Press of Florida.

Local Aid Coordinating Committee 2003: The Impact of Israel's Separation Barrier on Affected West Bank communities Report for the Mission of Humanitarian and Emergency Policy Group (HEPG) of the Local Aid Coordinating Committee, (LACC) May 4, 2003.

Seidman, D. 2003: "Erecting a Barrier to Peace". *Washington Post*, August 14, 2003.

Index

Index

Index